The Social Organisation of Death:

Medical Discourse and Social Practices in Belfast

Lindsay Prior

Senior Lecturer
Department of Sociology
University of Ulster at Jordanstown

MACMILLAN

First published 1989

Published by
THE MACMILLAN PRESS LTD
Houndmills, Basingstoke, Hampshire RG21 2XS
and London
Companies and representatives
throughout the world

Filmsetting by Vantage Photosetting Co. Ltd,
Eastleigh and London
Printed in Hong Kong

BRITISH LIBRARY CATALOGUING-IN-PUBLICATION DATA
Prior, Lindsay 1947–
    The social organization of death : medical discourse
    and social practices in Belfast.
    1. Belfast, Death, Social aspects
    1. Title
    306.9′09416′7
    ISBN 0–333–46434–6
    ISBN 0–333–46435–4 pbk

Contents

List of Figures

List of Tables

vii

Preface

This particular book about death began life as a doctoral thesis. Consequently it has undergone a number of transformations and, I hope, improvements since its inception. Death is not, of course, one of the most attractive of topics and I am not absolutely certain why I ever adopted it as a subject for study in the first place. I suspect, however, that from the very earliest stage it had something to do with my desire to investigate and examine a phenomenon which seemed to be incontrovertibly and unambiguously physical rather than social in its nature; that is, something about which there could be very little equivocation. In that sense death seemed to fit the bill. After all, one is either dead or alive; or so it would seem. Unlike various other phenomena such as suicide, or forms of mental illness such as schizophrenia, or even modes of behaviour such as drunkenness or aggression, death is unambiguous. It was, perhaps, to confirm my faith in this simple fact that I devoted my first day of field research to visiting a mortuary. (Fortunately, and given my initial abhorrence of such places, the building was empty of corpses).

One of the great joys of sociology is, of course, its capacity to encourage one to adopt a healthy degree of scepticism about the nature of the world, and the events and processes within it. And so it was with my study of death. Not that I ever questioned or doubted the status of death as a physical occurrence. No, what impressed me was the way in which in the mortuary (as in so many other locations) death was reduced solely to the status of a physical event. Indeed, death was regarded and organised first and foremost as a bio-physical fact, and the manifold nature of the materialist discourse which I first encountered in the morgue confronted me with a basic and fundamental problem. It was a problem which was pointedly raised by a rather sceptical pathologist who asked of me, 'what can sociology possibly have to say about the causes of death?'

I mentioned above that this book has undergone a series of alterations during the past number of years. One of the features which has remained constant, however, has been my reliance on, and debt towards, the ideas of a relatively small number of writers, all of whom throughout their lives remained critical of the claims of biology. The writers to whom I refer are Durkheim, his nephew Marcel Mauss, his associate Robert Hertz and, quite independently of the latter three, Michel Foucault. Among the enormous and multifarious achievements of all these writers was one which had a special appeal to me. Namely, their unmistakable and unparalleled ability to put human biology 'in its place'; that is, to regard it as a background to social life rather than as its determining force. For them, sociology was more than entitled to talk about and to question the accepted wisdom on such things as suicide, left-handedness, death, life, the causes of death and, of course, biology itself. I have therefore, and in a very modest way, sought to follow in their monumental footsteps and to examine physical death as an essentially social process. Consequently, I have chosen to focus on the forms of knowledge and schemes of social practice which surround the dead from the moment at which physical death is announced until the moment of disposal. Naturally, only some of those schemes of knowledge are rooted in the materialist modes of thought to which I alluded earlier, but, as will become clear from this study, materialist discourse determines virtually everything that occurs to the dead of the modern world. Indeed, it is the study of such discourse, together with the study of other related discourses on death which forms the rationale of the study.

As one might expect, in the course of completing this book (and the empirical work on which it is based) I have accumulated endless social and intellectual debts. Unfortunately, it would not be realistic to name every one of my creditors and I shall therefore restrict my acknowledgments to those to whom I owe a special thanks for the help which they very kindly gave to me during the various stages of research and writing.

I would like to open my list of acknowledgements by recording the help I received throughout the entire length of this study from the library staff of the University of Ulster at Jordanstown. Their assistance persistently underlined for me the indispensability of librarians to the academic researcher. I also received invaluable and generous assistance from the staff of the statistics section of the General Register Office, Belfast (1981–83) and from the staff at the Public Records Office of Northern Ireland. In addition, I would like to record my gratitude to each and every one of my informants, none of whom, I suspect, realised how invaluable their information actually was.

I am particularly grateful to a number of individuals for all manner of ideas and suggestions which they seemed happy to offer and which I was only too glad to accept. They are, David Armstrong, Mel Bartley, Robert Dingwall, Mike Hepworth, Robert Moore and Michael Shannon. A particular thanks is due also to Derek Carson who was usually rather puzzled by my interest in death, but who was always kind enough to answer my questions in full measure. My thanks to my friend Roger Byrne who produced the original sketches of the mortuary and of the funeral directors' premises which appear in Chapters 4 and 8, and last but by no means least, to my wife Pip for her unfailing help and encouragement. Finally, I should mention that some of the material contained in this book has previously formed the basis for a small number of journal articles. In particular, elements of Chapters 3, 4 and 5 have appeared in greater or lesser detail in: *Sociological Review* 1985, 31 (1), *Sociology* 1987, 21 (3) and *Sociology of Health and Illness*, 1985, 7 (2).

LINDSAY PRIOR

1 Death, Disease and the Body

THE SUBJECT, NATURE AND SCOPE OF THIS BOOK

This is a book about the ways and means through which death is socially organised in the city of Belfast. It is also a book about disease, medicine and the body. Indeed, the comprehension of death in the western world is so inextricably bound up with discourses on medicine and the body that it would be impossible to write a book about the one without extensive reference to the others. The bedrock of this particular study, however, is an analysis of the various responses which were made to 415 deaths which were registered in Belfast during 1981,[1] and I have sought to trace the numerous social, medical, legal, religious and (in some cases) political activities which were contingent on those deaths between the moment at which death was pronounced until the moment of disposal. Unlike many contemporary studies, therefore, the present one pays little attention to the study of dying. Instead it attempts to analyse the schemes of knowledge and social practice which the people of Belfast drew on to organise the deaths which fell within their domain.

In the process of researching the schemes of knowledge and social practice it became increasingly clear that death in Belfast, as in almost all other western societies, is organised in two distinct realms. The first is a public realm: a realm which is organised by the state and its agents and agencies. It is by means of these agents and agencies that death is certified and registered, that causes of death are determined and modes of death decided on. It is a world dominated by medical practitioners of innumerable kinds, by coroners and police and by the functionaries of the General Register Office. Indeed, it is here more than anywhere that death finds its hallmark and it is by means of the discourse through which these agents operate that death in the modern world is made visible. The latter is, perhaps, a point which deserves some underlining for, as I shall indicate below, the majority of contemporary writings on the subject of death either seek to support, or are based on the premiss that death in western societies has become a private, hidden and unconscionably secret affair.

In seeking to analyse and describe the public realm I have attempted above all to concentrate on the schemes of knowledge which state agents

1

and agencies routinely draw on to organise their affairs (as well as the affairs of those whom their decisions affect). And this focus on schemes of knowledge and their relationship to practice also provides the point of focus for the examination of private discourse. The latter, of course, accommodates a much more familiar world, existing as it does outside and beyond the state agencies which I have alluded to above. It is a world which encompasses the inexpressible sentiments which the deaths of friends and relatives seem to generate in each and every one of us, the ritual and ceremonial acts which ordinarily accompany instances of human mortality, the acts of disposal which are contingent on death and, inevitably, the world of the cemetery and the 'funeral home'. This private realm is not as tightly organised as the public one and at first sight it may seem to offer a boundless opportunity for the bereaved and those who surround them to express their emotions in forms untrammelled by cumbersome rules and regulations. Yet, in many respects, the practices of the funeral director, the priest and even the bereaved themselves are no more idiosyncratic than those of the pathologist, the coroner, and the registrar of deaths whose work normally precedes disposal and its associated ritual. Indeed, all of these agents work within and give expression to discourses on death which are, for the most part, ubiquitous in the world of western Christianity. Naturally, and as one would expect, the organisation of death in Belfast has its own peculiar and, at times, disturbing features, but in describing and analysing the organisation of my subject I have, for the most part, sought to follow a useful dictum of Malinowski's viz.

> to give a . . . complete survey of the phenomena, and not picking out the sensational, the singular, still less the funny and quaint . . . making no difference between what is commonplace, or drab, or ordinary, and what [is] astonishing and out-of-the-way. (Malinowski, 1922:10–11)

Malinowski, of course, would have railed at the notion of studying death as divorced from the social whole in which it is located and would no doubt have argued that 'death' is always part of a rich and elaborate social fabric from which it cannot be effectively separated. The argument is not to be lightly dismissed, but rather than locate death in the fabric of something called society or culture, I have chosen instead to examine it *via* the concept of 'discourse'. This latter term has become something of a shibboleth in contemporary sociology and before proceeding further it would be as well for me to state as precisely as I can how I intend to utilise it.

The analysis of discourse is cemented into a vast array of debates concerning complex epistemological and ontological issues. In this study, however, my use of the term is influenced (though not entirely determined) by the ideas of Michel Foucault (1970, 1972) who, among other things, saw in discourse the key to the problem of the constitution of reality.[2] Indeed, for Foucault the familiar objects of the social world (whether they be death, disease, madness, sexuality, sin or even mankind itself) are not 'things' set apart from and independent of discourse but are realised only in and through the discursive elements which surround the objects in question. Things, then, are made visible and palpable through the existence of discursive practices, and so disease or death are not referents about which there are discourses but objects constructed by discourse. As the discourse changes, so too do the objects of attention. A discourse moreover, is not merely a narrow set of linguistic practices which reports on the world, but is composed of a whole assemblage of activities, events, objects, settings and epistemological precepts. The discourse of pathology, for example, is constructed not merely out of statements about diseases, cells and tissues, but out of the whole network of activities and events in which pathologists become involved, together with the laboratory and other settings within which they work and in which they analyse the objects of their attention. Similarly with death; the discourse on death is composed not merely of what people say and write about death (though that is the most important source of data in this study), but of the entire range of practices, activities and settings which embrace death. Death, therefore, is constituted as much in the cemetery as it is in the pathologist's mortuary; as much in the General Register Office as it is in the undertaker's preparation room; and as much in the medical certificate of cause of death as it is in the funeral service.

As previously stated, I have chosen to divide the study of such discourse into two realms; the public and the private. Consequently, the book is presented in two parts. The first part concentrates on the state agents and agencies which are responsible for the certification, registration and explanation of deaths, whilst the second focuses on the world which lies beyond the realm of the formal state agencies and concentrates on the ways in which beliefs, sentiments and rituals of the living are structured around the dead. Before moving into the issues of substance, however, I would like to introduce some wider themes which cannot be suitably or adequately dealt with in the scope of the individual chapters which follow. The first set of themes is directly related to the sociology of death and dying, whilst the second is related to the nature of the human body as a site of social practice.

THE VISIBILITY OF DEATH

Some years ago Michel Vovelle (1976) published an article entitled 'The rediscovery of death', in which he documented the sudden flurry of publications on the subject of death which appeared in the western world from the 1950s onwards. Vovelle argued that the unparalleled focus of attention represented by these texts amounted to nothing less than the displacement of a deeply seated taboo on a subject which had lain hidden in the shadows of the western psyche since some unspecified point in the 19th century. Consequently, he claimed that the writings of such people as Gorer (1955), Feifel (1959) and Ariès (1967), not only provide us with accounts of attitudes to death in historically specific circumstances, but, in a dual representation, serve to signify a turning point in western sensibilities to death comparable to that which occurred during the 'twilight of the Enlightenment'. In other words, the 1950s marks the outer boundary of an era in which death was hidden in a veil of silence and secrecy, banished to the darker regions of everyday consciousness and repressed in a deliberate act of denial. It also marks the threshold of a new age in which death becomes a readily observed and much discussed object. An object cut free from the mask of silence which once disguised its true form.

This belief in the existence of a hidden death is one of the most widespread and popular in the current literature and it is very often conflated and intermingled with other related ideas about the place of death in modern western societies.[3] Ariès (1967, 1974, 1983, 1985), for example, in a series of works spanning three decades, argued that the modern age is hallmarked by the presences of what he termed 'La mort interdite'; that is, a form of death which has been banished to the margins of social life and isolated behind the walls of the hospital where 'a new image of death is forming: the ugly and hidden death, hidden because it is ugly and dirty' (1983:569). It is an argument which echoes the earlier claims of Gorer who maintained that in the England of the 1960s there was 'a squeamishness about reference to death, pain or mourning' (1965:114), which amounted to an act of denial.

These assertions about the denial of death are also conjoined with other claims. Thus, it is maintained by many writers that death has become an isolated event which, at best, is privatised in the limited emotional circle of the modern family. Elias (1985), for example, has recently spoken of the loneliness of the dying—a process which he traces to the rise of individualisation—whilst numerous other authors have harped on similar themes. Thus, Backer *et al.* (1982), Blauner (1966), Fox (1980) and Halper (1979), all comment on the processes through which death has been hidden, isolated and privatised in modern western societies. Indeed, if I understand them correctly, modern French historians have a term for the entire process. They call it the desocialisation of death (see Ladurie, 1979). All this, to say little of the related claims by such as Benoliel (1978), Engel (1977), De Vries (1981), Herzlich (1976), Hinton (1972) and Kubler-Ross (1970), about death being a bureaucratised, medicalised and hospitalised event which consequently has been 'dehumanised'.

All in all, then, death has had a bad press and its published image is a rather bleak one, reflecting as it does elements of repression, isolation, medicalisation and bureaucratisation. It is also, according to Chamboredon (1976) an image which reflects a contemporary critique of the modern technocratic world and an implicit idealisation of some pre-capitalist 'Gemeinschaft'. From our standpoint, however, it is an image which contains a suitable entry point into the study of the social organisation of death in Belfast. For the truth of the matter is not so much that death has been buried in the shadows of everyday consciousness for a century or more, still less that it remains suppressed but, that during that same period, it has undergone a series of transformations each one of which continues to have an impact on the way in which we understand, respond to and organise death in the modern world.

It is not my purpose to provide here an essay on the sensibilities to death in contemporary society. It is, however, important to note that our current relationship to death has not simply emerged in some mystical process of evolution, but is a product of quite definite and real transformations in the discourses through which the human condition is recognised and analysed. Indeed, when we examine the various disciplines through which that condition is represented we can see quite clearly that the analysis of death has always maintained a steady and sturdy footing in the consciousness of the West. In one sense, there is nothing new in thanatology. More important, however, is the fact that the transformations in the discourses which reflect on death have had serious and significant implications for the ways in which death and dying are organised in daily social affairs. Discourse and practice necessarily walk hand in hand, as it were, and one of the themes of this book is to demonstrate how this is so. Indeed, in order to elaborate on this line of argument a little further I would like briefly to return to the nature of Vovelle's 'rediscovery'.

It is true that Gorer's 1955 essay on 'The Pornography of Death' seemed to presage an opening of the flood gates as far as publications on the subject of 'Death' were concerned (though it was by no means the only publication on the subject during this period). And following Gorer it is possible to document the works of Feifel (1959), Glaser and Strauss (1965, 1968), Ariès (1967, 1974), Sudnow (1967a) and Kubler-Ross (1970), as particularly notable studies in the emergent field of thanatology. In addition, of course, there have been hundreds of publications on the subjects associated with death, grief and mourning, of which this is yet one more. But it would be wrong to conclude that 1955 marked, in any way, a rediscovery of death. On the contrary, what had been discovered was a new object of interest and new focus of study. That object was the *meaning* of death in everyday life and the sensibilities to death of those who surrounded the dying person. Indeed, we can, in part, establish the truth of this claim, merely by concentrating on the titles of the published works to which I have alluded. For, these latter works talk endlessly of meaning, awareness, attitudes and emotion—in short, of human sensibilities and their social variation. Feifel's work, for example, is entitled *The meaning of death*, Glaser and Strauss' is *Awareness of dying*. Ariès speaks to us of *Western attitudes to death*, Gorer of *Death, grief and mourning*, and Douglas of *The social meanings of suicide* (a fine contrast here to Halbwachs earlier 1930, study on the *causes* of suicide). Further confirmation of the true and ultimate objectives of these studies is also available in the prefaces and introductions which they contain. Gorer's (1965) work, for example, opens with an autobiographical introduction which centres on his own feelings about death. Feifel (1959) opens with the claim that 'far too little heed has been given to assessing thoroughly the implications of the meaning of death'. Ariès (1983) commences with a discussion on attitudes towards death and their association with an emergent awareness of self and other, and Kubler-Ross (1970) argues that her book will enlighten us about 'the final stages of life with all its anxieties, fears, and hopes'. Each one of these studies, of course, fitted snugly into the humanistic themes which were beginning to dominate the general tenor of social science research and in most fields of investigation during this period. But as far as death was concerned, the study of such everyday meanings did not emerge on to an empty stage, nor did it eclipse the objects of study which had preceded it. Instead, the analysis of meaning was added to an already substantial list of interests.

To claim that death was hidden in the folds of everyday consciousness for most of the 20th century is to ignore the fact that at least three disciplines had held such an object in their respective fields of focus for many decades. Demography, as the scientific study of populations had long recognised death as one corner of a triangular relationship on which all populations are built. Pathology, as a science of disease, had recognised death as a feasible and necessary starting point for the study of health. And sociology (with anthropology) had discovered in death something which both reinforced and reflected the nature of the social. None of these disciplines, however, had looked on the socially variable meaning of death as in any way important, but before I attempt to account for that apparent deficiency it will be as well briefly to examine the elements of the triad to which I have just referred.

It is quite clear that despite its central concern with death, demography did not speak of it *per se*. Instead it spoke of 'mortality' and rates of mortality and as such it reflects and reflected a significant point of focus in the modern world. That point is not the fate of the dying person or the individual body, still less the comprehension of death by the subjects involved, but the fate of the species. And the emergent attempts to register and measure patterns of mortality in western societies represent in many ways the essence of what Foucault (1979) referred to as a bio-politics of the population. Such a bio-politics was naturally as concerned with matters of natality and fertility as it was with morbidity and mortality and, according to Foucault, it marched through the modern world hand in hand with a second kind of power (one which was expressed in a political anatomy of the human body) to form a double-edged technology of life. Indeed, and for Foucault, it is as part of this technology of life that we meet the various apparatus of surveillance which are forever focused on our own bodies, namely, the mechanisms of registration, calculation, examination and physical control, each of which is:

> focused on the species body, the body imbued with the mechanics of life and serving as the basis of the biological processes: propagation, births and mortality, the level of health, life expectancy and longevity, with all the conditions that can cause these to vary. (Foucault, 1979:139)

In terms of this framework, then, the analysis of death was subsumed under a broader study which focused on the nature of 'populations'; the elements which generated their health and vitality as well as the things which encouraged their physical and moral degeneration. Consequently, and as we shall see from this study, the nature of 'mortality' was endlessly and meticulously broken down into finer and finer divisions viz. infant, childhood, perinatal, sex specific, age-specific and cause-specific mortality. And it was measured through ever more complex instruments, namely, crude death rates, infant death rates, occupational mortality rates, adult rates, male and female rates and standardised rates. Furthermore, and in tandem with this interest in the fate of populations arose a whole series of regulations, activities, organisations and occupations to collect, collate and analyse the associated data. The registration of births, deaths and marriages; the construction of official certificates and returns; the creation of an accounting mechanism in the General Register Office; the employment of registrars, statisticians and epidemiologists; and the development of rules concerning the disposal of the dead. Indeed, the social organisation of death is mainly structured in terms of such things and it is here rather than in any investigation of attitude or sentiment that we will have to commence our own inquiries.

In some ways, of course, this interest in the biological vitality of population can be linked to a wider discussion on the nature of 'things' in general. Perhaps, even, to a certain type of rationality. In this sense it fits in with the cognitive interests of 'science' and the associated desire for technical control and mastery of the world which Max Weber (1948) regarded as so characteristic of western capitalism—a characteristic later elaborated on by the members of the Frankfurt School of Social Research. In fact, it is a form of rationality in which the discovery of causal relationships plays an absolutely central role and where the formulation of laws and the accumulation of nomological knowledge is highly prized, but it is also, according to Weber, a form of thought in which the revelation of 'meaning' has no place. Thus, he states:

> If these natural sciences lead to anything in this way, they are apt to make the belief that there is such a thing as the 'meaning' of the universe die out at its very roots. (Weber 1948:142)

In many ways, then, the neglect of meaning is an essential feature of a much wider discourse on the nature of 'things'. It is also a feature of a particular discourse on the nature of scientific knowledge. In that context, demography, pathology and sociology merely express the epistemological and ontological precepts of their age. This is certainly true of the first member of the triad and it is, as we shall see, equally true of pathology. For, whilst demography concentrated on the scientific study of populations and, in its search for the laws of growth and decline, measured the mortality of men and women with increasingly complex tools, pathology as the science of disease also adopted death as an entry into the tangled world of causality. And, once more, it is Foucault who gives us an insight into the processes involved.

The rise of western scientific medicine has been analysed and reported on by a large number of commentators. Some of the more important investigations have been produced by Ackernecht (1967), Foucault (1973), Sigerist (1970), Singer and Underwood (1962) and Wightman (1971).[4] What is most striking about these various accounts is the fact that, in their different ways, they all emphasise the power and influence of clinical and experimental pathology in the development of modern medicine.

According to these accounts, the cornerstone of modern pathology is contained in Morgagni's 1761 manuscript entitled, *De sedibus et causis morborum*, which ushered into the modern world the concept of seats of disease and, by implication, the notion that one can pinpoint the axis of death and mortality within human anatomy. It was a thesis which formed the basis for the work of the Paris medical school—a subject which Ackernecht and Foucault examine in some detail—and which, in the words of Foucault, meant that:

From the point of view of death, disease has a land, a mappable territory, a subterranean, but secure place where its kinships and consequences are formed. (Foucault, 1973:149)

In other words, death and disease were seen as imprisoned in the living bodies of individuals. Consequently, the medicine of organs, sites and causes arose in harmony with the development of pathological anatomy, and henceforth, pathology concentrated on a somatic base which was extended from the bodily organs to the tissues by Bichat and from the tissues to the cells by Virchow. Furthermore, anatomy, having invaded pathology in the late 18th century, came to monopolise clinical medicine in the 19th. Thus, man the machine entered on stage and subsequently, this isolated, detached and mortal machine was viewed as a thing to be treated, reconstructed, repaired, improved and acted on. It was this very same machine which provided the space within which both the causes of disease and of death could be found; anatomical space became causal space. In fact, in its search for the causes of death, pathology conflated a number of diverse objects; and so disease, the body and causation itself, overlaid one another in a physicalist account of the human condition. Death and disease were to be located in the human body, diseases caused death, and the causal sequence which linked the one to the other were made visible in human organs and tissues. Like the demographers before them, then, pathologists treated their objects of study as 'things' whose essential nature could be comprehended and revealed according to the laws of human biology. And as with demography, this pathological vision of mortality had very real and lasting consequences on the social organisation of death. It justified the autopsy as a method of inquiry; it generated the need for the mortuary as a site of investigation; it structured the language of causation which was to be inscribed on the medical certificates of cause of death; and it justified an understanding of death and disease in terms of anatomical sub-systems. In short, it elevated the human body to a central place in the network of objects which could explain and account for death.

The analysis of disease and mortality like the analysis of populations was constructed according to the canons of positive science. Consequently, the emphasis of scientific study was placed on discovering the laws which organised the structure and functions of living organisms; the laws which defined the nature of population growth; the laws which explained the growth of healthy tissue, or the development of disease. But this quest for nomological knowledge was not, however, restricted to demography and pathology alone. In fact, the search for objective lawlike regularities in human affairs was nowhere more vigorously pursued than in the third and final member of the disciplines which analysed death: sociology.

There is no need to rehearse here the descriptions and arguments about the nature of late 19th- and early 20th-century sociology. Suffice to say that it was 'positivist', no matter how we may define that multivocal term, and that nowhere was this more the case than in the works of the Durkheimians. Indeed, Durkheim himself makes plain in his preface to *Suicide* that his aim is to study a specific form of death according to the canons of 'science' and that his study was constructed on the 'basic principle that social facts must be studied as things' (1952:37). By so doing, Durkheim hoped that the science of sociology would progress and the solutions to its problems would emerge. In fact the study of suicide provides an excellent example of the analysis and orientation towards death in the period under discussion, for it reflects above all an enduring and obsessive interest in causation. Not only, for example, is Durkheim's original work constructed in a framework of causality but Simpson's introduction to the English (1952) translation is written entirely in causal terms—a point which is evident from its very title: 'The aetiology of suicide'. This, apart from reference to the more obvious development of Durkheim's work by his follower Halbwachs (*Les causes du suicide*, 1930), or to the numerous social factor and causal studies which were published before the appearance of Douglas' *The social meanings of suicide* in 1967 (see Taylor, 1982). In fact, during most of this century, the study of death was the study of suicide, and that in turn was the study of social causation. Neither Halbwachs nor Durkheim, of course, exhaust the Durkheimian work on death and one of the finest essays on the subject was produced by Durkheim's associate, Robert Hertz. Hertz's 1906 essay, to which I will make reference throughout this study, was uncharacteristic of Durkheimian sociology in so far as it was not dominated by the search for causes. Instead Hertz took as the focus for his study the 'collective representations' of death and, in particular, a concern with the phenomenon of secondary burial. In many ways, and contrary to what I have so far argued, Hertz's study did analyse the meaning of death. But Hertz did not focus on the meanings of death and dying for the individuals involved so much as on the meaning of death for the collective conscience. Indeed, it was, if anything, the social 'functions' of death that Hertz took as his fundamental theme.

So what can be concluded from this short discussion and what are the implications for the study of death in the modern world? First, we have to recognise that death as an object of scientific discourse has always been visible and rarely, if ever, been hidden. But, in all probability, and for large parts of the 20th century, it has been visible only through an objective and scientific language which speaks of mortality, disease and causation, rather than one which speaks of attitudes, sentiment and awareness. And as Weber (1948) so correctly pointed out, such scientific investigations tell us nothing about the *meaning* of the world or of the objects within it. Second, it seems likely that in the 1950s there was a significant refocus of interest in death so that the object of attention switched from the study of 'mortality' and towards the examination of the meanings and sensibilities of those involved in the processes of death and dying; not just the sensibilities of the bereaved but also those of the dying themselves. Indeed, Feifel's key question for his 1959 work was, 'What does death mean to you?'

To these two simple conclusions I wish to add two further claims. First that the discourse on death which emerged through the language and practices of demography, pathology and sociology had important practical consequences for forms of social organisation; namely, that a whole series of mechanisms and organisations were established in the train of this discourse all of which concentrated on the recording, measuring and (causal) explanation of human mortality. Thus, the practices which we find in the General Register Office, the mortuary and the modern office of the Coroner are all explicable in terms of the 'scientific' study of death. In many ways, it is the elaboration of this theme which constitutes the premier part of this book. The second of the two claims alluded to above, is that as the focus of interest switched to an analysis of bereavement, meaning and 'awareness' of death, a new series of practices and organisations arose to accommodate and express this re-assessment of human sensibility. The most prominent of these is the modern hospice first founded in 1967, and directed towards 'managing the anguish of the dying patient' (Saunders and Baines, 1983). And no doubt, just as mortality was broken down into various categories and types during the last 100 years so too will the hospice be fragmented along similar lines of fissure (such as age, sex, disease and status group). The hospice, however, is only one expression of the new focus of interest and it marches hand in hand with the bereavement counsellor, the death education movement and the various voluntary agencies which have arisen to deal with the problem of bereavement. But perhaps most significant of all the changes which have occurred in the understanding of death during the past 25 years is the alteration in the definition of death itself. For, in the 1960s, death, once defined according to strictly physical criteria, suddenly became a point of ambiguity and equivoca-tion whereby the physical facticity of heart-lung death dissolved into a debate about the value of life and the essence of human qualities. That debate relocated the origin of the death in the brain rather than the respiratory system and the first test of death became one which questioned the receptivity and 'awareness' of the dying patient (Backer *et al.*, 1982. Gervais, 1987). Thus, death once so clearly defined as a physical fact became entangled in a discussion about the value of life. Indeed, it is an entanglement clearly evident in Veatch's (1976) discussion about the true and proper nature of death. It is a discussion in which he asks, 'What is significant about life that when we lose it, there is death?'

Veatch's question is not one which is easily answered. This is partly because it is imprisoned within physicalist assumptions and ignores the simple fact that death is primarily defined by the social practices which encompass it more than by the presence or absence of any given set of physiological processes. In that sense death is not, and never can be characterised simply according to biological 'facts'. Indeed, and as we shall come to see, physicalist accounts of death (as with physicalist accounts of other social phenomena), are somewhat weak in both descriptive and explanatory power. In the pages which follow, however, I shall concentrate on demonstrating how the comprehension and management of death in everyday social practices is dependent on the forms of discourse which surround it. And throughout the remainder of this book I shall seek to elaborate on this principle in a number of different ways.

THE VISIBILITY OF THE BODY

If death is best defined in relation to the social practices which encircle it, then, by implication it cannot be defined solely in terms of its anatomical and physiological features. Indeed, death is always, in part at least, defined by a whole array of legal, social, religious and political practices not withstanding the fact that such practices may be historically and culturally variable. Our comprehension of death and our reactions to death are therefore constructed in and through the numerous discursive régimes which circulate around the analysis and examination of human mortality.

The same might be said of the human body in so far as corporeality is also a product of the discourses which impinge on it and similarly cannot be reduced to a mere description of anatomical and physiological features. Indeed, these so called physical features of the human frame are themselves dependent on forms of knowledge and associated ways of seeing which seem to vary according to different cultures and historical periods. It is a point well made (though argued on the basis of widely different premises) by Ellen (1977), Marsh and Loughlin (1956), Manning and Fabrega (1973) and, most significantly of all, Foucault (1973). The body, therefore, does not and cannot yield its essential features to naked observation unmediated by forms of knowledge.

A discussion of the body and of corporeality in general is, of course, fundamental to this study because much of what we understand by death and most of the activities which we engage in on the occasion of death, have to do with the body. Death and the body are inexorably intertwined though they are not by any means co-extensive. The signs of death are normally discovered 'on' or 'in' the body, the causes of death are invariably located deep inside the body, the registration of death is contingent on the production of a body, the bereaved weep over the body, the funeral director prepares the body, and the clergy eulogise over an encoffined corpse. In fact, without a body the social processes which are contingent on death are severely and irreparably disrupted. This is perhaps why the definition of what constitutes a body can often be altered to fit the events at hand (mere parts of bodies or ashes can sometimes serve as substitutes for the whole), or why bereaved relatives are rarely satisfied with the 'facts' of death independently of the possession of a corpse. It is pertinent to enquire, therefore, into the ways in which the human body is perceived, understood and constituted at the hour of death, as well as into questions concerning the role of the body in the funerary process.

The body is a product of the theories and practices which surround it and as those theories and practices are multiple then so too is the body multifaceted. But before I venture into a resumé of the image of the body at death I wish to examine visions of the body as they occur within sociological discourse, for in many ways the comprehension of the human body in the domain of sociological discourse is representative of the ways in which the body is, and has been understood in wider domains.

Sociological Images of the Human Body

For many modern writers the fact of human embodiment is taken first and foremost as a problem of duality. In the words of Berger and Luckman (1967): 'On the one hand, man *is* a body . . . On the other hand, man *has* a body' (1967:68). And, grasping the fact of such a duality is considered essential to understanding the nature and the role of the body in social life. It is, for example, a theme emphasised in different ways by O'Neill (1985), Merleau-Ponty (1962), Sartre (1957) and Turner (1984). For sociologists, however, the study of the nature of the physical body is usually taken to be the preserve of a discourse other than sociology (anatomy, physiology, medicine or whatever). It is ordinarily assumed that sociology can only properly study such things as the social evaluation of the physical body, the ways in which the body is used as a means of communication, or the role of the body as a symbol system through which the world is ordered. Hertz (1973) in his masterful study of the dominance of the right hand in human cultures represents this position superbly:

Organic asymmetry in man is at once a fact and an ideal. Anatomy accounts for the fact to the extent that it results from the structure of the organism; but however strong a determinant one may suppose it to be, it is incapable of explaining the origin of the ideal or the reason for its existence. (Hertz, 1983:6)

Now, one of the great charms of Hertz's position is that it denies a primacy to physicalist accounts of social behaviour whether these be concerned with issues of 'race' or 'intelligence', or 'insanity' or 'competitiveness' or any other phenomenon so dear to those who seek to account for social life by non-social factors. In that sense Hertz was merely asserting the non-reductionist claims of Durkheimian sociology in general. Lurking within his analysis, however, is a secret acknowledgement that the 'facts' of the human physique truly do belong to the science of anatomy or some other such physicalist discourse, and that anatomy and physiology really can lay bare the truths of the human body. Perhaps it is too much to ask that Hertz should have seen that modern western anatomy is as much a socially determined vision of the human body (albeit a very powerful and useful one), as was, say, Hobbes' 17th-century vision of the body politic; or, that anatomy and physiology were and are as dependent on a social base as the evaluation of left-handedness or even death itself. But no matter, I cite Hertz mainly to emphasise the fact that sociology has relinquished discussions concerning the structure of the human frame to other discourses. Yet the visibility of the body is dependent on precisely these alternative discourses and the study of death cannot afford to ignore the ways in which the body is made palpable through the complete array of social and medical practices which impinge on it.

But how exactly does sociology view the human body and what implications do those ways of seeing have for the study of death? Chronologically speaking, the body in sociology (as in other scientific discourses) has been regarded first and foremost as a repository of human qualities. In this sense, madness, criminality, intelligence, race, mind, life, death and the myriad other qualities which human beings are supposed to possess are assumed to be located 'in' bodies. It is a theorisation of the body which I have referred to elsewhere as 'somatology' (Prior, 1987) and it is one which continues to dominate some areas of the social sciences (most notably psychology). This somatic vision of human behaviour and interaction is and has been necessarily associated with sciences of measurement. In its crudest form it manifested itself in the measurement of such features as facial angles, dimensions of the skull and its associated elements, resulting in such things as the production of the nasal index, the cephalic index and the measurements of anthropometry in general. It was, perhaps, in racial science more than anywhere that the intricacies and implications of this form of discourse could and can be most clearly seen (Stepan, 1982). Other features of the discourse, however, were or are to be discovered in such diverse fields as modern physical anthropology (Spencer, 1982), 19th-century physiognomy and phrenology (Young, 1970), as well as modern sociobiology (Rose *et al.*, 1984). Berthelot *et al.* (1985) argue that it was only with the emergence of Durkheimian sociology that sociology itself was able to make a decisive break from this form of biologistic thinking and that consequently the body as an object of inquiry 'was eliminated from the sociological field' (1985:142).

The elimination, of course, was only superficial and the body, at least in ghostly form, did reappear in the works of American sociologists. It was, after all, the human body that was socialised in the schemes of the Chicago sociologists and Talcott Parsons readily spoke of the 'organism' even though he was reticent about referring to the body. Yet, for the most part, the body which populated sociology texts was essentially a creation of biology. It was a universal and timeless body such as was represented in that indispensable and inimitable encyclopaedia of the human form, *Gray's Anatomy*.

This surrender of the body to the realms of anatomy and physiology was not, however, unconditional and total. For, in some senses, a discourse on what was 'in' the body was supplanted by a discourse about what was 'on' the body. In other words, the surface features of the human form rather than the internality of the body came to hold the attention of sociology. It is a switch of focus which is evident in many works published since the 1970s. O'Neill (1985), for example, opens his analysis with a distinction between the physical body and the communicative body. The lived body as he calls it is 'a medium of expression', (see also Benthall and Polhemus, 1975), and the ways in which the body is manipulated in social interaction is constituted as a legitimate area of concern. In this framework, bodies are viewed as things which are appropriated in concrete settings of social interaction so as to charm, cheat, influence, subordinate, exploit, love, hate or embrace humans in the course of their everyday lives. In retrospect we can see that Goffman (1959, 1970) was concerned with just this form of analysis—though he, of course, took 'self' rather than body as the true object of sociological focus—even in his discussion of physical 'stigma'.

This emphasis on the body as a means of expression has sometimes been taken further and linked to a consideration of wider structural forces which are present in all human societies. Mauss, for example, in a short essay published in 1936 spoke of the 'techniques' of the human body in walking, marching, swimming, running and so on (see Mauss, 1979). And he attributed the differences in the physical expression of such techniques to variations in the nature of collective life. And though it was not a prime point of focus, Elias (1978) also sought to trace links between bodily behaviour and aspects of social structure as human life manoeuvred itself through the 'civilising process'. The most recent expression of this way of thinking is, I suppose, that of Turner (1984) in so far as he argues that the modern body is structured through an ensemble of (mainly capitalist) social relations, the most compelling manifestation of which is to be found in 'consumer culture'. A line of analysis which is also pursued by Featherstone (1982).

But whilst some analysts have concentrated on the body as a medium of expression, others have decided to focus on the body as a sign system, that is, as a mirror or symbol system which can both be 'read' and/or utilised as a source for other symbol systems (see Shortland, 1985). This is, in fact, a line of analysis often chosen by modern anthropologists (Ellen, 1977) though one may find echoes of this way of thinking in 19th-century physiognomy and, most influential of all, of course, in clinical medicine. Such a semiotics of the body concentrates on the metaphorical relations which occur between the body and some aspect of social life. The body acts as both a classified entity and as a source of classification. It is both signifier and signified. The body is therefore seen to function as a cognitive map through which we can discover the order of things in the external world. A popular, though modified, form of this way of thinking is that contained in the works of Mary Douglas (1966, 1973) in which she argues that the socially constrained body furnishes a natural system of symbols through which the social world may be ordered.

> The social body constrains the way the physical body is perceived. The physical experience of the body, always modified by the social categories through which it is known, sustains a particular view of society . . . there is a continual exchange of meanings between the two kinds of bodily experience so that each reinforces the categories of the other. (Douglas, 1973:93)

Now it is not my intention to provide an exhaustive analysis of the ways in which the body has appeared in sociological discourse. That is far better done elsewhere (see Berthelot *et al.*, 1985). I have chosen to concentrate on a few sociological visions and to highlight some broad strategies for examining the body simply because they are images and strategies which reappear in other guises and other frames of knowledge. Thus, for example, the perception of the body as a receptacle of human properties is necessarily reflected in the mortuary where the body is seen as both a source of disease and a site of death. The recognition of the body as a mirror of human expression is clearly visible in the undertaker's preparation room where an image of peaceful and restful death is inscribed on the corpse. In the General Register Office the body is perceived as a source for the classification of pathological disorders, and at the funeral service the body is sometimes made visible as a symbol of political struggle.

It is, perhaps, because the body can be recognised and construed in such a diversity of ways, not to say acted on through such a diversity of practices, that few if any of the theoretical stances mentioned above seem to get to the heart of the problem of human embodiment. For the body is not, and cannot be 'this' or 'that' thing, and it cannot be adequately and fully described by reference to how any one interest group may monopolise and harness its 'properties'. Nor, indeed, is the body something immutable and unchangeable. In fact, what the body is depends on the very discourses which surround it. Thus, the body can be viewed and treated either as a productive force or a hedonistic agent of consumer culture (Berthelot, 1986). It can be a source of pathology or a source of sexual excitement. It can act as a framework of orderly classification, or a point on which to express rebellion against the prevailing order. Like Damiens' body (Foucault, 1977), it can serve as the locus of revenge and punishment, or like the bodies incarcerated in Bentham's Panopticon it can serve as a locus for reform and reconstruction.

In his *Discipline and Punish* (1977), and *History of Sexuality*, vol. I (1979), Foucault argued that the body always is and has been a product of the forms of power/knowledge which impinge on it. In particular, he argued that a form of political technology has encompassed the modern body so as to render it docile, disciplined and productive. It is a claim whose truth is suspect, but it is also a claim which underlines the fact that the reality of the human body is contingent on the myriad social practices which envelop it. As far as Foucault was concerned, of course, these practices fell into two distinct orders, each of which had functioned to render it visible in the modern world. Thus,

The great book of Man-the-Machine was written simultaneously on two registers: the anatomico-metaphysical register, of which Descartes wrote the first pages . . . and the technico-political register, which was constituted by a whole set of regulations and by empirical and calculated methods relating to the army, the school and the hospital, for controlling or correcting the operations of the body. (Foucault, 1977:136)

Death and the Body

As I have already stated, the presence of a body is a *sine qua non* of funeral procedure. Furthermore, the physical death of a human being presents one of the very few determinate points of life where the series of social, medical, religious and legal practices which serve to structure the human body, are actually synchronised. Death, therefore, presents an apt point at which to examine two aspects of the amorphous human form. First, the role of human anatomy in the articulation of social practices, and second the role of social practices in structuring images of the human form.

The articulation of concrete social practices on the human body is evident from the very moment at which physical death is perceived. The marks and signs of death are, as I have said, normally regarded as visible both 'on' and 'in' the body, and the body is ordinarily viewed as a container of all manner of facts, explanations and data on mortality. Pathologists, coroners, medical practitioners and the bereaved alike, more often than not regard the body as holding the secret of death's origins and so a whole series of events are necessarily triggered off by the cessation of the body's elemental physical functions. The discovery and explanation of death is not, however, a simple and straightforward affair, for the observation of tissue and organs is, as we shall see, forever mediated through discrete theories of disease and abnormality. Nevertheless, somatology is a framework of thought and analysis which dominates the modern approach to human mortality and is, of course, a part of that legacy bequeathed to us by the theoreticians of 18th-century Parisian medicine. More to the point, however, it is possible to see that from the very moment at which death is pronounced a dialectical process sets to work. A process through which theorisations of the body structure social practices, which in turn react back so as to shape our knowledge of the human form.

If causes of death can be located in bodies, however, it follows that the body must also serve as the starting point for the construction of the investigative system which surrounds the dead. It is, therefore, not just a system of medicine which circulates around the body but also a system of medico-legal investigation. The body thereby acts as the pivot for all manner of social and legal enquiries as well as functioning as a touchstone for decisions concerning cause and mode of death. Indeed, the body is a point on which a whole series of policing practices are pinioned; policing not merely in its modern sense of monitoring transgressions of the law, but also in its wider sense of regulating and furthering the interests of the state.

Yet the human frame serves as much more than a repository of explanations and a target point for policing. In fact, as significant as these is its role as the basis of a classificatory system. For the 20th-century body acts as much as a means for classifying diseases as it does for explaining human transcience. Thus, a mere glance at the World Health Organisation (WHO) nosology on diseases, injuries and causes of death (see Table 2.1, pp. 36–7), reveals a system of essentially anatomical orders through which diseases are categorised. Diseases of the respiratory system sit next to diseases of the circulatory system; diseases of the muscoskeletal system are nestled against diseases of the digestive system; and diseases of the blood-forming organs are settled adjacent to diseases of the nervous system. Of the 17 great orders of disease eight are clearly categorisations of anatomical site and a further two are sub-divided according to anatomical principles. The human body, then, acts as a foundation for the nosology. Yet, that same nosology acts as a prism through which the human body is refracted so that both the cultural significance of body parts and the basis of disease is made visible to the human eye. Moreover, and in so far as the nosology functions as an abacus for a state managed accounting mechanism, it is through this classificatory system that we come to gain our understanding of the distribution of death in the modern world. For it is after all not merely a classification of disease that we have here, but also the basis of the table which provides us with data on cause-specific patterns of mortality. At one remove, therefore, the 20th-century comprehension of social variations in patterns of health and disease are made transparent on human anatomy.

It is evident, then, that the human body serves as a foundation on which the modern state constructs its explanatory, investigative and descriptive apparatus. But we must not overlook the fact that this same human body also serves as a point on which private individuals can articulate their emotions, thoughts, practices and beliefs about death. As far as the bereaved are concerned, the body is first and foremost a site of personhood; a point at which persona, social existence and the idiomatic soul interconnect. It is therefore a site over which people weep, express sentiments of love and loss; over which they pray and eulogise, and through which they occasionally express affinities with the larger social, religious and political groups to which they belong. The body represents our primary and most fundamental source of contact with death. In a sense, the only portrait of death which we have is that which is inscribed on the livid corpse. The corpse is therefore not merely an object over which people vent their emotions but also one which is utilised to convey a representation of death and the hereafter. In Belfast, that representation is usually one of peaceful, restful and silent death.

Part 1
Public Discourse

Part 1
Public Discourse

2 Vocabularies of Causation

In a way the Kotas endow society rather than nature with the last word on whether a man has really died. (Mandelbaum, 1976:192)

DISCOVERING DEATH

In Belfast, whenever someone is thought to be dead, or close to death, a physician is invariably summoned. Only s/he can pronounce whether or not death has truly occurred.

The primacy of the physician in confirming death is echoed in the daily routines of the hospital wards where the majority of deaths occur. The 'Procedure Books' which encompass the rules of nursing are quite clear on the point, viz.

Last Offices
When the patient has died, the Doctor should be notified immediately and will confirm that death has actually taken place.[1]

And the pivotal role of the physician is equally well underlined in one of the very few 'procedure books' which is available to the general public on the question of death: *What to do when someone dies*.

Telling the Doctor
If there is any doubt whether someone is dead, treat him as being still alive. The first thing to do is to call the doctor . . . Even if it seems certain that the person really is dead, you should let his doctor know soon. (Rudinger, 1977:3)

The Department of Health and Social Security provides exactly the same advice in their leaflet, *What to do after a death*.

First things to be done
If death occurs at home, the following action should be taken: inform the family doctor contact the nearest relative if not already present. Inform the relevant minister of religion . . .[2]

The physician is supposed both to certify death and to state its cause,

25

or causes. In many respects this emphasis on the physician is peculiar as there is no statutory requirement that the cause of every death should be medically certified, but it would be regarded as most unusual for death rituals to proceed before certification has occurred. Indeed, the association between death and certification is so close that they have become synonymous. Thus, a medical practitioner attending a dying patient may confirm to the patient's relatives the certainty of approaching death by stating that s/he 'will be available at anytime in the next 24 hours for certification'.

In the everyday conversations which eventually take place on the subject of the deceased's last days and hours one of the items uppermost on the agenda will concern the question as to what the dead person died from, what diseases were present in the body of the deceased, the length of time which s/he suffered from such diseases and whether or not, given such diseases, the death was or was not a 'blessing'. And in reply to any queries about why and how a person died the most favoured response will be to provide an answer in terms of an illness or a failure of medication or therapy. For, in Belfast, as in most other parts of Western Europe, one dies from one's diseases rather than say of old age, malfeasance or misfortune.

As far as the organisation of death in Belfast is concerned; this reduction of death to its physical base is probably the most striking feature of all and in this chapter it is my intention to examine some of the central features of the official (and essentially medical) discourse within which death is analysed, understood and reported on. Needless to say, this discourse is inextricably bound up with the medicalisation and hospitalisation of death which has occurred throughout the western world during the last eighty or so years—features which have been widely commented on in the recent literature. Yet it is important to note that death and dying are hospitalised precisely because they are understood, first and foremost, as physical events. And the fact that it is now the doctor rather than the priest who is first summoned on the occasion of a death says much about the ways in which human mortality is comprehended in modern Ireland. Death is primarily regarded as an illness and an aberration rather than something which is natural and inevitable and the notion of someone preparing for their own death in the style of one of Philippe Ariès' medieval knights would be regarded as macabre in the extreme. This culture of medicalisation can, however, be directly traced back to and explained by the rise of specific ideologies and quite definite social interests. In fact, it is only with the rise of the physicalism which is embodied within modern pathology that human mortality came to be interpreted as nothing but a physiological event in the first place and it is to the nature and structure of this physicalist epistemology that we must now turn.

THE ANATOMY OF DEATH

Physiological phenomena are not the whole of death (Hertz, 1960 : 27)

The correlation of death with physiological signs is presumably as old as life itself, but the reduction of death to nothing but its physiological features is, one suspects, a comparatively recent phenomenon. According to medical historians it would seem that it was only during the 18th century that the desire to locate death with meticulous precision, to site it solely within the human frame, actually began. Alexander (1980) traces the visible origins of this obsession to the publication of Winslow's 1740 manuscript. *The uncertainty of the signs of death and the danger of precipitate interments and dissections*, whilst Ackernecht (1968) traces it to an earlier, 1707 text of Lancisi *On sudden death*. In any event it seems clear that the fear of premature burial together with an obsessive concern to determine the physical 'signa' of death are unequivocally contemporaneous with the rise of anatomical pathology.

The 18th- and 19th-century debate about death and premature burial tended to circulate around the issue of which anatomical site held the true origin of death. In Galenic medicine it was the heart which held the key to death. For Bichat, death could emanate from the brain or lung as well as the heart, whilst Orfila argued that death is diffused throughout the entire anatomical system (see Ackernecht, 1968). Thus, step by step a thousand deaths came to replace a single death and the signs of death were sought in tissues and cells as well as in bodily organs and specific anatomical sites. Henceforth, the moment of death was dissipated so that by the 20th century death was regarded more as a physiological process than as a single physiological event.

It is in terms of this legacy that modern debates on the nature of death seem to occur. The *definiens* of death are still sought in somatic sites and, indeed, Veatch (1976) goes so far as to suggest that we might locate the death of the soul in the quiescence of the pineal gland and social death in the dormancy of the neocortex. In more conventional circles it would seem that it is now the brain rather than the heart or lung which is supposed to contain the secret sign of death. And in line with this supposition the Harvard Medical School in 1968 supplanted death with

28

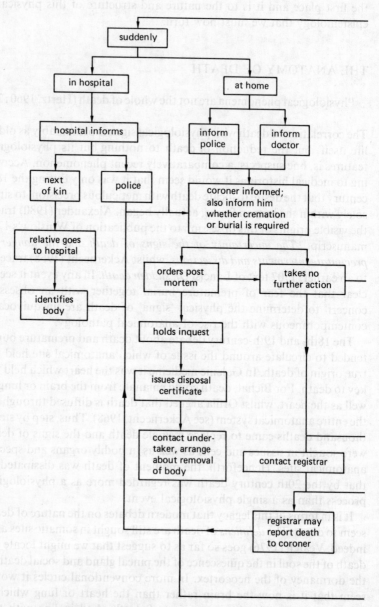

FIGURE 2.1 *What to do when someone dies*
SOURCE Rudinger, E. (ed.), Consumers' Association, 8th edn., 1977

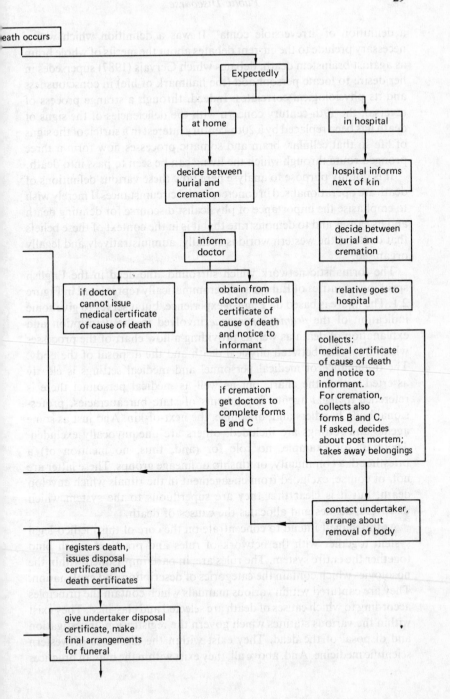

a definition of 'irreversible coma'. It was a definition which was a necessary prelude to the current debates about the merits of whole brain as against brainstem death: debates which Gervais (1987) supersedes in her desire to locate personhood (the hallmark of life) in consciousness and its physiological correlates. Indeed, through a strange process of reversal, the 19th-century concern with the deficiencies of the signs of death has been replaced by a 20th-century interest in a surfeit of the signs of life so that cellular, brain and somatic processes now form a three pronged route through which the living can be seen to pass into death.

It is not my purpose to analyse here how these various definitions of death are operationalised in concrete social circumstances. I merely wish to emphasise the importance of physicalist discourse for defining death and its causes and to demonstrate that it is in the context of these beliefs that death in the western world is socially, administratively and legally organised.

The formalistic network which surrounds the dead in the English speaking countries of Europe is diagrammatically represented in Figure 2.1. The figure is based on English experience, but it serves to give some indication of the *dramatis personae* involved in the description and explanation of death as well as providing a flow chart of the processes which intervene between physical death and the disposal of the body. The dominance of medical personnel and medical settings is clearly asserted within the chart, but as well as medical personnel there is reference to legal agents, incumbents of state bureaucracies, professional body handlers and, of course, the next-of-kin. And just as some agents and settings are included, others are unequivocally excluded. There is, for example, no role for (and, thus, no mention of) a priesthood, a community, or kinship or lineage groups. These latter are not, of course, excluded from engagement in the rituals which envelop death, but it is clear that they are superfluous to the system which discovers, defines and allocates the causes of death.

At this stage I intend to concentrate on the core of this medico-legal system together with the network of rules and practices which bind together the entire system. The rules are, in part, imprisoned within the nosologies which contain the categories of description and explanation. They are captured within various manuals which contain the principles according to which causes of death are selected and classified. They exist within the various statutes which govern the registration, investigation and disposal of the dead. They exist within the discourse of western scientific medicine. And, above all, they exist within the human practices which select, apply and adapt the rules and principles to organise social reality.

The hub of the entire system is in fact found within the medical certificate of cause of death. According to Schneidman (1976):

> In the Western world death is given its administrative dimension by the death certificate. It is the format and content that determines and reflects the categories in terms of which death is conceptualised and death statistics reported. (Schneidman, 1976:246)

The form of the medical certificate of cause of death which the physician is normally called on to complete has two components. The first component requires him or her to determine a causal sequence for the death and to unravel the relative importance of the respective factors embroiled in the causal network; thus:

I (a) Direct Cause (due to)
  (b) Intervening Antecedent Cause, (due to)
  (c) Underlying Antecedent Cause

The second component is simpler.

II Other significant conditions *contributing to death* but not related to the disease or condition causing it.

Leaving aside the fact that many diagnosticians elect not to analyse death at this level of detail, they normally state what they regard as *the* cause of death in the lowest line of Part One. And, in order to elaborate on the format of their reports and to examine the language of etiology which they use it will prove useful for us to examine a number of certificates which were completed for the Belfast dead of 1981.

CASE 1975
I (a) Coronary thrombosis (3 hours)
  (b) Congestive heart failure (5 years)
  Cause classified by GRO as I(a)

CASE 2918
I (a) Bronchopneumonia (3 days)
  (b) Pre-senile dementia (7 years)
  Cause classified by GRO as I(b)

CASE 1313

  I (a) Myocardial infarction
    (b) Coronary thrombosis
    (c) Hypertension
  Cause classified by GRO as I(a)

CASE 1293

  I (a) Bronchopneumonia
    (b) Chronic bronchitis
  II Ischaemic heart disease
  Cause classified by GRO as I(b)

CASE 3584

  I (a) Mesothelioma
    (b) Asbestos exposure
  Cause classified by GRO as neoplasia of unspecified site

CASE 3063

  I (a) Secondary haemorrhage
    (b) Duodenal fistula
    (c) Operation for periampullary tumour
  Cause classified by GRO as I(b)

Each one of these examples is written in terms of the discourse through which death comes to be known and recognised in the western world. Each one serves to demonstrate the fundamental axioms on which death is premised. Above all, they serve to illustrate the dominant belief that death is inherent in life. Death is not something which interpolates itself from the external world, nor is it a momentary, sudden, phenomenon, but something which exists within the living, active body. Thus, the hypertension, the chronic illnesses and the dementias are not so much acute causal conditions as long-term harbingers of death. In addition to this, of course, the terms and phrases on the certificates express the belief that the primary, fundamental and real causes of death are always medical causes sited in the human frame. Death, in every case, is pinpointed to an anatomical site. Death can in this sense be located in the lungs (case 3584), the duodenum (3063), or the heart (1313). And these certificates also illustrate the belief that although human beings die from many causes at once, it is always possible to isolate a single and precipitate cause of death. In fact, all of the examples demonstrate these three points especially well, but the last two examples serve to add a further dimension to our understanding of the ways in which death in Belfast is theorised. They illustrate how the social conditions which affect life (and, therefore, death) are either ignored in the selection of causes of death or are themselves medicalised. It is resonant of a process which recent German writers have referred to as *dethematisierung* (see Weindling, 1985) and to which I shall return later.

Over and above these considerations, we can also begin to see that the question as to what causes a death is intertwined with issues of moral responsibility and legal liability. Davis (1976), Elliott (1981) and Hart and Honoré (1985) all emphasise in different ways the important interconnections which exist between the allocation of cause of death and the moral and legal responsibilities which hinge on the ultimate allocation of a causal link. (This is especially clear in the cases of death caused by industrial disease.) The decision as to what causes a human death, therefore, is often forged through a multiplicity of competing interests and discourses; here legal, there medical, occupational, or economic. Thus, the primacy given to clinical discourse in allocating a cause of death may not only serve to obfuscate legal and ethical lines of responsibility, but also obscure the role of socio-economic processes in generating and sustaining specific patterns of health, illness and mortality. It is not simply the selection of a single cause of death which underpins such obfuscation, but also the selection of a single somatic point in the great chain of causation which underlies each and every death. In fact and in the words of Wightman:

> We are here at the heart of the matter; the whole history of medicine, from the most primitive to the most advanced is involved in the meaning of 'cause'. (Wightman, 1971:3)

It is because death is somaticised that it is also clinicalised. Thus in Belfast, as in other parts of Western Europe, death is viewed primarily as a medical problem. Death is conceptualised as an ailment which is amenable to intervention and therapy and so most of those who fall prey to death die in institutional care. In fact, in my 10 per cent sample of 1981 deaths, only 22 per cent died 'at home' whilst the remainder died in hospitals (58 per cent) or in nursing homes (13 per cent). It is, of course, this process of hospitalisation which has called forth the widest span of comments on the modern way of death. And it goes some way to explaining why most empirical studies on death and dying have been sited within the confines of the modern hospital (Glaser and Strauss 1965, 1968; Sudnow, 1967). But the hospitalisation of death is in many respects a surface feature of more elemental processes—the most important of which is the location of death in anatomical sites—and it is the physicalist epistemology within which death is understood and explained that forms the nodal point of the system.

A NOSOLOGY OF SPACES AND A NOSOLOGY OF SPECIES

Les sauvages n'ont pas de concept biologique de la mort. (Baudrillard, 1976:202)

In the Belfast of 1881 the major causes of death were those which were classifiable under three particular categories: Zymotic, Constitutional and Local diseases.[3] In 1981 the majority of deaths were allocated to causes which were classifiable as either Diseases of the Circulatory System, Diseases of the Respiratory System, or Neoplasia.[4] It would be tempting to translate the earlier terms into more modern language and to claim that it was essentially infectious diseases, tuberculosis, and respiratory and circulatory conditions which accounted for the bulk of mortality in late 19th-century Belfast. The temptation should, however, be firmly resisted for in the translation process we would lose many crucial and critical connotations of the terms in which the original nosology was written. Indeed, it would result in the eradication of an entire theory of disease. Thus, when Zymotic diseases were removed from the Registrar General's nosology in 1901,[5] it signified not simply a revision of terminology, but the last act in the expulsion of a theory of disease in which Zymotics had been embedded. In fact, the 1881 nosology contained elements of an epidemiology which has long since been eradicated, whilst the 1981 nosology expresses, quite forcefully, the elements of a pathology which has dominated medicine for over a century.

The 1981 nosology takes as its central point the human frame and builds on it an anatomical geography of disease. Thus, of the 17 great orders contained in the nosology, 10 are clearly related to anatomical seats (Table 2.1, see pp. 36–7). Mortality is distributed through a topography of the body. Diseases of the genito-urinary system sit next to diseases of the digestive system, diseases of the circulatory system next to diseases of the nervous system. The neoplasia (sub-divided by anatomical site) find their niche in a table which includes diseases of the musculoskeletal system, the respiratory system and the subcutaneous system. The causes of death are therefore not only discovered in human anatomy, but classified by human anatomy, the body serving as both a site for discovery and as a frame for understanding. This nosology, however, which at once presents a picture of the body and of disease, does not stand alone, detached and isolated from other aspects of medicine. On the contrary, it is itself a product of a complex discourse which sites diseases in bodies and seeks physical disorders in anatomical lesions.

I have already discussed the ways in which scientific medicine disclosed to us our vision of death and how that vision constructed death as a 'thing' amenable to scientific understanding. What I have failed to emphasise is the ways in which medicine's dependence on anatomical pathology resulted in a myopic vision of the social and material conditions in which human beings lived and worked and played. Consequently, it focused disease and mortality in a very narrow field. The initial processes, as Foucault (1973) described, involved an emphasis on the body and its organs, but as pathological anatomy became more adept at siting the seat of disease in organs, 'it would seem that the disease itself withdraws ever more deeply into the intimacy of an inaccessible process' (Foucault 1973:175). According to Foucault, the medicine of organs then came to an end and there commenced a medicine of pathological reactions which just happened to afflict this or that patient. It was at this juncture that death became dehumanised. Disease itself held the stage and not the patient and the therapeutic work of doctors was also, as Warner (1986) has recently argued, directed to disease rather than to a unique patient. Consequently, and as an adjunct to this, in the classification and enumeration of deaths it was diseases which were counted rather than mortalities. A new medicine of species was born.

It is from within this constricting ideology that the nosologies which provide the context for the Irish understanding and explanations of death are drawn. And the nosologies express a victory of a rationalised clinical and experimental medicine over a form of medical theorising which viewed mortality and morbidity in their socio-cultural contexts. Indeed, there once existed an alternative to this medicine of species. It was a medicine of spaces which, in a radically different form, has only recently been re-established and whose 20th-century origins have been traced by Armstrong (1983). It was a medicine which contained and developed its own nosological rules, and in order to discuss its structure it is necessary for us to return to the subject of zymotics.

TABLE 2.1 *The Distribution of Deaths by Sex, Age, and Nosological Category. Belfast 1981*

Nosological category		All ages	Ages at death											
			under four weeks	total under one year	1–4	5–14	15–24	25–34	35–44	45–54	55–64	65–74	75–84	85+
Total deaths	M	1986	21	37	9	10	40	37	46	142	363	607	518	177
	F	2062	17	25	8	7	6	9	24	91	239	458	737	458
I Infectious and parasitic diseases	M	3										2	1	
	F	9	1								2	1	3	2
II Neoplasms	M	411				1	1	3	4	37	97	140	105	22
	F	433					2	3	6	45	89	123	115	50
III Endocrine, nutritional and metabolic diseases and immunity disorders	M	4	1									2		1
	F	5	1							1		2		1
IV Diseases of the blood and blood-forming organs	M	5								1	1	1	1	1
	F	8								1	1	2	1	3
V Mental disorders	M	5								1	1	1	1	1
	F	3											1	2
VI Diseases of the nervous system and sense organs	M	22		2			1			1	1	2	6	5
	F	15					2			2	1	2	5	3
VII Diseases of the circulatory system	M	974					2	6	13	64	201	322	284	82
	F	1072							6	26	101	245	441	253

Cause	Sex												
VIII Diseases of the respiratory system	M	277	2	8	1	1	1	2	8	28	96	82	40
	F	297	1	5		1	2	5	7	19	51	102	103
IX Diseases of the digestive system	M	53			1		4		5	16	13	8	6
	F	61							2	8	14	26	11
X Diseases of the genito-urinary system	M	31						1	1	2	11	14	3
	F	46							1	5	10	18	11
XI Complications of pregnancy, childbirth and puerperium	M												
	F												
XII* Diseases of the skin and subcutaneous system	M												
	F												
XIII* Diseases of the musculoskeletal system and connective tissue	M	6								1	3	2	
	F	11									3	3	5
XIV Congenital anomalies	M	15	10	5									
	F	11	5	6	1								
XV Certain conditions originating in the perinatal period	M	14	13	1									
	F	8	7	1									
XVI Symptoms, signs and ill-defined conditions	M	3								1	1		1
	F	2											2
XVII Injury and poisoning	M	164			6	34	27	21	23	14	9	14	9
	F	80		1	2	3	5	6	8	11	4	21	16

*Deaths attributable to Classes XII and XIII are not distinguished within the Report for Belfast.

SOURCE Derived from: Registrar General Northern Ireland Annual Report 1981, Belfast HMSO, 1984.

When Farr introduced his nosology of diseases in the first Annual Report of the Registrar General for England and Wales, he explained that,

> The primary divisions of a *Statistical Nosology* should evidently be founded upon the mode in which diseases affect the population: whether they are generated and prevail only in particular localities (endemics), extend like cholera over nations (epidemics), or are propogated by contagion; whether they arise in an isolated manner (sporadically) from ordinary causes, and sources existing in the organisation itself; or whether they are caused by violent means.[6]

If we dwell on this quotation for a moment we cannot fail to note how the concept of a seat of disease is entirely absent from the classificatory logic. For once, the guiding principle of taxonomy is something other than anatomical space (though the concept of seats of disease did figure in the second tier of this nosology and became dominant in later revisions of the schema). Instead, the basis of classification is found in socio-geographical space, in material circumstances. So that, in a very important sense, it is social circumstances rather than living organisms which are held to embrace the origins of disease and mortality. In short, from our standpoint in the late 20th-century we cannot fail to note that this is an entirely foreign and somewhat puzzling conceptualisation of morbidity and mortality.

What, then, was zymotics and how did it relate to the nosological principles outlined above? Zymotics was a component of a theory of disease. It was a term invented by the English statistician Farr, and it was nestled in a discourse which saw the origins and nature of disease in living conditions (in the very broadest sense of that term), rather than in microbes. From our lofty standpoint it was a theory conceived in ignorance, but it also emphasised elements of the human condition which scientific pathology tended to ignore, namely, the conditions in which human beings lived and worked, the quantities of air which they breathed, the spaces between their bodies and their dwellings, the food which they consumed and the temperatures to which they were subject. In other words,

> the influence of civilisation, occupation, locality, seasons, and other physical agencies, either in *generating disease and inducing death*, or in improving the public health. [Emphasis added.][7]

Moreover, the 19th century nosologies in general and the concept of zymotic disease in particular were embedded in a broader debate between those who affirmed the virtues of contagionist, and those who affirmed the anti-contagionist theory of disease. And this latter debate was inextricably bound to an analysis of the socio-geographical conditions in which people routinely lived and worked. Among others, Coleman (1982), Eyler (1979) and Delaporte (1986) have recently examined the impact of these forms of theorising on 19th-century medical practice and highlighted the ways in which disease was always linked to the material circumstances in which people existed. It is a theme which clearly confronts us in the Annual Reports of the Registrars General of England and Wales, Scotland, and Ireland. The latter invariably include often lengthy accounts on the 'The Prices of Provisions and Pauperism', 'The Scarcity of Fuel', and 'The Weather' in their attempts to explain the annual variations in mortality. In fact, the Belfast report continues to carry a meteorological section even though no one quite knows why it is there or what relationship is supposed to exist between meteorology and mortality.

The specific principles on which 19th-century government nosologies were based was outlined by Farr in the fourth Annual Report of the Registrar General in 1841.[8] By the 1870s, however, those principles had been superseded by the ones encompassed in the germ theory of disease which, of course, provides the ground rules on which the contemporary understanding of disease is based. Consequently, the investigative programme of pathology (to seek out disease in the physical body), was strengthened, whilst those forms of investigation which sought the origins of disease in the social body were irrevocably weakened.

My purposes in digressing to consider the shape and form of 19th-century nosologies are twofold. First, to reinforce Foucault's (1973) point that conceptualisations of disease other than our own are possible. And, secondly and more importantly, to highlight the fact that contemporary European culture places a special emphasis on bodily, anatomical space and that it does so to the detriment of the consideration of social space. The living body has been given precedence over the social body and both the nosology used by the Belfast Register Office and the certificates which are completed by the clinicians and pathologists are dominated by the principles of anatomical pathology rather than those of social medicine. In contemporary Belfast, therefore (as in other parts of Europe), death is viewed first and foremost as a disease of living bodies.

This dethematisation or suppression of social spaces in nosological principles not only has fundamental consequences for our image of human mortality, but also for our conceptualisation and understanding of causal sequences. Yet in Belfast death is not only viewed as a process which occurs within bodies, but also as a phenomenon which is detached and decontextualised from all forms of human action. So that, paradoxically, although death is 'in' the human frame, it is understood as something which occurs independently of human agents and agency.

VOCABULARIES OF CAUSATION

Sociologically, as Max Weber put it, a motive is a term in a vocabulary which appears to the actor himself and/or to the observer to be an adequate reason for his conduct. This conception grasps the intrinsically social character of motivation: a satisfactory or adequate motive is one that satisfies those who question some act or program . . . The words which may fulfill this function are limited to the vocabulary of motives acceptable for given situations by given social circles. (Gerth and Mills, 1954:116)

For 'motive' read 'cause' and, in so doing, understand that the vocabulary of causation which we have been discussing is one which is historically peculiar; composed as it is in the language of pathological anatomy. It is a vocabulary in which the nosology acts as a lexicon. Yet we must not overlook the fact that behind the nosological principles lies humanity. It is a distant humanity and acts as a mere backdrop for disease, for treatment, for the geography of organs and tissues. And beyond that humanity lies a social, political and material world which equally fails to appear in the tables of disease through which the residents of Belfast come to understand the nature of death. The language of classification, therefore, squeezes out any agents of death which may be present in the socio-economic and socio-political structures within which men and women organise their daily existence. It even eradicates reference to the deceased themselves. Yet this exclusion of human actors and social organisation is not just a product of the structure and content of the nosology: on the contrary, human beings and human actors are classified out of the descriptive process which encompasses death at each and every level of understanding. Indeed, I have already cited two cases in which the erasure of social agents occurs (cases 3584 and 3083). In the first, the context in which the deceased was exposed to a carcinogenic agent was ignored. In the second, the iatrogenic agent was classified out of the causal sequence entirely and the death was plainly and unequivocally attributed to the presence of the tumour in the duodenum. But, in order to explore the nuances of this style of reasoning a little more closely I intend to examine some further cases of death. In the following paragraphs I have deliberately selected cases in which human actors were very much in evidence in the causal sequences which led to death and in each case I shall attempt to illustrate the principles by means of which these actors were systematically erased from the etiological accounts. As previously, the notation I (a) (b) (c) refers to the positions which the terms held on the original medical certificates of cause of death.

CASE 0229
    I (a) Multiple injuries. Fractures of 8 right and 9 left ribs with laceration of aorta and left lung, fracture of spine.
    Cause of death selected by GRO: laceration of left lung.

CASE 3731
    I (a) Paraquat poisoning
    Cause of death selected by GRO: toxic effect of other substances, not elsewhere classified.

CASE 2746
    I (a) Acute circulatory failure, due to,
      (b) Repair of ventricular aneurysm and coronary artery by-pass surgery, due to,
      (c) Myocardial infarction and coronary atheroma
    Cause of death selected by GRO: myocardial infarction

CASE 2114
    I (a) Multiple injuries: stab wounds to head, and bullet wounds of head and trunk
    Cause of death selected by GRO: Open wound to the head

CASE 3651
    I (a) Laceration of brain: bullet wound of head
    Cause of death selected by GRO: Intercranial injury

The banishment of human actors from the causal process is achieved in a number of ways. In the first two certificates the actor is directly excluded. The context of case 0229 is best summarised by saying that the deceased was a pedestrian who was hit by a vehicle which failed to stop at the site of the collision. Case 3731 was one in which a lorry driver, who was both depressed and recently declared bankrupt, deliberately swallowed paraquat and, regretting his action, sought urgent medical help to no avail. In neither case does the certificate make any reference in the causal sequence to human action. In both cases, however, an additional 'E code' was used by the GRO so that the external cause of injury or poison could be categorised appropriately.

In the words of the ninth revision of the World Health Organisation (WHO) *Manual of the International Statistical Classification of Diseases, Injuries and Causes of Death* (1977);

> The E code is now a supplementary classification that may be used, if desired, to code external factors associated with morbid conditions classified to any part of the main classification. (WHO, 1977 : xxix)

In other words, the E code serves to place the active subject(s) in parentheses. They are an associated, but not a primary causal agent in processes leading to death. And they are certainly not regarded as essential to either the classification of death or to understanding its nature. In case 0229 above the E code selected was 814 (Motor vehicle traffic accident involving collision with a pedestrian). But the code selected for 3731 made no reference whatsoever to human agency. Consequently, all reference to human wills, intentions and activities were sited tangentially to the deaths and the official interpretation of them and their principal causes inevitably reflects this deflection of attention.

Case 2746 points to the existence of an active subject directly. The deceased was undergoing a surgical operation at the time of death and the iatrogenic agent was therefore closely interlocked with the patient's demise. In the classification process, however, the active agent is coded out by selection of condition I(c) as the cause of death and again an E code was used to encompass the active subjects who impinged on the relevant circumstances. In this case the 'E' code was 998 ('Other complications of procedures, not elsewhere classified') which itself only hints at the existence of human subjects.

Cases 2114 and 3651 erase the active subject in more subtle fashion. Both these deaths are instances of what might be called sectarian assassinations. The first executed by a Loyalist paramilitary group and the second by the Provisional Irish Republican Army (PIRA). The certificates, of course, make no mention of this, but neither are they able completely to obscure the presence of human agents in the causal sequence. Instead, it is the very language of the etiology which serves to suppress human subjects. The reference to stab wounds and bullet wounds implies that someone stabbed, shot, killed, murdered or whatever, but it does not state this exactly. Indeed, the language of diagnosis so transforms the actional structure of the description as to place the active subject who did stab, shoot, kill, and the like, into the background. The precise codes which are used for these two cases removed the subject completely. Case 2114 is coded 873.8 ('Open wound of the head'), and case 3651 was coded as 854.1 ('Intercranial injury of other and unspecified nature'). In both cases an 'E' code was also cited, but in this, as in other cases, the code simply supplements the primary description and places human activity in brackets.

Naturally, at the inquests which accompanied each of these cases the human subjects who were involved in the circumstances which surrounded the deaths were summoned, interrogated, examined and implicitly if not explicitly blamed. But in no case was *the* cause of death altered by these deliberations. At no stage was the causal process deemed to be other than a medical process and at no stage was death ever perceived in other than physiological terms. On most occasions and for most deaths this line of reasoning is accepted without challenge. Occasionally, however, the political and emotional implications of explaining death in this way seep to the surface and pressure groups arise to challenge this official vocabulary of causation—as occurred with cases of children who died from 'plastic bullet' wounds.

The extinction of humanity does not, of course, occur within all frames of understanding and explanation. In fact, the human causes of death had to be cajoled out of the registers in which mortality was recorded. They had to be suppressed in the language of classification, or even coded out until very little of the alternative frames of explanation remained. The categories used by the Irish Coroners during the 19th-century, for example, were rooted in the existence and operation of human intentions, dispositions and moral designs. Active human subjects were embedded within the general categories of causes of death and within the specific accounts of their inquiries.

The interpolation of human subjects is in some ways evident in the nosology designed by Wilde in 1841 for the summary of Irish Inquest statistics.[9] Class I deaths: 'Deaths caused by violence, neglect, evil intent or design'; within which resided such categories as 'unskilful medical treatment', 'injuries inflicted by lunatics'; Class II deaths: 'Accidental deaths caused without design or intent'; Class V deaths: 'Deaths from immoderate use of ardent spirits'. But it is more readily evident in the specific accounts and verdicts which were listed by the Carrickfergus Coroner (who was the Coroner for Belfast) during the mid-19th-century. Among these we find the following causes of death: 'Intemperate living and drinking'; 'want of the common necessaries of life'; 'died from cold and whiskey'; 'killed by a lunatic named J.T., he being insane'.[10]

We can dismiss these categories and statements as the conclusions of men who were entirely ignorant of the 'true' causes of death, or, indeed, dismiss them as a by-product of an unsatisfactory nosology. Alternatively, we can see in these statements a radically different frame for understanding and explaining death. It is a framework in which human activity is located at the hub of the explanatory system and appears in contexts which would be regarded as inapplicable in contemporary nosologies. Thus, deaths from violence, for example, include deaths from starvation, industrial poisoning and 'want of breast milk'. In this way the socio-economic structure was written into explanatory categories rather than excluded as a source of valid and relevant causes. In the same fashion, and as I have already indicated, the Coroner wrote in iatrogenic factors as causes of death. In current nosologies reference to iatrogenic factors is deliberately suppressed and there is no provision made for omission to act or intervene. Indeed, from the introduction of the seventh revision of the WHO nosology, therapeutic misadventures have been attributed to the disease or condition requiring therapy and never to the therapeutic activity itself. Moreover, the present Coroner for Belfast restricts judgement to medical causes of death alone and has abandoned the use of such terms as homicide, suicide and misadventure (see Elliott, 1981). For him, the cause of death is 'always a medical cause'; the coroner's court 'does not exist to assign or remove liability'.

This same retreat into the categories of pathology is evident in the sole remaining hospital registers available for late 19th- and early 20th-century Belfast: the registers of the Lunatic Asylums. It is true that in the majority of cases the causes are written in the discourse of clinical medicine: pulmonary consumption, general paralysis of the insane, lupus, T.B., diahorrea, cancer and phthisis all appear in the registers. But they are inserted side by side with other causes which are derived from an alternative scheme of explanation. 'Died from obstinate refusal of food', 'exhaustion from acute mania', 'died from a piece of meat sticking in his throat', 'melancholic exhaustion', and 'senile decay'. These latter terms are, however, gradually squeezed out of the registers until disease categories alone dominate the pages. Of the 95 inmates who died within the Belfast Asylum in 1914 only 13 have deaths attributed to non-disease categories ('natural decay' and 'exhaustion') and by the late 1920s there were none.[11] Hence, those frames of understanding which located the principal causes of death in the creative or destructive acts of human subjects were gradually eradicated. The humanistic accounts of death were removed from the medical registers and effaced from the certificates. They may have lingered a little longer in the discourse of the Coroner's court, but their fate was ultimately the same.

CAUSES AND CONTEXTS

The singular features of the discourse through which causes of death are structured and analysed in modern Ireland can be best understood through the history of that discourse. History both reveals something of the origins of the discourse and also acts as a counterpoint to it. For there can be little doubt that the belief that death and disease are imprisoned in bodies is historically and culturally peculiar.

I have tried to indicate that anatomical pathology provides the source and origin of the modern Irish image of death and that anatomical pathology not only traced out a physical space in which clinical medicine could operate, but further provided an epistemological space in which causal logic could be formed. In the modern world, therefore, the techniques by which the causes of death are discovered are ideally those of biopsy and autopsy: a physicalist logic naturally requires a physicalist methodology. Yet, by delving into the interior of the corpse the explanatory horizon is restricted and limited. Indeed, the role of social relationships, of forms of social organisation, of material circumstances in generating morbidity and mortality are thoroughly ignored. Anatomical pathology precludes the study of what was known in the 19th century as social pathology. In fact, and on the basis of Coleman's (1982) and Eyler's (1979) work, there are good grounds for believing that death in the 19th century was perceived rather as a social disease than as an isolated physiological event and that Victorian medicine attempted to develop a political economy of death rather than an anatomy of disease.

It is no surprise, then, to discover that in contemporary Belfast only physicians can confirm and explain death. And given the premises of pathology, it is no longer puzzling why human agency is excluded as a valid source of explanation for death. For excluded it is, first in the nosological categories, then in the rules according to which causes of death are selected and, finally, in the language of etiology itself. Unlike, say, the world of the Azande (Evans-Pritchard, 1934), there is no room

TABLE 2.2 *Factors listed as 'cause of death' in the hospital register. Belfast Lunatic Asylum, 1871*

Cause of death	Number of deaths
Maniacal exhaustion	2
Mania complicated with chronic pulmonary disease	2
Mania complicated with paralysis	1
Mania complicated with epilepsy	2
Congestion of the brain	1
Pulmonary consumption	1
Chronic chest disease	1
Epileptic mania	1
Alcoholia mania	1
Exhaustion from diahorrea	1
Dementia and scrofula	1
Phthisis pulmonals	3
General debility	1
Chronic bronchitis	3
Senile debility	1
Exhaustion from acute mania	1

SOURCE PRONI. Hos 28/1/4/1.

for malfeasance, sorcery or the supernatural here. Nor, indeed, for an analysis of human relationships. And, yet, the strangeness and singularity of this image of death occasionally slips free of the straightjacket which pathology has imposed on the corpse. Indeed, it emerged in 1981 and is evident in the following report drawn from the *Belfast Telegraph* of 1 December 1981. It concerns a statement made in the Coroner's court in Hillsborough, County Down. A representative of the Northern Ireland Office is speaking about the Republican Hunger Strikers, ten of whom starved to death during that year and in whose wake many more died.

Mr Robert Carswell, QC, appearing for the Northern Ireland Office told the jury of two women and nine men, it is necessary only for you to decide the medical cause of death. It is not for you to explore questions about why the deceased embarked upon their hunger strike or what they sought to achieve by doing so'.

3 Categories of Death

Uncleanness or dirt is that which must not be included if a pattern is to be maintained. (Douglas, 1966:40)

CATEGORISING DEATH

During the early morning of 23 January R.M. was asleep in bed when two gunmen burst into his house and murdered him. On the night of 18 November R.K. shot himself in the head, having previously told his wife that he could not 'face up to his responsibilities'. On the evening of 14 December A.G. (a schizophrenic) poured petrol over himself and ignited it. He died in hospital the following day. And on the afternoon of 13 October an apparently fit and healthy 21-year-old male collapsed and died suddenly whilst playing football in the street.[1] The anatomical cause of death was never determined. Were these natural or unnatural deaths? And how is it possible to distinguish the one kind from the other? Indeed, is it necessary so to do?

The answer to the last of these questions is an unequivocal 'Yes'. For, in Belfast decisions concerning the mode of death rank in importance with decisions concerning the causes of death. This is not perhaps surprising, since in most societies decisions concerning the modalities of death are regarded as fundamental to the status passage of the corpse, and in all societies they seem to affect the organisational responses which are contingent on bodily disposal. Categorising the dead is, therefore, fundamental even though the basis of categorisation can take many forms. Thus, in some societies a distinction is made between good and bad death, in others between social and physical death, and still others between natural and unnatural death.

It is the last distinction which dominates in Belfast and one of the problems faced by the sociological researcher is to determine the principles according to which the distinction is made. In analysing the problem one is necessarily drawn into an examination of the classificatory logic which operates in Coroners' courts, as well as into the discourse of death which is expressed in Coroners' verdicts. The logic of classification is, of course, fabricated on case histories, on the bodies of those who have been murdered, injured, poisoned and asphyxiated. And so it will be instructive to note who it is that suffers from unnatural death

and how the investigatory apparatus of the Coroner is distributed across
the population of the dead.

MODES OF CLASSIFICATION

Ways of categorising death are numerous and in sociological and
anthropological literature a number of categorisations have been
consistently isolated for investigation. Of these the distinctions between
'good' and 'bad' death, social and physical death, and natural and
unnatural death are the most common.

Anthropological studies contain a wealth of detail on the distinctions
which are drawn between 'good' and 'bad' death. The most notable of
the earlier works on this subject was probably that of Hertz (1960), but
following Hertz a large number of anthropologists took up and
developed the distinction. The works of Huntingdon and Metcalfe
(1979) and Bloch and Parry (1982) are among the most recent in a long
line of these developments. And, according to the latter:

> The 'good' death is thus one which suggests some degree of mastery
> over the arbitrariness of the biological occurrence . . . By contrast, in
> nearly all of our examples, those deaths which most clearly demon-
> strate the absence of control are those which are represented as 'bad'
> deaths and which do not result in regeneration. (Bloch and Parry,
> 1982:15)

The most oft cited example of a good death is that provided by
Lienhardt (1961) concerning the death of the Dinka spearmaster. The
central theme of this death is the voluntary choosing of the time, manner
and place of death, but it would seem that most societies hold some views
on the nature of good death and bad death. Parry (1982) gives examples
from Hindu society, Middleton (1982) from Lugbara society, Watson
(1982) from Cantonese society, and Loraux (1982) cites the warrior
death of 5th century BC Greece as a further example of good death.[2] In
western society the notion of a good death was most closely embodied in
the *Ars Moriendi* (O'Connor, 1942; Ariès, 1983), and despite the fact
that manuals for dying are no longer fashionable there is no doubt that a
timely death in which ritual can be properly attended to and power and
influence can be appropriately redistributed remains the preferred mode
of death (see Glaser and Strauss, 1968).

As well as distinctions between good and bad death a further division is sometimes drawn between natural and unnatural death. According to Simmons' survey of primitive cultures:

> The fact of the naturalness of death even for the aged has not been generally accepted by men. Of 47 tribes on which information could be obtained, in 17 death was not regarded as natural; in 26 others the possibility was only partially admitted; while in only 4 did it appear that death was frankly recognised as a natural occurrence. (Simmons, 1970:219–20)

Similar results were evident in Bendann's (1930) study of death customs, as well as in Frazer's earlier (1913) study of beliefs concerning the dead. The tendency in western culture, however, has been to adopt the view that death is inherently natural and only in special circumstances should it be regarded as unnatural. Thus the Brodrick Report (1971) on death certification and coroners contains the following assertion:

> In a philosophical sense all deaths can be regarded as natural, since death is the natural end of all men. Even in medical terms it is possible to regard all deaths as natural in the sense that they result from the failure of one or other of man's vital organs. (Brodrick 1971:6.14)

Jervis (1957), the legal manual for Coroners, contains a similar statement on this issue:

> All deaths can in a sense be regarded as natural. This is true in a philosophic sense in that it is part of man's lot to die. It is also true in a medical sense in that in all cases death is brought about by one or other of man's organs. In order, therefore, to distinguish between one sort of death and another it is necessary to consider not the terminal cause of death but the cause which was the real cause of death. (Jervis, 1957:83)

It is probably this distinction rather than the previous one which has played the major role in the categorisation of deaths in the western world (see, Brodrick, 1971:88–106), and it is certainly the one which dominates the classification of death in Belfast. There is, however, one further oppositional form within which death is understood and which I would like to say something about. It is that between social and physical death.

The contemporary form of this distinction is embodied in the classification of somatic versus brain death where sociability is seen to reside in human consciousness and the absence of such consciousness is regarded as being equivalent to death (see, Backer *et al.*, 1982; Glaser and Strauss, 1965), but the nature of this last distinction is a widespread and long-standing one. Fortune (1932) cites examples from Dobuan society concerning those who lie dying from a swollen stomach— 'he is as one alive, but he is dead'—and Sigerist (1970) cites examples of this distinction in the Christian world as it expressed itself in the treatment of lepers, and he also provides instances of the distinction as it appeared among the Kubu of Sumatra where those with contagious diseases were treated as socially dead long before physical death arrived. Harvard (1960) overlaps the social/physical distinction with that between the natural and the unnatural and claims that in the medieval world two definitions of the unnatural were in operation: (1) natural (physical) death as opposed to unnatural (civil) death which occurred on outlawry or on taking holy orders; and (2) natural (non-violent) as opposed to unnatural (violent) death.

Such overlapping of the unnatural with the violent persists in the modern world and looms large in Coroners' judgements, though the manner of the relationship between violence and unnaturalness is rather uncertain.[3] However, it is clear that in a wide variety of cultures there are many systems of classification for death and that, as Hertz has shown, they structure both perceptions of, and responses to the dead. The classification system which I shall concentrate on takes naturalness and unnaturalness as its central terms. The terms and the principles of classification are articulated through a series of political, clinical and legal contexts, and in order to comprehend the meanings of the terms and the practicalities of their utilisation I intend to turn to a closer examination of both the contexts and the verdicts which emerge from them.

THE CONCEPT OF UNNATURAL DEATH

Considering the significant role which the concept of natural death has played within the legal systems of the United Kingdom it is somewhat surprising to discover that the distinction between a natural and an unnatural death has never been embodied in law. Examination of the relevant Acts of Parliament relating to the work of Coroners shows that there are a great many issues on which the law is equivocal—not least of which is the status of verdicts. The nature of these equivocations is best demonstrated through an examination of both English and Irish law.

Until the passing of the Criminal Law Act (1977) English law as it related to Coroners was guided by the Coroners Act 1887 (50 and 51 Vict.). This required the Coroner to investigate a death whenever there was found:

> the body of a person who there is reason to believe may have died a *violent or unnatural death* or a sudden death the cause of which is unknown or has died in prison or in any place or circumstance which, under another act require an inquest to be held. [Emphasis added.]

But although the term and the concept of an unnatural death figured in the statute (and even more so in the practice of constituting verdicts) the act failed to provide any definitions. Nor did it provide a statement on the verdicts which could be brought in a Coroner's court. In fact it presumed what was subject to investigation and as the Brodrick Committee (1971) reported, the phrase 'violent or unnatural' was particularly unsatisfactory and yet indispensable to the work of the Coroner. Because English law contained no statements on appropriate verdicts there developed a set of rules for procedure. The Coroners Rules of 1953 contained a number of recommendations for verdicts, and we can perhaps glean something of the meaning of the terms natural and unnatural from the verdict categories. Fourteen verdicts are listed: Murder, Manslaughter, Infanticide, Killed himself, Attempted or self-induced abortion, Accident/Misadventure, Execution of sentence of death, Justifiable or excusable homicide, Natural causes, Industrial disease, Want of attention at birth, Chronic alcoholism/addiction to drugs, Aggravated by lack of care/self-neglect and Open. And, as one can see, this *pot pourri* of socio-legal and medico-legal distinctions contains a great many overlaps and ambiguities, not least of which are those contained in the term 'natural causes'.

In Ireland things were no clearer. The equivalent Coroners Act in Ireland was that of 1846 (9 Vict.) which also neglected to specify verdicts, and even neglected to mention naturalness. Despite this fact, however, Irish Coroners tended to draw exactly the same distinctions in practice as did their English counterparts. By 1959 Northern Irish law had advanced to a position where verdicts were specified in name if not in meaning and five possible categories were listed: Natural causes, Accident/misadventure, Died by his own act, Execution of sentence of death, and Open. These categories were once again replaced in 1980 by a system where the Coroner only provided a statement of 'findings' on the causes and circumstances of a death (Elliott, 1981), though in practice the findings were and are written in the discourse of the verdict system.

These ambiguities of meaning were, for the most part, left untouched but Jervis did attempt to confront the issues of denotation head on. The ninth edition attempts at least nine definitions of the term unnatural, not all of which are positive. They include: violent death with and without human intervention—a peculiar death; one that is not natural—a death from homicide, drowning, poisoning or accidental injury; an unexpected, exceptional or extraordinary death—a death which cannot be satisfactorily explained by medical science; a suspicious death—a death which is not due to disease or old-age. And from this range of definitions as well as from various discussions on the concept which Jervis contains it becomes clear that all attempts to specify the meaning of unnatural death tend to reach an ambiguous end, so that in effect the only means of gaining any insight into the term is to study the manner of its use; that is, to study the contexts of death in which the term natural has been used, as well as those in which some other term has been used, and to assume that what is not referred to as natural is thereby unnatural. By carrying out such an exercise we will see the nature of the categorisation process at work and we will notice that despite the prevailing ambiguity there is a logic in operation which lies beyond and behind the statute law and on which the law itself rests.

THE BODY NATURAL AND THE BODY SOCIAL[4]

An inquest is always on the body of the deceased and according to Hunnisett (1961) the body has been awarded a pivotal position in inquest procedure ever since the office of Coroner was first instituted. A body for Coroners' purposes, however, is as much a theoretical as it is a physical entity (see Jervis, 1957:69–73).

The centrality of the body to Belfast Coroners past and present can be evidenced in numerous ways. The depositions of the Carrickfergus Coroner (who was the Coroner for Belfast during the last century), for example, are clearly marked in heavy print, 'An Inquest on the Body Of . . .'. The jurors were expected to view the body 'there and then lying dead', the local doctor surveyed the body, the Coroner himself examined the body, the relatives identified the body, and all this observation was organised in terms of a statute law which sited the body at the hub of the investigative process. These various observations were designed to discover the nature of death as it rested 'in' the corpse, but any reading of these same depositions will quickly make apparent that the inquest was as much an enquiry into social relationships as it was into the somatic causes of death. In other words the jurors, the coroner and the doctor were as much concerned with the social characteristics of the deceased and the history of his/her social relationships as they were with the appearance of the human organism. Thus, JJ who was found suspended from a rope in a cowshed on the morning of 10 August 1888 was subjected to a primitive form of social autopsy through which it was determined that 'for the past number of years [he] had been in a silly harmless way'. Whilst CC, 'there and then lying dead', apparently died of a broken heart 'consequent on grief for the loss of her son'. G.M., on the other hand, was 'well known' and had often threatened to cut his own throat before being found drowned on the morning of 5 June 1894. And deliberations such as these are equally evident in contemporary enquiries. Thus, in my own, albeit crude, analysis of Coroners' summary statements on 98 inquests held in Belfast during 1982 (representing 50 per cent of all inquests), the Coroner referred to a wide range of personal detail from the past lives of his subjects and left virtually no aspect unobserved. For example, in only 34 cases was the summary statement written solely in terms of the immediate circumstances surrounding the deaths, and these were mainly deaths from road accidents and homicides. For the remainder, the Coroner's eye passed over such things as : drinking and eating habits (cited in 24 cases), physical living arrangements (17), previous illnesses (16), family relationships (7), emotional states (6), sleeping habits (5), political beliefs (4) and leisure interests (4). This was apart from the routine collection of data on marital status, occupation, social class, age, place of residence and place of death. And whilst this cannot be regarded in any way as a rigorous and exhaustive analysis of the issues which Coroners routinely examine, it does provide some measure of the breadth and depth of their vision. The most forceful expression of this vision, however, was undoubtedly that represented in the demands of Weisman and Kastenbaum (1968) for the psychological autopsy: that is, a meticulous reconstruction of the psychological and social factors which surrounded the death of any given individual.

Foucault, albeit in another context, has spoken of the political significance of inquiries such as these as well as of the significance of the 'case' and the 'case history' in general. He states:

the child, the patient, the madman, the prisoner were to become, with increasing ease from the eighteenth century and according to a curve which is that of the mechanisms of discipline, the object of individual descriptions and biographical accounts. The turning of real lives into writing is no longer a procedure of heroization, it functions as a procedure of objectification and subjection. The carefully collated life of mental patients or delinquents belongs . . . to a certain political function of writing. (Foucault 1977a:192)

In the Coroner's court, then, medical and social evidence is in a sense fused in an exercise of power so as to make sense of sudden death. It is to the nature of this social evidence which I shall now turn, for there is little doubt that the social characteristics of the dead were and are used to reach satisfactory conclusions about the naturalness or otherwise of death.

The study of unnatural death has, for most of the 20th century, been dominated by the study of suicide. Indeed it is hard to think of a study of unnatural death in the sociological tradition which has not been concerned with suicide (though both Bohannan (1960) and Lane (1979) have carried out studies with a somewhat wider compass). This domination by suicide of sociological studies of unnatural death has created a legacy of misunderstanding and misperception about sudden death which it is hard to overcome. These misunderstandings have been compounded over the years by the persistent belief that unnatural death and social, or personal, 'disorganisation' exist within some kind of causal nexus. Indeed when Durkheim picked up the problem of suicide in the 1890s it was already neatly ensconced in a tradition which saw in suicide rates a sound index of the moral weakness of social groups. And Durkheim did little to disabuse the world of such a notion. On the contrary, by linking suicide rates with divorce rates, single status, widowhood, urban life and social integration in general, he more probably bolstered claims that 'social disorganisation' and unnatural death were somehow linked. Indeed the empirical element of Durkheim's investigation is well summed up in the following statement:

We have thus successively set up the three following propositions:
    Suicide varies inversely with the degree of integration of religious society. Suicide varies inversely with the degree of integration of domestic society. Suicide varies inversely with the degree of integration of political society. (Durkheim, 1952:208)

For a large number of researchers who followed Durkheim these generalisations were taken as truths to be confirmed, rather than theses to be questioned (see Riley, 1983). And it is certainly the case that such people as Halbwachs (1978), and other researchers in the same tradition saw these variations in the light of a causal model in which age, sex, marital status, area of residence and so on were assumed to be the variables which caused people to commit suicide rather than as cues by means of which sudden deaths were interpreted as suicides by significant others (see Douglas, 1967).

Suicide, of course, is not coextensive with unnatural death, but the kind of evidence which the suicide researchers amassed, taken in conjunction with the pejorative connotations of the term unnatural—suggesting as they do, elements of deviance—tempts one into the belief that among those deemed to have died unnaturally one would expect to find a preponderance of people in socially marginal positions; that is, for the single and widowed to appear more frequently than the married, for the unemployed to appear with greater regularity than the employed, vagabonds and hawkers to appear more frequently than accountants and priests, and altogether those who lived in peripheral social roles to be overrepresented compared to those who, in Durkheimian terms, could be considered as being well integrated into social life. Such expectations are not, however, fulfilled in this study, but I can demonstrate the existence of a distinct social profile among the unnaturally dead. And I will do so not so much in order to explicate the components of some causal model for unnatural death, but rather to demonstrate two features concerning the nature of medico-legal classifications. Firstly, to show that social characteristics are used as interpretative cues for investigating *prima facie* cases of unnatural death and, secondly, to demonstrate the way in which investigative and inquisitorial power is distributed across the society of the dead.

By social characteristics I mean, of course, to refer to such variables as age, sex, social class, marital status and religious affiliation. The analysis of the ways in which such factors are associated with unnatural death will not provide an answer to our central problem concerning the meaning of 'natural' and 'unnatural' death, but it will go some way to demonstrating that the way in which death is assessed does have a relationship to basic social attributes.

Eighty-eight of the cases included in my 1981 sample of the dead were certified by the Belfast Coroner. And, needless to say, certification by such a source suggests some element of impropriety about the deaths in question. In a few cases it may have been nothing more than the fact that the deceased had not been seen by a medical practitioner during the 28 days preceding death. More likely it was because there was something unexplained or unexpected about the death. In any event the Coroner usually investigates only those cases which represent a *prima facie* instance of unnatural death and it is in this sense that we can ask some initial questions about who it is that dies such deaths.

I commence the analysis with what appears to be a simple and uninteresting observation, namely that in the Coroner's court male subjects are disproportionately represented on the case register. Table 3.1 indicates the extent and strength of the association between gender and a *prima facie* claim to unnatural death.

TABLE 3.1   *The relationship between sex, age of deceased and certification by Coroner in sample of 415 deaths. Belfast 1981*

			Certified by Coroner		
	Females			Males	
Age	%	N	Age	%	N
0–19	33	6	0–19	50	10
20–59	46	28	20–59	52	29
60+	11	189	60+	22	153

At this stage we could no doubt advance a series of *post hoc* explanations as to why this association exists. We could try to explain it in terms of the social distribution of violence, or through postulating that men die suddenly with a greater frequency than do women, or we may even be tempted to attribute the differences to varying life styles, consumption of alcohol and so on. It is impossible to dismiss every one of these reasons as being without foundation in fact, but it is clear that they cannot account for the distinct patterns which emerge in the analysis of the sample population. Table 3.2, for example indicates the distribution of cases for (1) all non-violent causes of death and (2) for deaths from circulatory conditions in which most 'sudden' and 'unexpected' deaths are to be found. Thus, if we exclude cases in which death was caused by Injuries and Poisons—eliminating the WHO (1977) causal category which contains homicides and other forms of violence— the percentage of males certified by the Coroner diminishes, but a significant over-representation persists. And male predominance even persists if we control for diseases of the circulatory system. Indeed it seems more plausible to conclude either that male deaths are more likely to be regarded as unnatural *per se* or that males are, in general, more likely to die 'suddenly and unexpectedly' which is itself a socially structured judgement.

TABLE 3.2 *The relationship between sex of deceased and certification by Coroner in (1) all cases of non-violent death and (2) deaths from circulatory disorders, in a sample of 415 deaths. Belfast 1981*

		Certified by Coroner			
Death from non-violent causes					
Females	% 13	N 215	Males	% 21	N 176
Death from circulatory disorders					
Females	% 19	N 106	Males	% 31	N 110

This marked prevalence of a socially dominant group raises the possibility that judgements concerning unnatural death are always more frequent among those segments of the population which are, so to speak, over-valued, and always less frequent among those segments which are undervalued. If this were the case, then we might expect there to be an over-representation of Protestants among Coroners' cases in Northern Ireland (there is, of course, usually a predominance), an over-representation of middle class dead, an over-representation of those in the economically active age-groups, and in so far as marriage is taken to be an index of integration and stability, a relative preponderance of married people.

TABLE 3.3 *The relationship between occupational class, age and certification by Coroner in a sample of 415 deaths. Belfast 1981*

	Certification by Coroner				
	Non-manual			*Manual*	
Age	%	N	*Age*	%	N
0–19	0	1	0–19	46	15
20–59	56	18	20–59	46	39
60+	15	98	60+	16	244

Public Discourse

Unfortunately, and as Tables 3.1 to 3.4 indicate, the patterns which emerge from the data are not as neat and clear cut as one would like. The relationship to age, for example, is a clear one. Table 3.1 demonstrates that those in the economically active age-groups have a far greater chance of having their deaths investigated by the Coroner than do the over 60s. Moreover, we cannot account for this pattern by controlling for violent deaths. On other fronts, however, the picture is obscure. There is, for example, no clear relationship between occupational class and the expenditure of investigatory resources. And although there is a relationship between marital status and certification it waxes and wanes according to the age distribution of the sample population. (Nor does the distribution of investigatory resources bear any relationship to the denomination of the deceased).

TABLE 3.4   *The relationship between marital status, age and certification by Coroner in a sample of 415 deaths. Belfast 1981*

	Certification by Coroner					
	Married				*Single/Widowed*	
Age	%	*N*		*Age*	%	*N*
20–59	40	37		20–59	59	17
60+	19	126		60+	13	192

Marital status unrecorded in 43 cases

Age and gender, then, do seem to have an effect on whether or not a death is investigated by the Coroner. Though we have to recall that not all deaths so investigated result in the conclusion of 'unnatural death', and most of those who go before the Coroner are deemed to have died naturally. As I demonstrated in an earlier paper (Prior, 1985a), however, an age and gender bias in the distribution of 'unnatural causes' verdicts does exist in Irish Coroners' courts and seems to have persisted throughout most of the 20th-century. In other words, being a male in the 20–59 age group increases one's chances of being regarded as having died unnaturally. There are, of course, all manner of contingent reasons why a death is or is not regarded as unnatural and it is impossible to analyse such reasons in a quantitative fashion. But there is one piece of evidence which can be taken into account – place of death. Those who die 'unnatural' deaths are more likely than not to be found dead at home or in the street, rather than in hospitals or nursing homes. The oddities of place are therefore taken into account in assessments concerning the naturalness or otherwise of any given death, but once again we would be foolish to believe that a factor of this nature would in itself contain the hallmark of the phenomenon or, indeed, serve as a useful predictor of unnaturalness; it does not, as Table 3.5 shows. Indeed, despite all of our data on the subject, we have still taken only a few steps towards a thorough understanding of the initial problem. At this stage we can say only that the unnaturally dead are more likely to be drawn from males in the economically active age groups. The hallmarks of unnaturalness, however, reside far outside of these characteristics and within a classificatory system whose logic it is now necessary to examine.

TABLE 3.5   *The relationship between gender, place of death and certification by Coroner in a sample of 415 deaths. Belfast 1981*

Females			Males		
Place of death	%	N	Place of death	%	N
At home	26	65	At home	34	62
In hospital/ nursing home	9	150	In hospital/ nursing home	18	117
Elsewhere	63	8	Elsewhere	85	13

(column header: Certification by Coroner)

THE LOGIC OF CLASSIFICATION

I stated at an earlier point that the sociological study of unnatural death had been dominated by the study of suicide, and attention was drawn to the way in which causal sequences had been read into the social characteristics of victims; Durkheim (1952), Halbwachs (1978), Baechler (1979), all follow this causal path. What was not mentioned was that the other important trend in research took the social ascription of motives as the central problem, and sought to understand how suicide was imputed to some dead and not to others. This second trend was instigated by Douglas (1967), and Garfinkel (1967a), and pursued at later dates by such investigators as Atkinson (1978) and Taylor (1981). Atkinson, for example, claims that suicide is imputed on the basis of (1) notes and threats (2) mode of death (3) location and circumstances of death, and (4) biography of the deceased. Whilst Taylor lists (1) state of mind prior to death (2) mental and physical health (3) social problems

(4) life history and (5) what he calls normality of place. Both researchers were keen to underline the fact that the social ascription of suicidal motives was achieved on the basis of individualistic and subjectivist modes of interpretation, and both authors cite instances of the occasional eccentricities involved in such a process. But what they failed to point out was that this problem of motives is a secondary process and is in fact dependent on some earlier decision to site any given death in terms of a categorisation system which is built on the dichotomy between the natural and the unnatural. In other words, a death must first of all be allocated to the unnatural realm before it has any chance of qualifying for the title of suicide. And the categorisation process at the base of such a decision lies not in the eccentricities of individual investigators, but within a public system of discourse operated by Coroners. The constitutive rules of the classificatory system are not, however, always discursively available. They are drawn on and utilised almost unconsciously and exist as an element of what Giddens (1979) has referred to as practical consciousness. It is to the examination of these constitutive rules that I shall now turn.

W.D., aged 59, lived alone and died sometime during the middle of May. About a month later his decomposing body was found on the floor of his living room by police who were investigating a burglary at the house. Death was attributed to a coronary thrombosis and the Coroner concluded that it was a natural death.

P.R. was 32 years old. He collapsed at home and died in hospital the same day. No anatomical cause of death was discovered, but the Coroner nevertheless attributed death to 'a defect in conduction of the heart' and concluded that it was, after all, a natural death.

W.I. lived alone. He was an alcoholic and his landlady found him dead in bed at 19.00 hours on 17 October. The cause of death was determined as hypothermia and the Coroner concluded that the death was unnatural.

Baby T died on 21 June in the City Hospital. He was 12 hours old. The cause listed was 'unexplained', but as with other unexplained infant deaths there was no inquest and the death was regarded as entirely natural.

On the face of things, these are peculiar, puzzling and perhaps even suspicious deaths. In two cases at least they cannot be satisfactorily explained by the canons of medical science and their unexpected and sudden character mark them all down as plausible candidates for unnaturalness. And one assumes that it was precisely for such reasons as these that they (the adults at least) were subjected to scrutiny by the

Coroner. Yet scrutiny revealed only naturalness and the reason why this was so holds the key to the nature of the Coroner's categorisations.

It is clear from these four examples that suddenness, strangeness of place or time or other problematic features of a death are not in themselves unnatural (despite the claims of Jervis). Yet the practical rules by which these deaths were classified *are* embedded in the case summaries and are part of the framework through which Coroners organise their findings. The rules and the framework, however, are not explicitly formulated and operate as something akin to what Goffman (1974) has called primary frameworks.

Goffman in fact distinguishes between two types of framework. The first he calls natural, in which events are seen as the result of unguided, unmotivated and purely physical processes. And the second he calls social, in which human agency, will, motivation and purpose are embedded. The same set of events can be interpreted in either a natural or a social framework, and both may incorporate concepts of causation, though with entirely different meaning.

Referring back to our examples, we can now see that three of the four deaths in question were slotted into a natural framework because disease and illness, which are seen as purely physical processes in western culture, were believed to be present in the bodies of the deceased. Disease naturalised their deaths and did so by eliminating human agency, so that with the naturalisation of the deaths the efficacy of any agents who may have been involved in the events preceding death was removed. Where disease exists, motives, will, purpose and agency are held to be absent, and this decontextualisation or dethematisation of disease marks death as natural.

This equivalence of disease and naturalness is not, however, the only principle which has been involved in the Coroner's classificatory system. The 19-century Coroner, for example, maintained a further source of naturalness, namely, God. 'Visitation of God' was a common cause and mode of death prior to the 1887 reforms, and such visitation covered all kinds of deaths where human agency was apparently absent from the causal process, and especially those where disease was not present (though it was also used to account for the apparent arbitrariness of mortal illness). This slot, once occupied by God, seems now to be occupied by the concept of 'Accident', and the use of this term brings in its train special problems. Figlio (1985) has argued that accident is a concept which arises only with a contract society, that is, a society in which human relationships are embroiled within and viewed as components of formal contracts rather than as freely motivated and casually constructed events. Figlio, of course, was interested in the examination of industrial 'accidents' where the recourse to chance as a source of explanation often benefitted employers. But in researching the social basis of the concept of accident we must not overlook the fact that it is a concept which could only gain widespread acceptance in societies where the doctrine of Providence had withered, that is, in those societies where the image of an omnipotent and omnipresent God had disappeared.

However, and to return to the issue at hand; if the insertion of an acting human subject into an explanation turns the death into an unnatural event, then the presence or absence of intent (malice) has further consequences. Deaths in which intent is present are usually categorised as suicides, homicides, infanticides or acts of war; whilst unintentional events are usually called accidents or misadventures. The problem is that the removal of intent leaves the death in Limbo whereby proximate causes stemming from human intervention are recognised but are, at the same time, robbed of their guided quality. 'Accident' is therefore something of a sociological hybrid which places death in a purposive setting but removes efficacy from the human agent. It is therefore a term which is especially suited to the explanation of occupational diseases and 'industrial accidents', and its use is also clear in cases of therapeutic misadventure where deaths are, by the very rules of contemporary nosologies, classified according to the underlying disease condition which necessitates the intervention of medical treatment rather than to the treatment itself. The social ascription of intent, then, has significant sociological, legal and moral consequences. And the erasure of intent, and the placing of social action in parentheses often serves to garb the death in a false cloak of naturalness. Indeed, it would seem that accident verdicts are frequently unsatisfactory attempts to come to terms with human agency, for when one examines the detail of the cases involved one realises that it is often possible to categorise the deaths in more precise language—for example, as due to industrial processes, lack of warmth, activity of the police, or negligent (drunken) driving. Coroners can, and do, attempt to mask the presence of social structure and the social action which lies behind the cases in which they are involved by using both the adoption of natural frameworks and the catch-all of the accident verdict.

One group of deaths which exhibits the interplay of these numerous considerations and which demonstrates the ways in which frameworks are central to the classification, perception and response to death is that of sudden infant deaths. Sudden neonatal and postneonatal deaths used to be categorised as unnatural, but in more recent times they have been reclassified as natural deaths despite the fact that they remain puzzling, unexpected and unexplained events (see Knowelden, 1985). In the pre-1941 era such deaths were described much as in the following cases which I have drawn from the Coroner's case books of 1888 and 1921.

Samual Tipping. Age: 7 weeks.
Son of a Linen Finisher.

Died on the morning of July 14th from being accidentally overlain.

Patrick Rice. Age 3 months.
Son of a Labourer.

Found dead in bed on January 19th, and that the cause of death was asphyxia due to bedclothes accidentally getting over his face.

The mothers of these children were understandably at pains to point out that being overlain was not possible, or that the coverings over the baby were so light as to negate any possibility of the baby being smothered, or even that the straw bedding could not in any sense account for the baby's death. Such denials of negligence were readily accepted by the Coroner, but as disease was not found to be present in the bodies of these children their deaths could not therefore be allocated to the natural realm. On some very rare occasions sudden deaths were mistakenly attributed to a disease category (status lymphaticus) in which event they were naturalised and all references to human agency were thereby removed. But it is only in the most recent samples of deaths that such cases of mortality are consistently regarded as natural—though they still cannot be accounted for. This somewhat late recognition of naturalness is primarily due to the medicalisation of the deaths in terms of a syndrome (SIDS), which was first recognised in the 1950s but not officially reported on in the UK until 1965 (see OPCS, 1982).

Such a reclassification of infant deaths provides a model for understanding the way in which deaths are classified into either one of the two great orders and we can safely assume that any form of death which is today regarded as unnatural would quickly be reallocated to the natural realm were it to be attributed to disease factors (and the converse of this is also true). But this supposition raises a further set of questions concerning the locus of causes and what is and what is not, in the words of Jervis, a 'real' cause.

THE DETHEMATISATION OF DEATH

The deletion of human agency naturalises death and the deletion of intent morally neutralises it and relegates it to a limbo in which the proximate causes are agreed on, but the contingency of the event is left to 'chance'. The erasure of agency from explanations of death does not, of course, occur solely in the discourse of the Coroner's court. To the contrary, and as I have shown in the previous chapter, it seeps through the entire network of rules and practices through which death is comprehended in western society. Thus, social actors, and social action are consistently deleted from the categories into which death is sorted, as well as from the nosological rules of modern medicine, and even from the language of aetiology itself.

This naturalisation of the categories for death extends far beyond the language in which individual deaths are explained. I have already demonstrated how, to the Irish Coroner at least, active human subjects were once encompassed in the very taxonomy of death as well as within the specific accounts of his enquiries. Deaths due to 'unskilfull medical treatment', 'want of the common necessaries of life', 'intemperate living and drinking' all figured in the published accounts of the last century. And this terminology was used in the context of a discourse which linked death, disease and illness to the social, economic and political environments in which they occurred. The same concern to draw links between disease and socio-economic conditions is equally evident in the 19th-century reports of the Registrars General (to which I have already made reference), where the statistical summaries of mortality are prefaced with lengthy remarks on the 'Prices of Provisions, and Pauperism', the availability of fuel and the severity of the weather, as well as on all manner of conditions which affect the well being of the human body.

It would seem, however, that this form of humanistic reasoning was eventually buried beneath the claims of modern pathology. Henceforth, human mortality and its attendant illnesses were increasingly described in the framework of 'disease'. Indeed, in the present age the Coroner's office claims only to comment on the pathological causes of death without reference to its broader context. Such a strategy marches closely in step with the demands of a clinical medicine which has consistently sought to expel humanistic terms and humanistic thinking from the nosologies through which death is sifted. These days one would be hard pressed to discover such phenomena as senility, hunger or poverty cited as causes of death in any influential nosology concerned with the aetiology of disease, and certainly not in the Manual of the International Statistical Classification of Diseases, Injuries, and Causes of Death.

This suppression of social action and social structure in explanations of death is evident, for example, in descriptions of deaths due to the use of 'plastic bullets' by the Northern Ireland police. The fate of one such victim was initially explained in the following manner:

Cause of Death:

I (a) Bruising and Oedema of Brain associated with Fractures of the Skull.

Such a relegation of the socially relevant cause to the realm of somatic conditions was deemed to be unsatisfactory by the relatives of the deceased. A redefinition of the cause of death, brought about after legal action, resulted in the following conclusion: 'Died as a result of injuries received after having been struck by a plastic bullet, and we believe her to have been an innocent victim', which, within the constraints of permissible language, highlights the markedly different frames of thinking adopted by the parties involved. Similar concerns arise in other cases, such as those described by Weir (1983) and Scraton (1984). In like manner many of the cases taken up by the pressure group *Inquest* display features of the struggle to choose a socially relevant cause of death drawn from a framework other than the clinical one which is so much favoured in contemporary Coroners' courts. And the power and importance of clinical discourse to redescribe cases of industrial disease is also apparent in many studies (Davis, 1976).

So, despite the claims of those Coroners who maintain that accounts of death are set in a language which is neutral and objective, it is clear that the description and explanation of death occurs in a setting and a discourse which is beholden to pathology. Pathology hands down to us our prevailing concepts of disease, illness and death, together with explanatory principles which disembody and decontextualise the latter from social and economic circumstances. It is a discourse geared towards the technical principles of calculation and control, and one which consequently restricts human agency to ever diminishing circles of influence.

I commenced this chapter with a quote from Mary Douglas which pointed us towards the realisation that disorder can only occur in a framework of order, pollution only in a framework of purity and, by implication, unnaturalness in a framework of naturalness. The order of

things, however, is not natural. We do, of course, order the world
according to categories that we take for granted, but when we are
confronted with an alien way of organising experience we come to
recognise the arbitrariness of our own classificatory schemes. It is a
point well made and well emphasised by Foucault in his 1970 work,
which he opens by describing a classificatory system for a Chinese
encyclopaedia imagined by Jorge Luis Borges. The classification is
significant, says Foucault, simply because of the impossibility of
thinking it.

It is not so impossible to conceive of natural and unnatural deaths, but
the division is still arbitrary and dependent on a peculiar understanding
of the distinctions between disease and society. Thus, by siting death
within a world of illness and disease the Coroner can normalise and
naturalise the cases of death which come before him. Any deaths which
escape naturalisation by being sited in a context of disease can be
cleansed of all references to their human origins by the use of the concept
of accident. Chance and disease in tandem are thereby used to account
for the sources of death in the modern world; and scientific medicine
comes to control and regulate all that we know about our manner of
dying.

4 The Pathology of Death

DEATH, DISEASE AND THE MORTUARY

Cause and mode of death are the twin pivots around which the public discourse on death circulates and one of the most important organisational settings in which causes and modes of death are determined is the mortuary. It is there, more than anywhere, that the true facts of death are supposedly revealed, and it is there more than anywhere that contemporary theorisations of disease are visible.

The Oxford English Dictionary lists eight entries for 'mortuary', but none of them refer to it as a socio-medical institution. Even within the social sciences there is considerable ambiguity in the use of the term, so that it can refer to 'a building in which bodies are stored', or 'a place belonging to the dead', or simply 'anything associated with death', (Huntingdon and Metcalf, 1979). Yet none of the meanings fully grasps the nature of a phenomenon whose uniqueness rests in the fact that it is not simply a building where bodies are stored (though many mortuaries serve only this purpose), and still less is it a building where bodies are disposed of, but that it is a site where the investigative and explanatory power of the state is exercised over social beings. Indeed, I have previously argued (Prior, 1987) that the mortuary is, above all, a product of two great sets of forces. The first is that which generated the development of the modern state together with its ever growing concern with the minutest details of the lives and deaths of its subjects; what Foucault (1977) has referred to as the development of Panoptic technology. The second set of forces is that responsible for the development of clinical medicine and its consequent emphasis on the clinical gaze. Both of these forces converge in the mortuary and thereby manufacture it as a site for discovery and explanation. In a sense the mortuary is the place where the investigative powers of the state and the explanatory principles of scientific medicine intermingle to police the dead. Here, however, I wish to emphasise and elaborate on theorisations of disease rather than of policing, and to describe how the mortuary is locked into the wider discourse on death, disease and causation with which we are directly concerned.

THE MORTUARY AS AN OBSERVATIONAL SITE

According to Ministry of Health Building Note Number 20, 1963 (MOH. 20), a mortuary is required so that:

(a) bodies may be kept until burial can be arranged; (b) the pathologist may investigate the causes of death, and make other scientific investigations; and (c) bodies may be viewed or identified by relatives and friends. (MOH. 20, 1963:1)

In fact, and as the sketch plan of the mortuary below indicates (Figure 4.1), there is provision for more than these three functions in any mortuary. Storage and dissection naturally loom large, but in addition there are offices where records and reports on the social identity of the deceased are kept, a chapel where religious services and viewing can take place and, in this case, a spectators' gallery from which the lines of affinity between death and disease can be studied.

In the ideal mortuary, the spatial arrangement of these functions should be such that each one is isolated from the other. Convenient and separate access should be arranged for the medical staff, visiting relatives, and undertakers, and 'the layout should ensure the correct internal arrangement of the rooms and the isolation of the several entrances for the different users; it should be made impossible for visitors to enter any other part of the mortuary by mistake' (MOH 20:15). Within the storage area there should be a space for each body, isolated, marked, and recorded in the written documents around which the mortuary circulates. Indeed, it is on these physical spaces that the therapeutic and administrative practices through which the system operates are articulated.

The internal isolation of parts also reflects the external isolation of the building from others in a complex. A mortuary is normally sited away from the hospital as a separate building in its own grounds. The entrance is screened from public view both to 'avoid upsetting the patients, and to deter the inevitable curious onlooker' (Knight 1984:3). Its location usually remains unreferenced, secret and unknown to the public. This isolation of the mortuary not only signifies the separation of functions which are performed within it, but further expresses the isolation of death in general. The modern mortuary is no longer a part of life and, like the cemetery before it, is frequently expelled beyond the city boundaries. Yet the activities which are carried out in this isolated and circumscribed world continue to have an important impact on the activities of the living.

For those who work in the mortuary one of the most fundamental of all issues relates to the identification of deceased persons. Identification of bodies and parts of bodies is work which dominates the daily routine of the mortuary and it is the process in which the interests of the state and

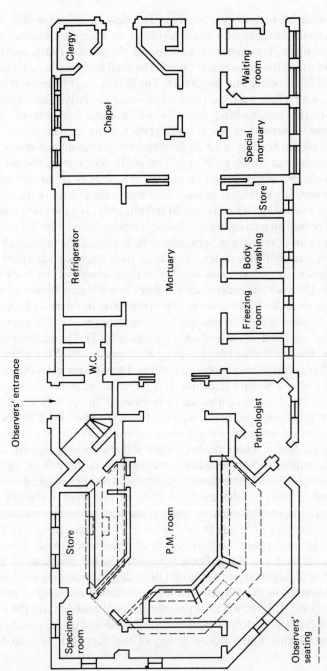

FIGURE 4.1 *Plan of Royal Victoria Hospital Mortuary*

the interests of pathology converge. The first questions which the attendant asks of those who bring bodies to the mortuary concern the name, age, place of residence of the deceased, the place of death, and the context in which the cadaver was found. The dead body has to be located in terms of time, place and procedure. The details must be entered in a Register, which forms a focal point of mortuary activity. The Register represents the bureaucratic space in which facts are ordered and systematised. According to Knight (1984), 'The central point of mortuary record keeping is the Register, which records all movement of bodies in and out of the mortuary' (1984:31). The corpse should be given a reference number, and an identity tag. 'It is essential that each body is positively identified as soon as it enters the mortuary' (Knight 1984:34). According to Emery and Marshall (1965:34), the body is and must be 'passed on by a continual chain of responsibility'. For the police also, the issue of identity is paramount. Rule one of the investigating officer's mortuary forms states, 'You must have the body identified to you in person so that you can identify to the pathologist the body on which the Coroner has ordered an autopsy'. It is not only bodies which cry out for identification—storage spaces must also be referenced. 'Each individual space should be marked for identification . . . it is usual to record the occupant of each space' (Knight 1984:5). The cadaver and the space it occupies thus adopt a 'thing-like' quality which is evident in many other forms of mortuary interaction. The cadaver is an object, a repository of disease and infection. It is a container, a shell; at once a solution to a riddle, and an obstacle to knowledge. In the daily life of the mortuary it is most commonly referred to as 'it'. The object becomes objectified in the acts of persistent observation. In the acts of discovery to come, the disease within the body itself will also be investigated, and thereby identified and on occasion marked clearly on the corpse. In the cases of those dying from radiation the forehead must be marked with a red adhesive disk; in the cases of those dying from Category A pathogens, the corpse must be clearly marked as being infectious. Identification thus proceeds from the outward surface features of the cadaver, to encompass first its social characteristics, and then its pathological features. Identification constitutes *the* problem of the mortuary and, according to Simpson (1975:20), the pathologist should 'exercise himself in the subject even when the actual necessity of proof does not arise'. It is, however, a two dimensional problem: on the one hand concerned with identifying the cause of death and on the other with the social identity and social location of the deceased. It is in the relationship between these two aspects of a single problem that the interests of the state intermingle with those of modern medicine.

As well as recording the identities of the corpses, the Register must also record the identities of those who bring and remove bodies from the building. The Mortuary book must, in addition, record the names of those who execute the autopsy on the body, as well as those who may be present as observers. Any specimens or organs removed from the cadaver must also be referenced and identified through the accounting mechanism. In most cases these issues of identification are regarded as routine. The corpse is known, the name is known, the age, the place of residence, the site of death are known and need only be recorded.[1] On entry to the mortuary, the body is usually weighed and measured, and the details recorded in the mortuary book. A visual inspection of the body is made in a search for abnormalities, and in these acts of measurement the secrets of death are often revealed. But for each 'case' there is a 'history', and this must also be noted down. The police and the relatives, as well as general practitioners, can all serve as potential sources of information for the biography of the uncertified corpse, though it is only after extensive observation of the dead that the living will be questioned about the history of the case, and it is assumed that in this regular alternation of speech and gaze the true causes of death will emerge unblemished. But it is clear that in the interrogatory scheme of contemporary pathology the pathologist is forever forced out beyond the livid body, and beyond the mortuary walls, into the social, occupational and political world in which the deceased once lived, and it is in this alternation between the cadaver and its social history that we can locate the field in which a political anatomy of the body and a vocabulary of causation is elaborated.

Though identity is central to the daily routine of mortuary work, it constitutes but one of many fundamental concerns, not least of which is the attention paid to the visual appearance of the corpse throughout the time in which it exists within the mortuary. At first the visual appearance of the corpse is considered in an attempt to discover the 'abnormalities of anatomy'. According to Knight (1984:157), 'external examination is the responsibility of the pathologist, who should examine the whole body surface for abnormalities'. At this preliminary stage the appearance of the body is of importance only in so far as it may yield some clues as to the cause of death. This emphasis on the visuality of pathological features is sustained throughout the post-mortem examination, but once the necropsy has been completed visuality reappears in a different context. For, after the medical examination, one of the most important jobs of the post-mortem technician is to restore the body to as good a condition as possible before it is returned to the relatives. The technician must have due regard to the effects of incisions on the later appearance of the corpse. The empty body shell must be reconstituted. 'Special efforts should be made with children and babies to restore the body as carefully as is humanly possible' (Knight, 1984:177). In reconstitution, a 'natural' appearance should be aimed at, the cheeks slightly reddened, and a restful pose should be created whenever relatives need to view the body. For it is, after all, on the dead body that our contemporary image of death and the hereafter is inscribed.

This network of identification, observation and restoration is also productive of a sentimental order. The introduction of relatives of the deceased into the mortuary occurs in specially managed settings. 'Viewing' usually takes place in the chapel, and according to MOH 20, 'The room should be attractively decorated and subdued lighting is recommended' (1963:53). In the normal routine of the mortuary, scant attention is paid to the emotional loss which death involves, but, in viewing, the technicians have to make emotional readjustments. Spontaneous bursts of emotion are regarded as a nuisance, and on occasion there is 'terrible trouble with relatives' who throw themselves on the body—women are regarded as especially emotional. MOH.20 (1963) approved the use of a glass partition from behind which viewing could take place, but in recent years the sentimental order has been somewhat reassessed. Knight (1984) suggests that relatives should be allowed to approach the body closely if they wish, and that the technician should permit parents to pick up and hug the dead baby when appropriate—an embrace of death which seems to signify a rearrangement of the bonds which exist between the living and the dead.

The mortuary, then, deals with many aspects of social being even though it centres on the physicality of the corpse. It is a socio-medical institution designed to seek answers to pathological problems in bodies, but it also has to concern itself with the social biography of the deceased, as well as with the emotional relationships created by the individuals who fall within its scope. The mortuary and the world beyond its walls co-exist in an uneasy relationship. The causes of death and the sources of abnormality are sought within the observational space which the mortuary creates, but the aetiology of death, and even the criteria of normality and abnormality cannot be discovered within its boundaries. In the next section I shall seek to demonstrate the truth of this claim.

THE NORMAL AND THE ABNORMAL

For many of those who move through the mortuary doors, the building is little more than a store house, a temporary resting place where the cadaver awaits the arrival of its next professional manager – the funeral director. But for others there follows a journey into the dissecting room; for it is only in the dissecting room that diseases are revealed and abnormalities are displayed. The dissecting room exhibits special and peculiar problems for sociological analysis, yet it is in this room that the practice of dissection and the discourse on pathology interpenetrate so as to locate the causes of human mortality. Here one witnesses two orders of dissection: the physical dissection of flesh and bone, and the theoretical/conceptual dissection which has long preceded the former. Both forms are said to rest on observation, and one of the prime problems of the mortuary as a locus for discovery is the way in which apparently neutral observation is structured. But it is not necessarily the sole problem, or even the most important, for there is a second theme which permeates the work of the dissecting room, and it is that of abnormality. The mortuary not only dissects, it also normalises and in so doing gives a vivid expression to a 20th-century theorisation of disease.

The privileged position of observation is readily asserted in pathology and anatomy. According to Willis (1950) pathology is largely an 'observational science', dependent on thorough examination and accurate description. The centrality of seeing is embodied in the very terms necropsy—to look at the dead, and autopsy—to see with one's own eyes. Even within anatomy itself, the act of seeing is highly valued. According to Zuckerman (1963), 'topographical anatomy is essentially a visual discipline'. One must see in order to understand. This act of seeing is, of course, the very hallmark of the scientific medicine which was developed by Bichat, Broussais, Corvisart, Laënnec and Virchow. Disease is located in bodies, organs and cells. There is no disease without a seat, no functional disorder without structural lesion. In the post-mortem records which have been preserved from the 19th century this golden rule is echoed loudly through the autopsy reports, even though it sometimes creates considerable problems for the observer. Here, for example, is an anonymous pathologist from the Armagh Lunatic Asylum seeking the signs of mania and epilepsy which had killed the patient: the extract demonstrates the dilemma:

According to Trousseau functional lesion cannot occur without tissue modification . . . Yet in this case death was preceded by a continuous series of epileptic seizures and post-mortem exhibited no symptoms which would have demonstrated the fact that epilepsy either caused death or was present during life. (PRONI. Hos/27/6/1)

The improbable: a disease without a seat, a cause without tissue modification. But what was it that was being observed, and what was the body on which the pathologist worked? In what sense could it, and can it, be seen?

In *The Social System* (1951) Parsons draws our attention to an important consideration of which anatomists seem to have been only dimly aware. It is that:

The body is no more a concrete ontological real entity than society. *Pari passu* the organism, as a boundary maintaining physio-chemical system, is in absolutely no sense more or less real than the system of action. (Parsons, 1951:542)

Opening up corpses may dissipate ignorance, but the seeing is nevertheless structured in accordance with theoretical presuppositions. The body does not merely confront the observer as a stark and undifferentiated mass, but as a predefined system. The body of *Grant's Anatomy* (Basman, 1971), for example, is dissected by regions and described by systems; the systems traverse and interlace the regions. The cadaver is apportioned into anterior and posterior, superior and inferior, the medial and the lateral. Its components are named and standardised in the *Nomina Anatomica*, they are normalised through the aegis of statistical anatomy, and its racial type is classified under the aegis of racial anatomy. But the textbook describes only average conditions of the body, 'the commonest may have less than fifty per cent incidence' (Basman 1971:10), and not only the anatomy of the corpse is pre-dissected by a conceptual system, so too is its physiology. One cannot see without prior analysis. According to a JAMA (1965) editorial on the autopsy, for example, one cannot see in the absence of the 'prepared mind, without which observations are quite sterile'. In other words the conceptual scheme constructs the object. The image of the body and its constituent organs alters with each conceptual revolution. The brain of Morgagni, or Golgi, is not therefore the same brain as was studied by Alzheimer, and that in turn is a different brain from the one which confronts the contemporary neuropathologist (Lantos, 1983). In the same way the physiology of the heart is not to be discovered in the heart but in the theoretical analysis which fashions the observations. Here the heart is viewed in terms of fibres, there in terms of cells (see James, 1982).

Now, according to both Ackernecht's (1967) and Foucault's (1973) analyses of 19th-century pathology, it was the problem of disease and its localisation which constituted the major feature of the discourse – the capacity to 'correlate symptoms with lesions', as Boyd (1943) put it. In the 20th-century, however, it is not the localisation of disease which puzzles pathology; in a sense it is not even disease *per se*, but rather the features of normality and abnormality. Muir expresses this principle as follows:

> Pathology . . . deals with anything abnormal, and the abnormalities in structure may not be attended by disease. (Muir, 1924. 1941:1)

Disease, then, has been edged off the centre stage and placed neatly in the wings. And here is Willis (1961) on the same theme:

> An orderly and systematic method [for pathology] should be carried out in three stages (1) recognition of any normal anatomy present (2) simple description of how the specimen differs from normal (3) pathological interpretation of the differences. (Willis, 1961:676)

This domination of pathology by the concept of the normal is also evident in the mortuary. Indeed, 'the pathologist in the mortuary does a dissection for the purpose of looking for abnormal anatomy' (Emery and Marshall 1965:1). Abnormalities of the external frame must be sought first. On dissection the organs must be weighed. According to Emery and Marshall (1965), 'one of the most important items of the dissecting room is the balance', for normality cannot only be seen, it can also be measured. The quantification of the normal constitutes one of the building blocks on which the mortuary rests. The normal brain, for example, weighs 1400g +/− 300g (male), 1300g +/− 300g (female). The normal male heart weighs 300g +/− 40g, the liver weighs 1600g +/ − 200g; the testes weigh 25g +/− 5g. The hypertensive heart is heavier than normal, the underutilised thyroid, on the other hand, has a low weight. And in this process of weighing, pathology expresses one of its most fundamental assumptions, viz. that the abnormal is nothing but a quantitative variation on the normal.

Disease is not caused by the acquisition of a new and different set of properties by the affected cell, but rather by quantitative alterations in existing functions and structures. (Grisham and Nopanitaya, 1977:1).

This thesis, which according to Canguilhem (1978) was introduced into France through the work of Comte, Broussais and Bernard, constitutes a dogma of pathology. 'There is nothing peculiar to disease', states Muir (1941), and so the components of the abnormal and the pathological can be discovered by measuring functions, or examining organic structure. This principle, moreover, forms not only a framework within which abnormalities can be assessed, but also reflects a nosography which directly confronts and contradicts that of the ontologists and thus serves to underline the central role of the mortuary and the laboratory in the architecture of modern scientific medicine. For, if the abnormal/pathological is nothing but a quantitative variation on the normal/physiological, then the mortuary can indeed release all the secrets of organic degeneration. There is no call and no need to look over the shoulder of the corpse to the world which exists outside the mortuary walls. But what if the pathological is something qualitatively different from the physiological? It would then constitute another type of normal, albeit measured in relation to another context. Thus, Canguilhem concludes that there is no fact which is normal or pathological in itself, and that in order to decide such issues one must look beyond the body:

> It seems very artificial to break up disease into symptoms or to consider its complications in the abstract. What is a symptom without context or background? What is a complication separated from what it complicates? When an isolated symptom or a functional mechanism is termed pathological, one forgets that what makes them so is their inner relation in the indivisible totality of individual behavior. The situation is such that if the physiological analysis of separated functions is known in the presence of pathological facts, this is due to previous clinical information, for clinical practice puts the physician in contact with complete and concrete individuals and not with organs and their functions. (Canguilhem, 1978:44–45)

Thus, it is always the intermediary of clinical practice, supplying as it does the environmental context in which an individual patient lives, which enables us to utilise the concept of the pathological. An organism which is detached, isolated, and decontextualised cannot generate its own evaluative principles. For Canguilhem, then, disease is another way of life and not a variation on the dimension of health. Such an ontological conception of disease—a conception whose basis was most effectively analysed by Faber (1923)—has, however, rarely been entertained in the pages of 20th-century pathology texts. In fact, following the post-war surveys of levels of arterial blood pressure and glycosuria found in the general population (and which demonstrated the ubiquity of abnormal rates—see Armstrong, 1983), the empiricism of modern pathology was vindicated, and the sharp distinctions drawn by the ontologists between health and disease finally collapsed.

Given the nosographical principles which pervade the mortuary there can be little doubt that it provides a mechanism for discovering the normal and the abnormal. It is equally beyond doubt that the findings of modern pathology have to be meshed into a set of broader social, moral and political concerns before adequate causal accounts of pathological states can be constructed. The inquisitorial exercises which occur in the interchange between pathologist and practitioner, police, or relatives constitute an element of this wider vista. In this interchange it becomes clear that the external context in which any given pathology is sited can provide not only some principles through which normality can be judged, but also some elements of an aetiological scheme. That is to say, in the search for the causes of pathological conditions the body proves to be deficient, and pathology is forced to look outside of the human frame for its causal factors. Thus Robbins *et al.* (1981), in their discussion of neoplasia, talk in a language of 'predisposing' factors and conditions: geographical and racial factors, age, nutrition, social and cultural influences. But rather than see this redirection of vision as a result of a conceptual switch, or a reconstruction of problematics, they talk of 'advances in knowledge' which have blurred the distinctions between nature and nurture—even in the consideration of 'genetic' diseases. In the same manner, we can see in the later editions of Muir's *Pathology* a rewriting of the aetiology which was offered in the first edition, so that he came to regard the environmental context in which pathologies and abnormalities occurred as 'predisposing and auxiliary causes' of pathological states. From both cases it is clear that at some point in the 20th century the somatic scheme of causation proved deficient in explanatory force and consequently the vocabulary of causation was redrafted.

The discovery of *the* cause of death is not, however, just a concern of mortuary pathology. It is also a concern of the political and legal agencies of the modern state within which the mortuary operates. In the language of pathology primary causes are necessarily sited in somatic structures and functions, but this emphasis on soma has always to be related to a network of legal, moral and political interests which lie beyond the mortuary gates. In fact, in order to formulate valid explanatory schemes, the findings of pathology have to be interwoven into a pre-existing field of political and legal practices, and within this field the human body is not and cannot be regarded as the alpha and omega of human existence. In order to demonstrate this simple point I am going to consider a case of death. It is in many ways unfortunate that this case is drawn from the register of forensic pathology, for it may be argued that in this instance the cause 'really was' located outside of the body in a way in which deaths from natural causes are not. The fact is, however, that it is only in cases of unnatural death that pathology is forced to spell out, exactly and precisely, its aetiological logic. Deaths from coronary thrombosis and carcinoma of the lung, are rarely elaborated on, and such conditions are regarded as self-sufficient causes which call for no further elaboration. But, as we know, the elaboration is there, it does exist within the textbooks; it is merely that no one sees fit to spell it out.

CASE 2722

The medical causes of death were given as:

(a) Acute Renal Failure.

(b) Hypothermia.

In itself this was regarded as an unsatisfactory explanation of the death by both the pathologist and the Coroner, so other investigations were instigated. The Coroner summed up his findings in the following manner, and it is instructive to note the detail.

The deceased was 91 years of age and lived alone. She was mentally alert, but very independent and refused offers of residential accommodation, meals on wheels, and attendance at day centre. A home help called on weekdays except public holidays, and her next door neighbour also called every day. A niece called twice a week to help with the shopping, and the local social services supervisor also called regularly. There was ample food, and several electric fires in the house, but despite pressure to heat the house she would only allow the room which she was using to be heated. The home help did not call on St. Patrick's Day, and when she arrived at about 7.30 a.m., next day she found the deceased lying unconscious on the cold kitchen floor. She was admitted to the X hospital and died five days later.

Given that the Coroner is concerned as much with the distribution of moral blame as with the analysis of cause, we can nevertheless see from this example that he focuses on a great deal more than mere somatic structure and function in the quest for causation. Personality traits, material artifacts, personal relationships and means of subsistence are all called on in order to make sense of the medical conditions listed above. Frequently it is argued that factors such as these are separate from cause, and that there is a distinction between cause and verdict, or cause and mode of death, but in reality the distinction does not hold. All of the aforementioned conditions are part of the great chain of causation which led to death, and the example underlines the ways in which the origins of death are understood by reference to factors which lie well beyond the boundaries of the mortuary. In other words, the vocabulary of causation is elaborated within a dual field: a medical field which seeks causes in bodily lesions, and a politico-legal field which seeks causes in social relationships. It is in the mortuary that these two fields are interconnected so as to formulate an official (state) account of life, death, disease and health.

PATTERNS OF OBSERVATION

The Anatomy Bill of 1829 delineated the unclaimed bodies of work-house, prison and hospital inmates as the most appropriate for feeding the voracious demands of the anatomy schools, and according to Knight (1980) it was the poor and the criminal who were first subjected to the pathologists' scalpels—perhaps in the hope of locating the causes of organic and social pathology within a single system (see Smith, 1981). Gradually, however, autopsy was used as a weapon in the analysis of all forms of disease and bodily disorder, and the use of the pathologico-anatomical method was thereby extended to cover a wider population. Indeed, this form of investigative power was eventually imposed on medicine itself in the form of medical audits and attempts to measure the accuracy of information contained in death certificates (see Chapter 5). It seems unlikely, however, that the elaboration of observational power represented by the use of the survey and the audit occurred in a random or arbitrary manner. Investigative resources generally (as criminologists are often keen to point out), are frequently structured in accordance with all manner of social and political interests, and there are few grounds for believing that the resources of pathology are any different in this respect.

In fact, it is more plausible to suspect that the observational method embodied in the autopsy is applied to populations in quite precise and specific ways, and though we may all have a chance of ending up on the mortuary slab, it is not necessarily an equal chance.

Who then, falls under the pathologist's gaze? In Belfast during 1982 there were approximately 900 cadavers sent to the city mortuary for storage or dissection. Of these some 680 fell under the tutelage of the city Coroner and it is this latter population which is of concern here. In fact, by imposing the tools of sociological observation on a population which has already fallen prey to the tools of pathology it becomes possible to discover the social characteristics of those who slide across the mortuary slab.[2] In this section, therefore, I hope to demonstrate some of the emergent patterns which arise in the exercise of observational and investigatory techniques.

In the discussion so far I have attempted to emphasise the fact that forensic pathology, as with other forms of social practice, is exercised within a specific ontological and epistemological field. Consequently, and in the light of this I have tried to discuss the role played by such basic concepts as identity, cause of death, normality and abnormality in modern pathology and its techniques of investigation. In addition to these basic concepts, however, there are others which I have not so far mentioned, and of the unmentioned concepts by far the most important are those of the natural and the unnatural. Forensic pathology is concerned with the investigation of unnatural death (see Brodrick, 1971), and it distributes its resources accordingly. Moreover, in tandem with a concern for the 'unnatural', is an interest in 'suspicious', 'sudden' or puzzling deaths. For the most part, the elements which determine what is and what is not unnatural, puzzling or suspicious depend on the very detailed circumstances of each death, but they also depend in part on certain rules-of-thumb concerning what is and what is not a proper age to die, or a proper place in which to be found dead, or a proper manner of dying. And, above all, they depend on whether or not fatal disease is 'found' to be present in the corpse. As far as *prima facie* cases of puzzling, suspicious or unnatural death are concerned, however, it is the rules-of-thumb which tend to determine selection for autopsy. The precise nature of such rules is not easy to uncover, though as far as death and dying are concerned there is some qualitative evidence (Sudnow, 1967; Glaser and Strauss, 1965) to suggest that medical resources for the dying, at least, are distributed according to principles of perceived social status, estimated social value and so on.

The distribution of autopsy as a method of investigation would pose little or no problem were it the case that all cadavers sent to the public mortuary were subject to dissection. Such is not, however, the case, despite the fact each one of the cadavers in the mortuary serves as a pointer towards a sudden, suspicious or unusual death. (For it is after all, only the 'unusual' deaths—that is, those which cannot be certified by a general practitioner or a hospital doctor—which are sent before the Coroner.) Yet, and despite the fact that there is a certain level of commonality among the deaths which are processed by the Coroner, not all of them are investigated in the same manner. There are, of course, all manner of contingent reasons why one body is autopsied whilst another is left untouched, but in addition to these reasons I intend to argue that there are broader trends of a social nature evident in the manner in which autopsy is applied. In fact, in the paragraphs which follow I shall attempt to advance two claims: that the use of necropsy is socially variable; and that the resources used for the investigation of death are structured as much in accordance with social and political values as medical or diagnostic concerns. Both points can be best made by examining the social characteristics of the population which falls within the jurisdiction of the mortuary technician.

In terms of the classificatory system as represented in the *Manual of the International Statistical Classification of Diseases, Injuries and Causes of Death* (WHO, 1977), the overwhelming majority (55 per cent) of the 168 deaths in the 1982 sample were eventually attributed to malfunctions of the circulatory system; some were attributed to the presence of neoplasia (3 per cent), some to respiratory conditions (7 per cent), some to disorders of the digestive system (6 per cent), and some to violence (23 per cent). For the purposes of this study I have defined a violent death in the widest possible terms, that is, as any death which carries an 'External cause of injury' code in the General Register Office (GRO) code sheets. The injury codes, or 'E' codes indicate that on the medical certificate of cause of death some mention has been made of an external injury, or poisoning or other activity which contributed to or was associated with the death.

In some senses, as I shall demonstrate below, the diagnostic factors associated with the deaths do have an influence on the decision as to whether autopsy is or is not an appropriate method of investigation for the death, but over and above these diagnostic criteria there appears to be some evidence for believing that non-clinical factors also play a part in the crucial decision.

The first and most prominent point of focus for pathology is the age of the deceased. As Table 4.1 shows, there is a strong correlation between

TABLE 4.1   *Distribution of autopsy by gender and age in a sample of 168 mortuary cases, Belfast, 1982*

| | Autopsied | | | | | |
| | Males | | | Females | | |
Age	%	N		Age	%	N
0–19	100	7		0–19	75	4
20–59	82	34		20–59	85	13
60+	60	58		60+	54	52

age and selection for autopsy. The numbers in the youngest age group are rather too small to provide us with firm conclusions, but it is nevertheless clear that autopsy is not an investigative method as widely utilised on the over-60s as it is on those in the economically active age groups. In part, of course, this is due to an accentuated interest in violence as a cause of death, but, as Table 4.2 suggests, even when we control for diagnostic category there is still a significant correlation between age of deceased and autopsy. Moreover, it is important to keep in mind that the deaths contained in Table 4.2 all occurred under roughly similar circumstances—that is, swiftly, suddenly and unexpectedly.

TABLE 4.2   *Distribution of autopsies by gender and age in 92 cases* of death from circulatory conditions.*

| | Autopsied | | | | | |
| | Males | | | Females | | |
Age	%	N		Age	%	N
20–59	64	14		20–59	75	8
60+	55	38		60+	45	31

*Table excludes one autopsied male aged seven years

I would argue first, then, that one social factor which enters into deliberations concerning autopsy is age. Age, of course, can also be viewed as a biological variable and in the modern world death is more likely to visit those in the very youngest and the very oldest categories than those who find themselves in between. Yet, the way in which we respond to the deaths of people in various age groups is inherently social. Infant deaths in the 19th-century would never have warranted the attention which is currently paid to them, and even in our own society the way in which we respond to the death of a new-born infant is markedly different from the response due the death of an older child (as I shall demonstrate in Part II). I would argue, therefore, that these tables reflect to a certain extent a difference in the social evaluation of the deceased. Thus, the deaths of infants and children are regarded as worthy of maximum investigative resources and the deaths of those in the working age groups as worthy of substantial resources. For the old, however, the extent of investigative coverage is not so great (and remember that this is a very special population), and I would argue that this is not simply because we expect the old to die, but rather that we have less interest in the myriad factors which presage their demise. It is after all, only comparatively recently that 'old age' *per se* was rejected by the World Health Organisation as a satisfactory cause of death (see (WHO, 1968).

Tables 4.1 and 4.2 also indicate the presence of another variation. It is a variation related to gender of deceased. This latter is by no means as large as the first and in any case we must take into account the fact that there is an inevitable correlation between age and sex. Nevertheless, we can see that for the over-60s, where the largest number of cases lie, the association between gender and selection for autopsy is a real one. In the higher age groups, at least, men are more likely to be autopsied than women and this kind of evidence squares neatly with the Coroner evidence which I discussed in Chapter 3.

The impact of violence on selection for autopsy is demonstrated in Table 4.3. As one would expect, a person who has died a violent death has a far higher chance of being autopsied than one who has not. Even here, however, there are some interesting variations with regard to sex and occupational class of deceased (though there were some cases which could not be satisfactorily classified for occupation). The tendency which is shown here to autopsy manual workers more than non-manual workers runs against the general trend of expending extra resources on the 'socially valued'. In fact, only for the violent group does the former tendency actually hold. Autopsy, it appears, is an instrument wielded predominantly on working class subjects.

In the light of this evidence I would argue that such factors as age, gender, occupation and marital status, in particular, are widely utilised as signifiers of potential pathological states. In other words, social factors are interwoven with clinical criteria in the selection of cases for autopsy and so, in its search for the origins of death, forensic pathology tends to reserve the scalpel as an investigatory instrument for distinct and specific segments of the population. In this respect it reflects the broad principles of selectivity which are utilised by the Coroner, and in the history of such selectivity ideas concerning the status of 'natural' and 'unnatural' death, 'sudden' and 'suspicious' death, and 'normal' and 'abnormal' death all serve to play a part. In addition, medicine itself constantly maps out new and specialised objects of clinical focus—here, for example, SIDS, there the premature death. And explanations of death once regarded as entirely satisfactory, such as 'immaturity' (in the case of infants) or 'cardiac debility' and 'myocardial failure' (in the case of adults) come to demand ever more exact specification. Such concepts as these, however, are grounded as much in social as in medical or legal discourse, and the investigative patterns evident in the mortuary reflect the social theorisations which are embedded in this vocabulary of human mortality. Above all, it is the corpse which serves as a point at which various forms of social, medical and legal interests converge. Indeed it is on the corpse that these interests and theorisations are articulated and it is through the interplay of such interests that a vocabulary of causation emerges to account for death and disease in the modern world.

TABLE 4.3 *Distribution of autopsies by diagnostic category, gender and occupational class in a sample of 168 mortuary cases. Belfast 1982*

			Autopsied		
Violent deaths			*Non-violent deaths*		
Male	%	N	Male	%	N
Non-Manual	100	6	Non-Manual	42	19
Manual	90	20	Manual	69	52
Female			Female		
Non-Manual	80	5	Non-Manual	50	22
Manual	78	9	Manual	58	31

THE DISEASED BODY

Foucault (1973) opens his study of the clinic with the following claim about the relationships which exist between disease and the human body.

> For us the human body defines, by natural right, the space of origin and of distribution of disease . . . But this order of the solid, visible body is only one way—in all likelihood neither the first, nor the most fundamental—in which one spatializes disease. There have been, and will be, other distributions of illness. (Foucault, 1973:7)

This discourse on the body, however, did not simply attempt to spatialise disease, it also attempted to define the space within which causality operated. Thus, the organ was not only a site of disease, but was, in addition, a causal site. It is this framework which is manifested in Muir's first edition of *Pathology*, and which was subsequently modified in an attempt to incorporate non-somatic factors into the aetiological scheme. As an example of this shift, it is instructive to analyse the changes which occurred in the aetiology of neoplasia. For, in line with the somatic principles mentioned above, 19th- and early 20th-century pathology located two forms of causal relationship: the first sought the origins of tumour growth in abnormal development, and hereditary transmission; the second located the origins in 'irritation'—an ill-defined concept which had only the vaguest reference to exogenous factors. Yet, from the late 1920s onward, there was a radical shift of vision in two respects. First, the principle of monocausality was rejected so that Muir, who was able to speak confidently of *the* cause of tumours in the first edition of his textbook, was forced to state in the third that, 'there is no one cause; there are many causes'. Secondly, pathology let into its ranks a Trojan horse called the carcinogenic agent. The latter is significant because it changed the point of focus from the internality of the body to the external world and, after initial experimental work had identified specific chemical compounds as carcinogenic agents, the pathologist's gaze was redirected out of the mortuary and into the world beyond: initially to the chemical world and thence to the social world. The early steps were somewhat tentative and Boyd (1943), for example, mentions 'social cancer' only briefly, but by 1950 Willis was able to devote a full section of his *Principles* to occupation, social class and tumours. This redirection of vision, however, cannot simply be seen as an advance in knowledge, for the evidence which related tumour growth to occupational activities had existed for well over a century, yet it was not satisfactorily integrated into the prevailing aetiological scheme until the prison house of assumptions which had been constructed around the discipline of pathological anatomy had finally been burst asunder.

Not only does the mortuary give expression to a theory of causation, however; it also reasserts medicine's reliance on a physicalist concept of disease. A concept which defines disease *via* the system of anatomy; and one which regards disease as a 'thing' whose presence can be made visible in the human form. It is a theorisation of disease which is blind to the fact that the latter is defined not just according to visible anatomical presence, but also according to clinical signs, forms of therapy, aetiology, distribution in the population at large, relationships with other diseases in a system, as well as pathological characteristics. Indeed, neither death, nor disease, nor the causes of death and disease can be located solely in human anatomy.

It may be objected that in studying the mortuary, and by taking forensic pathology as the test case, I am examining something of a medical dodo; that forensic pathology is the 'last outpost of the autopsy' (Wright and Tate 1980), and that it is the biopsy which now dominates pathology. The biopsy, of course, merely replaces the body with the cell as a causal space; but, more importantly, it is still true to say that pathology continues to revere autopsy as a prime technique of validation. Thus, in 1982, the Royal College of Physicians and the Royal College of Pathologists argued that in order to improve the reliability of medical mortality data, the number of deaths certified by means of necropsy ought to be significantly increased, thus reasserting their trust in this basic method of discovery and validation.[3] It is, after all, only autopsy which can reveal the nature of the 'silent diseases' which lurk within human anatomy.

5 Accounting for Death

THE GENERAL REGISTER OFFICE

Whilst the mortuary acts as a site where the causes of death and disease are discovered, the General Register Office (GRO) acts as a site where causes are tabulated and where patterns of mortality are revealed. It is in the GRO that the decisions made in the mortuary are summated and classified according to the various sections of the WHO nosology. In other words, the examination of the physical body is followed by an analysis of the social body and, in the language of Foucault (1979), a bio-politics of population supersedes a political anatomy of the human frame. In both cases, however, it is the individual corpse which acts as the point of articulation for social practices and medical theories. In both cases death is individualised, and in both cases the physical nature of death is given primary emphasis.

In this chapter I intend to analyse the processes through which the patterns of mortality which exist in Belfast come to be known and recognised, and to inquire into the epistemological basis of the material which is contained in the Annual Reports of the Registrar General; that is, to examine how an official agency of the state makes sense of the mortality which it surveys. In following through such an examination, I hope to analyse both the frames of knowledge and the social practices through which mortality data are sifted. And I shall argue that, in large measure, the picture of mortality which we receive from the annual reports is a product of the concepts and rules through which the raw data are collected and processed. For ease of analysis, however, I intend to concentrate on the organisation of just two types of data: medical cause of death and occupation of deceased.

Commenting on the patterns of death which occurred in Northern Ireland during 1981, the author of the Annual Report (DHSS, 1984) stated:

> Heart Disease continued to bear by far the greatest proportion of the total deaths; other diseases having a high proportion were cancer, cerebrovascular disease (mainly cerebral thrombosis and cerebral haemorrhage) and respiratory diseases. (DHSS, 1984:22)

The evidence on which this statement, and others like it, was based

87

was of the type which I have already discussed in Chapter 2, namely, the data contained on medical certificates of cause of death. And Table 2.1 illustrates quite clearly the ways in which death in Belfast was distributed across the various nosological categories; that is, 2046 deaths attributed to circulatory conditions, 844 to neoplasia, and 574 to respiratory conditions and so on.

This knowledge concerning the distribution of death and disease is often disseminated to the broader population through various newspaper reports and summaries. And the journalistic style of the latter often results in the production of such headlines as: 'Heart Disease Biggest Killer', 'Heart Disease and Cancer claim most victims', and the like. In fact, the popular image of death and its causes is largely fashioned through this disseminated information. More importantly, however, the data contained in the Annual Reports also forms the nub of many professional and epidemiological discussions of human mortality as well as the foundation of many popular or lay interpretations of death. In fact, the figures contained in the Reports are often taken and used as a basis for discussions on the causes of heart disease, the role of diet, occupation, physical exercise and the effects of living conditions on human health and mortality in general. Thus, both the Black Report (1980), and the Health Education Council's (1987) Report on health inequality used data of this type to formulate conclusions on the relationships between occupational class and human mortality. But, as I hope to demonstrate here, there is a danger in using the data thus, a danger which only becomes apparent when we examine the precise ways in which data are constructed.

MORE VOCABULARIES OF CAUSATION

Since 1864 the civil registration of deaths has been mandatory in Ireland. Informants are required to register a death within seven days of its occurrence. Normally a medical record of the cause of death will be completed either by a medical practitioner or a Coroner. In my sample of 415 deaths, about 21 per cent were registered by the latter. I have already discussed the format of the certificate and it is important to note at this point that the medical practitioner is required to state only the 'underlying cause of death', and to record the sequence of morbid events which is pertinent to the case at hand. A Coroner's certificate contains a similarly structured section for the medical cause of death (as do still-birth certificates), but has in addition a section where the Coroner can record his 'findings', that is, an account of what s/he regards as the relevant context in which the death occurred; though, as I have indicated previously, unlike medical investigators in many other countries, those in Northern Ireland do not provide 'verdicts' of the kind found in the English system.

On the presentation of either a medical certificate or a Coroner's certificate, the Registrar will record further details of the dead person on a death certificate. And it is necessary to note that all information relating to the age, sex, occupation, marital status and usual residence of the deceased is recorded on this second certificate. Put together, these certificates constitute the raw data from which statements about the nature, patterns and trends of mortality are made. Indeed, the bio-politics of population is founded on these documents.

I have already discussed and explained the discursive context within which causes of death are to be found, and in that discussion I have shown how emphasis is placed on locating physical lesions in anatomical sites. I have also demonstrated how the nosology within which mortality statistics are compiled and enumerated, reflects this basic and fun-damental premiss of pathological anatomy. In that sense, the body is the fulcrum of the investigative and bureaucratic system which surrounds the dead. More importantly, however, it also acts as the fulcrum for the investigative apparatus of much of modern epidemiology which tends to rely very heavily on the data which are provided in death certificates (see Black, 1980). But before I move on to discuss the work of the GRO in processing these data, I would like to digress somewhat in order to investigate a fundamental and crucial aspect of this investigative system—namely, the extent to which, within the rules and principles of pathological anatomy the data contained on death certificates are 'accurate'.

The problem of accuracy of cause of death certification is recognised as a component of the wider problem of diagnosis which is itself a well documented concern within clinical practice (Koran, 1975). The iden-tification of a cause of death has, however, its own peculiarities. The standard procedure for studies of the accuracy of cause of death certificates is to compare the statements cited on the death certificates with some other source of evidence—case notes, consultants' opinions and, most important of all, necropsy reports. Such comparative studies are designed on a prospective or retrospective basis and, invariably, wide discrepancies are discovered among the information contained in the various data sources. Normally necropsies are assumed to hold the true cause of death and the evidence obtained from them is then utilised as a

plumb line against which deviations in diagnoses are measured. A
concern to establish the parameters of error was first exhibited in the
pioneering studies of Cabot (1912) in Boston, and Karsner *et al.* (1919)
in Ohio, but persistent enquiries into the matter have established degrees
of agreement between death certificate diagnosis and some other source
of diagnostic evidence ranging from 93 per cent to only 35 per cent (see
Britton, 1974). And even larger variations have been noted for the
diagnoses of particular pathological conditions. In fact, Prior (1985b)
listed 54 separate studies on certification which contained evidence of
variability in the allocated causes of death between two or more records.
Taken together, the information contained in those 54 references casts
some doubt on the reliability of the raw data. Indeed, Cameron and
McGoogan (1981a), on the basis of their audit in Edinburgh, arrive at
the following conclusion:

> Comparison of certified clinical diagnoses with autopsy findings
> showed that, while the major cause of death was confirmed in 61% of
> cases, many diagnoses were wrong . . . Accuracy was particularly
> poor in some clinical categories: notably cerebrovascular disease and
> infections. In these, the diagnosis was more often wrong than right.
> *Thus, death certificates are unreliable as a source of diagnostic data.*
> (Cameron and McGoogan, 1981a:273) [Emphasis added].

It seems likely, then, that clinical perception is subject to the same
kinds of distortion and selectivity as social perception, and that medical
facts can no more be treated as things than can other orders of fact. The
investigation of the social contexts of diagnoses is a theme which lies far
beyond the limits of this study, but I would still like to say something
about the potential sources of such diagnostic error or inaccuracy as
they occur in concrete social settings.

In Belfast, as elsewhere in the western world, each deceased carries a
medical history. It is a history which is carefully inscribed in the records
departments of the hospitals and general medical practices which are
distributed throughout the city, all of which contain a register of the
minor and major ailments which affect the physiology of the living. I
have already noted how the construction of such histories is characteristic of certain forms of what Foucault (1977a) calls political technology.
In allocating a cause of death, this medical history of the deceased forms
the prime source of evidence and exists as the first point of reference for
the certifying agent. There are, however, many cases in which a medical
history of the deceased is too inadequate to form a valid medical opinion

as to the cause of death. This is often the case with peri-natal deaths and still-births. For example, of the 66 still-births which were registered in Belfast during 1981, 20 had 'cause unknown' cited as the only diagnostic evidence. It is also evident in the fact that since 1979 when the World Health Organisation cited Sudden Infant Death Syndrome (SIDS) as a valid cause of death, the percentage of infant deaths attributed to other causes, such as interstitial pneumonia, has declined (see OPCS 1982).[1] For most adults, however, there is seldom a scarcity of information on previous medical conditions. In fact, there is often a surfeit of data on the dead and dying and it gives rise to a further complication.

The fact that clinicians are often required to cite *the* cause of death can often create difficulties because, for many individuals, several pathological conditions will be present at the moment of death. Indeed, it may sometimes be the case that it is the simultaneous occurrence of diseases which causes death rather than any single affliction. This problem has also been noted in the medical literature (see Prior, 1985b). And as far as the Belfast death certificates are concerned, it is a difficulty manifested in the fact that some 71.8 per cent of them contained more than one piece of diagnostic information, and almost 10 per cent contained four or more items of information, though only one of these items can be selected for coding and tabulation.

These difficulties of diagnosis leave aside other significant conditions which may affect the choice of cause of death. Thus, it is sometimes the case that certifying practitioners deliberately seek to suppress clinical data on the grounds of social sensitivity as, for example, when someone dies of alcoholism or even of a cancer. And other forms of social pressure may also impose themselves on the certifying authority, as may be the case with deaths caused by asbestosis (Cutler, 1982, 1983), or other forms of industrial disease. (In fact, Davis (1976) instances a somewhat instructive case involving decisions about the role of pneumoconiosis in causing death and the way in which different medical interests impinged on the final decision.) Or it may simply be that the certifying doctor prefers not to chose a category of disease or illness which is notifiable to the coroner on the grounds that this would create excessive administrative burdens, or distress to bereaved relatives (see Royal College of Physicians and Royal College of Pathologists (RCP), 1982). Finally, and most importantly, it is sometimes the case that the commonplace interests within which practitioners work causes them to view the certificate more readily as a medico-legal document than as a source of clinical data. In these cases the completion of the medical certificate becomes 'just another administrative exercise and almost any description will do'. In such circumstances the certifying doctor may choose rather vague terms of diagnosis such as bronchopneumonia, or heart disease.

It is, I suspect, in this last set of considerations that the crux of the difficulty lies and one is reminded here of Garfinkel's (1967b) discussion of 'good' organisational reasons for 'bad' clinical records. It is a discussion in which Garfinkel demonstrated that although clinical records are ostensibly maintained for clinical purposes, they are practically used as elements of a potential legal contract. Designed, in other words, to indicate that the 'right' thing was done to the 'right' person at the 'right' time. So too, perhaps, with death certificates. Only in this instance, the record is designed to indicate that, irrespective of the specific cause of death, the death itself was an ordinary, disease-based and natural phenomenon. The vocabulary of causation is thereby drawn from a framework of medico-legal, rather than clinical or epidemiological interests.

The upshot of all this is that the primary data on the medical certificate of cause of death are sifted through a mesh of clinical practices, medical theories and commonplace social interests. And the utility of medical certificates as a data base for epidemiological research is restricted by the operation of such practices, theories and interests. The proposals offered for dealing with such weaknesses invariably take the form of advocating improvements in organisational procedures. Thus, the RCP (1982) Report suggests that the number of autopsies performed in hospitals ought to be increased by 20 per cent and that senior rather than junior staff ought to be made responsible for completing certificates.

There can be little doubt that such changes as these would reflect back on the overdiagnoses or underdiagnoses of such conditions as cerebrovascular disease, brain tumours, or infections, but such alterations of practice cannot, of course, change what Alvin Gouldner has called the 'domain assumptions' on which the diagnoses are made. So the location of underlying cause of death solely within the human frame, which is a *sine qua non* of western scientific medicine, the emphasis on anatomical lesions and the selection of just one cause of death remain as three central principles within which our comprehension of human mortality is structured.

In this chapter, however, we shall have to bracket off a consideration of the practices, interests and theories which give rise to the clinical data, and simply note that there are sufficient grounds for believing that the recording of precise anatomical causes and sites of death is a process fraught with error. Instead, we shall examine those processes which more properly fall within the realm of sociology, namely, the study of the organisational procedures which are contingent on the collection of such mortality data. But, first it is necessary to say something about the collection of biographical data.

THE BIOGRAPHY OF DEAD PERSONS

Having considered the nature of the clinical and pathological data which are made available by the certificates, it is now necessary to say a few words about the quality of the biographical data which is collected and recorded by the registrar. Almost every major study which has investigated the registration process has concentrated attention entirely on the quality of the medical data. It is usually taken for granted that the accompanying data on which social variations in mortality are based are subject only to technical errors of coverage or classification. Thus, the Brodrick Committee (1971) charged with reviewing the law and practice relating to the certification and registration of deaths focused totally on clinical and legal issues and entirely ignored the processes which surround the collection of non-medical data.

By the term biographical data I mean to refer to data sufficient to complete the death certificate proper (as distinct from the certificate of medical cause of death). The collection of this information is left to the local registrar, and is completed on the basis of common-sense understandings of social structure held by the registrar and the informant, a series of rules pre-given to the registrar, and innovative schemes which the registrar will devise in order to complete the task efficiently. Out of these pre-given and post-hoc rules and understandings, the biography of the deceased is constructed.

The collection of these data provide an insight into the issues which 20th-century medicine has come to regard as central to understanding the distribution of disease. On these certificates we see inscribed the perimeters of social space, so that age, residence, sex, occupation and, in the case of still-births, parity, age at marriage and so on, all figure in the certificates. It is an indication that 20th-century medicine is aware of the social space within which disease moves and operates, even though it is reluctant to allocate any causal efficacy to such factors. Thus the physical causes of adult deaths are understood against the background of age, sex and occupation, whilst peri-natal deaths are understood against the social circumstances of the mother, rather than, say, in terms of factors which may or may not be present within the fetus itself. At this stage, however, I shall restrict my comments mainly to the collection of occupational data.

In the conversations between registrar and informant, the biographical data is composed. Categories of age and sex are rarely regarded as presenting specific problems even when the details of age may be vague. In response to a question about the age of the deceased a respondent may simply reply, 'he was born about the turn of the century', or, 'he retired in 1965'. In order to be helpful, or in order to complete the task at hand, a registrar will overlook such ambiguities and out of the conversation with informants s/he will negotiate appropriate answers concerning sex and age. In a similar fashion the details relating to occupation will also be constructed and here the registrar will be guided by a number of rules which are provided by the GRO in note form: do not record 'unemployed', record the last known occupation; in the case of a married woman, record husband's occupation and so on. The registrar and the respondent will be required to come to some satisfactory conclusion within these rules even though the terms and structure of the discussion may be extrinsic to the deceased's life experience; s/he may have worked for only a short while ('He had a labouring job just after the war'); s/he may have held many 'occupations' at once, or a series of occupations such that it becomes difficult for the informant to say with certainty what the last 'proper occupation' was, or a wife may have been the only partner involved in the occupational structure and so on. In fact, in some parts of Belfast the whole concept of an 'occupation' would be extraneous to normal experience. Nevertheless, each and every death certificate will have some response fitted into the occupational title: labourer, grocer, butcher, company director, tinker, tailor, soldier, sailor. Yet, in so many respects, these words have meanings which can vary markedly from one context to another. And this perhaps accounts for many of the variations in responses which are noted when death certificates are compared with census data. Thus, Hembright (1969) claimed that agreement in responses between a sample of these two sets of records was in inverse proportion to the number of response categories available for use. Whilst Leete and Fox (1977) in a comparison of fathers' social class at birth registration with fathers' social class on Census Day 1971, found that 19 per cent of their birth registration sample had to be re-allocated to an alternative social class on the basis of the Census data.

Biographical details are, then, collected in an *ad hoc* fashion. But these details, once collected, have also to be managed, processed and organised into their bureaucratically acceptable forms. The processing of such data is often viewed as a neutral and technically objective process which has little impact on the raw material, but in the following sections I shall demonstrate that there are good grounds for believing that more than mere technical rearrangement of the primary information is involved. In fact, these details have to be further embellished before the patterns of mortality, which I referred to at the beginning of this discussion, are able to emerge.

CONSTRUCTING PATTERNS OF MORTALITY

The medical certificate of cause of death and the registration certificate contain between them all of the information which is required by the GRO. For the purposes of statistical aggregation and tabulation, however, the information has to be coded on to code sheets before it is processed by machines. In order to achieve this, the words and phrases on the certificate have to be translated into digital sequences suitable for computer processing. In the space which opens up between the words and the translation is sited the interpretative work of the clerks of the GRO. And into this space are inserted the elements which go to make up their own understanding of death and social structure, though, in formulating such understandings they are required to work within the confines of various manuals and rule-books.

The key compilation mechanism involved in the translation to which I have just referred is the *Manual of the International Statistical Classification of Diseases, Injuries and Causes of Death* (ninth revision, 1977). The Manual contains 999 codes (with sub-divisions), for all manner of diseases and ailments. It also embodies the conceptual and technical framework within which mortality data are supposed to be tabulated and assembled. Revisions of the Manual invariably mean revisions of the rules under which the assembling occurs. New terms may be introduced, as with SIDS in 1979, or old ones deleted as with 'congenital debility' in the sixth revision (1948). New coding rules may be listed as in the seventh revision, which required that all deaths due to self-inflicted injury be coded as suicides (thus increasing the suicide rates by fiat), or that iatrogenic factors be ignored in the coding process and that only the medical conditions which necessitated treatment be used for coding processes. The most far reaching of these kinds of changes, however, occurred in 1912 when cardiac causes of death came to be regarded as more fundamental than causes located in other anatomical sites. It was a rule which, in the twinkling of an eye, altered our image of the human condition at death.

> Where two or more local diseases, neither of which is included in the preceeding list, are certified together, that of longest duration should be preferred. . . . Exceptions to this rule are as follows.
> (a) any disease of the heart (90–95) or kidney (130–133) is to be preferred to *any disease of the respiratory system (104–114)*[2]

These ground rules of precedence and preference which are contained in the Manuals have, of course, to be operated by coders, though coders are not mere robots for applying the rules and regulations contained in the nosology. In fact, coders are active subjects in their own right and they play a fundamental and creative role in the assembling of mortality data. In order to describe this role I am going to consider some specific examples of the coder's art, but before I commence I would like to say something about the social context of coding.

Coding death certificates is an indispensable precursor to obtaining quantitative data on the patterns of mortality which epidemiologists and social scientists use as research material. The work involved is regarded by those who do it as routine and excessively boring. It is mainly carried out by women who are employed in the lower clerical grades of the state bureaucracy. They are given very little formal training in the procedures necessary for carrying out their normal work and are not required to have any kind of medical knowledge. Both those who do the work and those who use the product of the work undervalue the importance of the procedures involved in coding. Yet, mortality data cannot be correctly understood as long as they are divorced from an understanding of coding work, or from the wider organisational context of its production.

I have already stated that death certificates contain many items of diagnostic information, and the coder is expected to place these items in a hierarchical order of diagnostic significance and code correctly. In my own sample of 415 certificates only 28 per cent contained one piece of diagnostic information, whilst the remainder contained between two to eight pieces. Whenever a certificate contains more than one item the coder is faced with a series of possible selections and in the examples below I have tried to explain the principles of primacy which coders operate in this selection procedure. In each case the symbols I (a), (b), (c), and II refer to the positions which the terms held on the original documents and the numbers refer to the appropriate codes.

CASE 1463
 I (a) Terminal bronchopneumonia 485
   (b) Secondary deposits in brain 191
   (c) Primary carcinoma of prostate 185
 II Chronic Obstructive Airways Disease 496
 Coded As: 185

CASE 3088
 I (a) Coronary Thrombosis 410
   (b) Ischaemic Heart Disease 414
 II Myxoedema
 Coded As: 410

CASE 2259
 I (a) Intraventricular haemorrhage 431
   (b) Rupture of cerebral artery 430
   (c) Damage to arterial wall by long standing hypertension 401
 Coded As: 431

CASE 3063
 I (a) Secondary Haemorrhage 459
   (b) Duodenal Fistula 537
   (c) Operation for Periampullary tumour 239
 Coded As: 537

CASE 059
 I (a) Unknown (intrauterine death) 779
   (b) Cord around body stricture 762
    umbilical cord at umbilicus mild pre-eclampsia 760
    mild polyhydramnios 761
 Coded As: 761

CASE 0229
 I (a) Multiple Injuries: Fractures of 8 right and 9 left ribs (807) with
    laceration of aorta (901) and left lung (861), fracture of spine
    (805).
 Coded As: 861 with an 'E' Code of 814

CASE 0155
 I (a) Aspiration of Gastric Contents (934) and pulmonary oedema
    (508) during induction of anaesthesia (995) for elective cholecys-
    tectomy for chronic cholecystitis (575)
 Coded As: 999 'E' Code 879

CASE 1315
I (a) Poisoning by alcohol (305) and chlordiazepoxide (librium) (969)
Coded As: 969 'E' Code 853

CASE 1560
I (a) Barbiturate (Nembutal) and Valium Poisoning 967
Coded As: 967 'E' Code 950

CASE 11
I (a) Pericarditis
   (b) Uraemia and Pneumonia
Coded To: Uraemic Pericarditis 585

CASE 12
I (a) Meningitis
   (b) Tuberculosis
Code To: Tuberculosis Meningitis 013

The first and primary rule for coders is to code to the last stated condition in Section I, as was done in the first case. The rule is stated thus:

General Rule. Select the condition on the lowest used line of Part I unless it is highly improbable that this condition could have given rise to all the conditions entered above it. (WHO, 1977, vol.1: 703)

Although coders have no medical training and cannot reasonably be expected to know when to apply this rule, they do operate it quite frequently in accordance with knowledge derived from a number of sources. Such sources include the Manual itself, mimeographed sheets which state orders of diagnostic preference and acceptable and unacceptable diagnostic links, past coding experiences, 'common-sense' medical knowledge and conversation with other coders. Hence in case 3088, the coder is aware that 410 takes precedence over 414 and codes accordingly, thus overturning the diagnostic order. The same is true of 2259 and, surprisingly, case 3063 where I(b) overturns I(c). This last case also demonstrates another principle of cause of death allocations, namely the frequent exclusion of human agents in the causation process. Here the coder has to code out the iatrogenic factor and reduce the cause to the condition for which the surgical operation was undertaken.

The operation of this first form of primacy is regarded as a legitimate practice of coders and is intended to standardise coding results between different offices. Even here, however, there exists a certain amount of (illegitimate) variability so that coders sometimes overturn the diagnostic order only under certain conditions as, for example, on those certificates relating to people aged under 70.[3] The second form of primacy is exemplified in case 059. Here the coder is unable fully to understand the nature of the sequences involved in the still-birth and so reverts to the utilisation of the general rule given above, coding to 761.3. In actual fact there are two more likely possibilities to this certificate. The first suggests that mild pre-eclampsia plus stricture of the umbilical cord compromised the oxygen supply to the fetus, leading to intrauterine anoxia (code 768). And the most likely is that the stricture and compression of the umbilical cord was the underlying cause of death (code 762.6)—though the coder never considered such a choice. I shall refer to this form of primacy as primacy of the rule over the diagnosis.

The asserting of rules over the diagnosis can have quite misleading effects on our understanding of causation, and some of these have been documented by Cochrane and Moore (1981) in relation to the coding of pneumoconiosis. They quote the following example where the operation of the coding rule (which states that where there is more than one sequence terminating in the condition first entered on the certificate, coders must select the underlying cause of the first mentioned sequence), results in a death coded to chronic bronchitis rather than to pneumoconiosis.

I (a) Heart Failure
  (b) Pulmonary Heart Disease
  (c) Bronchitis, emphysema, and pneumoconiosis Death caused by
      an industrial disease
  Coded As: Bronchitis

The third form of primacy is illustrated by case 0229. The deceased in this case has died from multiple injuries, but for the sake of the coding operation one condition has to be selected. Selection therefore dominates over description, and the coder selects 861.2. The operation of this form of primacy would be common to many road accident victims, and to cases where the diagnostician fails to set out a logical sequence of causal events.

The fourth principle is provided in certificate 0155 which has affinities with case 059, above. Once again, it is difficult for the coder to comprehend the chain of material events which led to death. Unlike case 059, however, it is clear that the operation of the general rule would, in this case, be incorrect. The coder has therefore to impose her understanding on the jumble of events which is recorded on the certificate, and she has to do this in the absence of a clinical training. The codes which are eventually selected, however, skate over some rather important issues—999 refers to complications of medical care not elsewhere classified, and E879 to an accident. In fact, the medical cause of death is quite clearly something to do with the administration of the anaesthetic, and is therefore classifiable as such. Furthermore, the use of the E code for 'accident' rules out other possibilities such as, misadventure (a separate event in the WHO nosology). Though, interestingly, within the framework of the nosology the attribution of such a death to negligence, or manslaughter is not even possible.

This last point also impinges on cases 1315 and 1560, where the coder has to decide on the mode of death as well as on the cause of death. The first of these two cases was coded as an accident and the second as a suicide. They were both cases of poisoning, and in each instance the deceased was a single woman (one aged 59, and the other 60), and both were 'found dead'. The only significant difference between the two descriptions which accompanied these deaths was that in the second case, the following phrase occurred: 'The deceased lived alone and had been feeling depressed from time to time. . .'. It is on the basis of this master clue that the suicide code was chosen. The use of these codes, together with the use of alcohol codes (for deaths associated with alcohol), and special codes to mark the mention of hypertension, constitute particularly good examples of what Garfinkel (1967b) has called 'ad hocing'. For now, however, I would simply like to underline the fact that we are here witnessing the manufacture of rates for different modes of death and not just the manufacture of rates of disease.

The final form of primacy is that of recombination. It is instanced in cases 11 and 12 which I have borrowed from the International Classification of Diseases (1977:710). Here the items of diagnostic information have to be recombined to form a more plausible underlying cause of death. Such acts of recombination require of the coder particular confidence in the translation of clinical data.

In outlining these principles of primacy it has not been my intention to spot 'mistakes' and errors in the work of the GRO, but rather to illustrate the role of that office in manufacturing patterns of mortality. In other words, to show that the GRO is not simply a clearing house for the clinical decisions which have been made at the bedsides of the dead and dying, but an active producer of data in its own right. It is there that we can see the interplay of social practices and medical priorities; the presence and manipulation of nosological principles and the articulation of medical theories on individual corpses.

THE SOCIAL BASIS OF DISEASE

The primary impetus for introducing and refining the procedures contingent on certifying the dead undoubtedly came from forensic medicine. The Brodrick Committee (1971), for example, quite openly stated that it was a concern about undetected homicide which gave rise to its investigations. And exactly the same concern, 'that vastly more deaths occur annually from foul play and criminal neglect than the law recognises',[4] formed the foundation for the investigations of the Parliamentary Select Committee of 1893. In a very real sense, therefore, the registration system is one which is primarily concerned with the policing of the dead. But on to this system there has been appended another set of concerns and interests. They are interests which stem from what might be termed social medicine.

In Chapter 2 I made reference to a 19th-century medicine of social spaces which, I claimed, was superseded and displaced by a medicine of species which took as its fulcrum the human body. This latter is with us today, but throughout the 20th century it has been supplemented by a new medicine of spaces. It is a medicine whose characteristics have been meticulously traced by Armstrong (1983), and which is touched on in the works of Wright and Treacher (1982), and Arney and Bergen (1983). It was this medicine of spaces which was responsible for placing still further demands on the registration process. And it did so in such a way that it became necessary to register not just the diseases which were present in the cadaver at death, but also the nature of the social space in which the diseases occurred. The registration of age, together with the registration of sex, place of residence, marital status and occupation, thus assumed a new importance in this newly directed medical gaze. Of these points of focus it is the very last which I am interested in analysing here for, in many ways, occupational space has, during the current century, come to be regarded as the most fundamental of all.

The necessity of social class analysis in mortality studies arises out of the situation whereby social, economic and political causes of death are excluded from consideration through the operation of the systems of relevance embodied within western scientific medicine. The nosologies, having written out the socio-economic contexts in which death occurs, force epidemiology to write the social structure back in to our understanding of death through a consideration of such things as the social class, occupational or geographical distribution of mortality. In fact, Antonovsky and Bernstein (1977), in a review of literature concluded that:

> Social class subsumes a large set of more directly causative biological and behavioural variables . . . [It] is thus a powerful 'zeroing-in' variable because it points to high risk cases. (Antonovsky and Bernstein 1977:459)

This reintroduction of social structure into medical data is particularly clear in such documents as the Black Report (1980), and the various OPCS studies on medical and population subjects. At this point it would be useful to consider the nature of the social classes into which individual cases of mortality are fitted.

The social class distribution of mortality is known only in and through the data which the Register office has collected and processed. These data are a product of various interpretations, and I have already alluded to the interpretive exchanges which occur between the registrar and the respondent in the attempt to allocate an occupation to the deceased. But in addition to these initial exchanges, the coder has to interpret the respondent's/registrar's decisions into acceptable and satisfactory codes, all of which are drawn from the OPCS (1980) manual.

The social theorists who lay down the terms, concepts and rules of categorisation for social class analysis work within a tradition which was first established by Stevenson in the 74th Annual Report of the Registrar General in England (see Szreter, 1984). Stevenson, who commenced with studies of infant mortality, produced a scheme for the social grading of occupations on the grounds that occupation was associated with 'culture'. Mainly on the strength of an equivocal terminology and dubious social theorising (for example, that occupation reflects cultural differences), Stevenson proposed the existence of five social classes. (1) Upper and Middle Classes; (2) Intermediate between 1 and 3; (3) Skilled Workmen; (4) Intermediate between 3 and 5; (5) Unskilled Labourers. Variations in mortality rates were to be observed against these gradings and, although Stevenson's classification was the most influential one of its type, it was not the first social class scheme to be used as a grid against which mortality patterns could be plotted. The prize for that must be awarded to the second Registrar General for Ireland, Dr Grimshaw (see

Humphreys, 1887). Strangely, Stevenson took his findings on variations in mortality to act as proof of the validity of his initial guesswork on social classes, and eventually became entangled in an absurd network of tautologies (Stevenson, 1928).

Leaving aside Stevenson's tautologies we can see clearly within his system the operation of numerous assumptions which belie the whole of his and of subsequent schemes of this type. At best it is guilty of reducing that system of socio-economic relationships called class, to mere occupation—though in practice it arbitrarily interjects other cultural factors, such as education and training, into the categorisation. More seriously, it orders occupations into a hierarchy which may be entirely unrelated to the understandings of occupational hierarchy which exist among the population at large. In fact, Goldthorpe and Hope's (1974) analysis of the social grading of occupation, which was based on systematic scaling procedures, when compared with that of the OPCS produces significant discrepancies in the overall distribution of occupations. Bland (1979) concluded from his comparison of the two schemes that the OPCS scheme contained enormous areas of overlap within each class, and:

> It turns out that we need to change the definition of social class for about 33% of the male population in order to remove overlap . . . and we cannot use class IIIN at all—it has no-one in it at the end of the rearrangement. (Bland, 1979:286).

Finally, it is necessary to note that the OPCS scheme frequently groups together people whose life styles and socio-economic relationships are markedly diverse. In 1970, for example, own-account hedgers, ditchers and turf-cutters were categorised with cabinet ministers. And the OPCS 1980 scheme links marketing executives with laboratory technicians, and parish priests with permanent secretaries of the civil service. When we trace the history of specific occupations and their place within the class system we encounter further instances of arbitrary relocations. Male clerks, for example, were classified in Class I for the 1911 Census of England and Wales, in Class II for the 1921 Census, and Class III for the 1931 Census. The latter resulted in a shift of half a million males into the lower social class (see Leete and Fox, 1977). And Davis (1980) has described the changing occupational classification of nurses in both the English and the United States censuses (see also Jones and Cameron 1984). These re-arrangements of the working population occasionally give rise to class mortality patterns which are clearly recognised as epiphenomenal, as was the case with the 'W factor' results of the Registrar's General 1951 Occupational Mortality Study. And other instances of possible artefactual effects have been cited by Bloor *et al.* (1987).

It is plain, then, that the terms and concepts embroiled within social class analysis, together with the classificatory principles which are produced by state bureaucracies are instrumental in generating information on class variations in mortality. The social theorising enmeshed within the general scheme is not, however, the only theorising which impinges on our understanding of class mortality patterns. Coders of occupational data are also social theorists in their own right and their understandings and reconstructions of the data, and of the coding rules, have an impact on the final product.

The coders of occupational data in Northern Ireland code to the instructions contained in the OPCS Classification of Occupations, 1980. The manual contains 350 codes for 161 occupational groupings and the coder is required to translate the literary description of an occupation into a numerical code, and allocate in addition, (1) a code for social class, and (2) a code for employment status.

In order satisfactorily to achieve this task the coder has to reduce the brief and often ambiguous terms used on the death certificate to a recognisable term used in the OPCS classification, and then to infer on the basis of her own images of social class, economic activity and political relationships, the social class to which the occupation belongs. Here are some illustrative examples.

Case 1
    Occupation: Retired Farmer
    Coder's Decision: Code 107:
    Employment Status, Self-Employed. Social Class II.

In order to reach these decisions the coder has to fill in the gaps which the original description creates, and she does this by calling on her own knowledge of social structure; that is, she makes use of her awareness that Northern Ireland has an agricultural structure in which small family-owned farms predominate, and that there is no large class of agricultural labourers, tenant farmers and so on, in order to carry out the task at hand. Yet, none of this information is incorporated in the ambiguous term Retired Farmer. It is really in the next case that the nuances of the classificatory system truly emerge.

Case 2
Occupation: Teacher, wife of J.M, Farmer.
Coder's Decision: Code 166:
Employment Status, Employee. Social Class II.

In this instance the coder is required to suppress the information conveyed by the title of Teacher and reduce the wife's employment to the husband's. And, in this case there is an additional coding rule which states that farmer's wives must always be coded as employees. The position of women in the classificatory system is strangely marginal, for not only are their occupations reduced to those of their husbands, as was done here, but in the case of the still-birth certificate there is no space allocated for the recording of mother's occupation whatsoever, even though this may be of more relevance to a still-birth than that of the father. The analysis of problems associated with the distribution of women within the class and occupational system is, however, beyond the scope of this brief enquiry.[5] I only wish to demonstrate the existence and application of specific rules concerned with the employment of women.

Case 3
Occupation: Grocer
Coder's Decisions: Code 101:
Employment Status, Self-Employed. Social Class II

Case 4
Occupation: Butcher
Coder's Decisions: Code 186:
Employment Status, Employee. Social Class III.

This pair of examples provides interesting contrasts in the coder's decision-making processes. In Case 3 she envisages a corner shop proprietor and codes accordingly, but in Case 4 she envisages someone employed in an industrially structured slaughterhouse. In neither case, however, is the relevant information readily available to the coder.

Case 5
Occupation: Retired Dressmaker
Coder's Decisions: Code 210:
Employment Status, Employee. Social Class III.

In this instance the coder assumes knowledge of the district in which the dead person lived, knowledge of the textile industry in Belfast and so on, in order to exclude the possibilities that the deceased was self-employed, a manufacturer of dresses, or such like.

Case 6

Occupation: Managing Director
Coder's Decisions: Code 111:
Employment Status, Self-Employed. Social Class II.

This is always a troublesome category and is recognised as such by the OPCS Manual (along with such terms as clerk, engineer, instructor and manager), covering as it does a veritable wealth of interpretations. In this particular instance the coder recognised the details of the case from a newspaper report and coded on the basis of that knowledge.

Case 7

Occupation: Government Servant
Coder's Decisions: Code 139:
Employment Status, Employee. Social Class III.

The possibilities for coding such a title are numerous – it could refer to clerical, administrative or industrial work, each of which would involve quite different codes and decisions about social class. In Belfast the term 'government service' is often used as a euphemism for policeman, prison officer and soldier. It is a term whose use is especially prevalent among those who register still-births and who lay themselves open to attack through disclosure of occupations. The chosen code (above) of 139 is in fact the code for prison officer and the coder has arrived at such a code on the basis of the respondent's address.

It is, then, through such mechanisms as these that the coder imprints her images of class and social structure on the data at hand. And without such imprinting the task would remain forever incomplete. But just as significant as coder's decisions is the underlying taxonomy of class and occupation on which the procedures ultimately rest—the classification system can generate almost as many anomalies as the coding process itself (see Brewer, 1984).[6]

PATTERNS OF MORTALITY

The images of human mortality which the GRO offers to us are, therefore, themselves fashioned in accordance with a set of classificatory logics and social practices. And there can be little doubt that the aetiological logic embodied in the WHO nosology can have a significant effect on our perception of such things as the prevalence of heart disease (see Bartley, 1985), suicide or SIDS. In fact, the emphasis placed by the WHO nosology on the significance of circulatory conditions, and especially heart conditions, as against respiratory conditions is probably one of the most important sources of these artefactual effects. In a similar manner our knowledge concerning the class distribution of mortality is moulded and fashioned by the principles and alterations embodied in the OPCS taxonomy and its predecessors. In this sense, our image of mortality and its distribution is very much a socially constructed image, and the basis of death in disease is, so to speak, made visible by the GRO. However, whilst the visibility of death is primarily dependent on the taxonomies which are used to collate the raw data on human mortality one must not underestimate the significance which coding practices have for our comprehension of that mortality. Indeed, coding data is not merely a technical operation or neutral re-arrangement of facts, but a reconstruction of data in its own right.

Beyond the multifarious practices which are manifest in the coding office, of course, are bodies; dead bodies. It is individual corpses which are represented by the certificates of death and it is isolated cases of mortality which are slotted into the coding frames. In that sense, the GRO is a component of a much wider system which differentiates the dead. In fact, it is part of a system which individualises death, disease and social conditions, and then refracts all of these things through the numerous tables which are reproduced in the Annual Reports. These latter are then drawn on as a resource for understanding patterns of mortality rather than viewed as a partial and partisan discourse on the human condition at death. And what is represented in that discourse is a specific and peculiar vocabulary of death, a vocabulary which speaks to us of individualised and isolated death as well as a bio-politics of collectivities. Indeed, it is to the examination of the private discourses and practices which surround those isolated dead that I now wish to turn.

Part II
Private Discourse

6 Segregating the Dead

A DISCOURSE ON SEGREGATION

'In establishing a society of the dead, the society of the living regularly recreates itself', said Hertz (1960:72) and that single statement illuminates much about the nature and meaning of the processes and procedures which link the living to the dead. Hertz's statement, however, embodies two separate claims which it would be as well to disentangle at the start for, by using the term recreate, it would seem that Hertz was suggesting that the society of the dead not only serves to regenerate, but also to reflect the society of the living. And in many respects the whole of the second part of this book involves little more than an elaboration of these two assertions so that the chapters which follow are mainly concerned with examining both the manner and the structures in which such recreation and reflection occur. First, however, I shall seek to demonstrate the ways in which these principles operate in specific and concrete circumstances and I shall attempt to do so by concentrating on the distribution of death within the cemetery, the hospital and the city. By embarking on such an investigation I hope to show that the ways in which the dead are organised within these three fields not only reflect the social world of the living, but, in the act of reflecting, provide a basis and a structure through which that world is sustained and reaffirmed. As a corollary of this it will, I hope, become apparent that discourses on death are manifest not only in what people say and do, but also in how they arrange things, and particularly in the ways in which they arrange the dead. Indeed, the analysis of discourse cannot be restricted to the examination of spoken or written language alone, for a discursive régime is spread across many different types of statement, only some of which are linguistic. In this sense, aspects of physical design, for example, are as solid a form of discursive enunciation as are texts or speech. In fact, buildings transpose themselves as statements and architectural forms not only offer the material settings within which discursive formations unfold, but also act so as to constitute the objects to which the discourse is addressed. Thus, the structure of the Nightingale hospital ward, for example, is constitutive of a specific theory of disease; the structure of children's hospital wards speak to us of changing images of the child as well as of disease (see Prior, 1988) and, more to the point, the architecture of the cemetery

111

gives expression to a society's most fundamental beliefs about death and the hereafter. My primary theme in this chapter, however, is segregation; the segregation of the living from the dead and the segregation of the dead from each other. The acts of differentiation and segregation which occur in the creation of the society of the dead tell us much about the world of the living. These acts are, in many respects, most clearly expressed within the cemetery. The cemetery will, therefore, constitute the starting point of a journey which will traverse both geographical and social space. These spaces will sometimes be seen to merge and sometimes to open up to reveal the social worlds which are constituted within, and refracted through them. The cemetery, however, is usually the end point of a voyage which commences elsewhere—in that dense network of social, political and economic relationships which sustain the living. To that end, this chapter also touches on the structured world within which the living fall ill and in which they die. The segregated cemetery is itself a reflection of a segregated city and interposed between the city and the cemetery is that invention of modern medical practice, the hospital. The hospital also segregates (albeit according to different principles), and thus plays its role in structuring the differentiated world of the dead.

THE ARCHITECTURE OF THE CEMETERY

The ideal village of Dobu is a circle of huts facing inward to a central, often elevated mound, which is the village graveyard. (Robert Fortune, 1932:1)

There is an ossuary at Cooley in Co. Donegal—human remains still within. Nearby are the ruins of two churches. The spatial proximity of the mortuary and the churches expresses a once deep affinity between the socio-religious world of the living and the silent world of the dead.[1] Surrounding these structures is a low, perimeter wall of much more recent date and within the enclosed space one finds evidence of numerous, narrow, rectangular plots marked off by roughly hewn stones. The stones mark the presence of anonymous corpses beneath. On the higher ground there are more familiar and more elaborate graves: many with carved stones containing the biographical details of the deceased and some surrounded by iron railings and locked gates.[2] The entire complex stands isolated on a hillside overlooking the town of Moville. Between the ossuary and the small rectangular plots is a space.

The physical distance is hardly noticeable, but the cultural distance is unbridgeable. For the culture in which the ossuary was built laid at least some emphasis on a collective post-mortem identity: a collective judgement perhaps, or a collective resurrection, or maybe nothing more than a collective resting place. The later culture, however, has sought to mark out individual identity and private, personal space in ever bolder strokes. The modern dead lie quarantined in their strictly defined and very private plots.

There is, in fact, a triple isolation here; first of the church from the cemetery, then of the cemetery from the village, and finally of the persons from each other. And this triple process characterises much about the place of death in contemporary Irish society, for somewhere in the development of Irish culture the centrality of the graveyard was lost. First the perimeter walls were built so as to hide the noiseless dead; and in Belfast at least, these walls were often prohibitively high, as can be seen from those which surround Clifton House and Friar's Bush cemeteries. Then the cemeteries were segregated from the life of the towns and villages and expelled beyond the city boundaries, so that, in their day, every one of the 19th-century cemeteries was developed outside of the city limits. (It is, perhaps, no accident that both the existing Belfast city mortuary and the municipal cemetery lie on the outer edge of the city's borders.) Within the cemetery itself there was a further distribution of death which, this time, was a product of the principles of individualisation and privatisation; an individualisation expressed through the multiplicity of private plots which populate the cemetery. It is, in fact, the regimented and orderly spread of individual graves which, more than any other feature of the graveyard, affirms the contemporary predication of death on personal identity. Indeed, it is this personalisation of death which has attracted the attention of the modern analysts of death such as Ariès (1983, 1985), and McManners (1981a), and it is an expression of what the French historians have referred to as the 'desocialisation' of death (see Ladurie, 1979). There is, however, one further secret which is held within the architecture of the cemetery. It is, to use another term much loved by French historians, the 'dechristian-isation' of death. It is a phenomenon characterised by the absence of the church from the burial ground and, more positively, by the municipal-isation of the cemetery in general. Such municipalisation,[3] coupled with the processes of segregation and privatisation, tie together the modern way of burial and in some respects it is possible to pinpoint the origins of these alterations with remarkable precision (see Etlin, 1984). In the United Kingdom, for example, the relevant year is 1843, the year in which Chadwick published his report on interment in towns—a wide ranging investigation of the medical and moral consequences of funerary customs and burial. It was this report which recommended the removal of the dead from the rooms of the living as rapidly as possible after death, the provision of a single grave per person and the municipalisation and regimentation of the cemetery—each grave and each occupant being separately numbered. It is often stated that Chadwick advocated the expulsion of the dead from the world of the living on sanitary grounds alone, but as the following recommendation indicates, medical reasons came only third in the list of considerations.[4]

That on several special grounds, *moral, religious, and physical* . . . the practice of interment in towns in burial places amidst the habitations of the living, and the practice of interment in churches, ought for the future . . . to be entirely prohibited. (Para. 249. [Emphasis added.]

The processes of municipalisation, segregation and privatisation are evident in virtually all modern western cities, but in Belfast the themes of segregation and privatisation are often overlaid with novel and complicating factors. Of these the most important is that particular form of sectarianism which pervades all aspects of the city's life—the sectarian split between 'Catholic' and 'Protestant'. This latter is one of the most fundamental of all factors to affect the social organisation of death in Belfast. It imposes itself on burial patterns, funeral processes and burial rites; though the precise edge of sectarian fervour does not always cut through these various practices with equal sharpness. In burial, the dominant pattern is expressed through the provision of separate Catholic and Protestant graveyards. This religious apartheid is, in many respects, represented by the traditional roles fulfilled by the Milltown and City cemeteries. The former was, and continues to act as burial ground for Catholics under the control of the ecclesiastical authorities. The latter, on the other hand, was traditionally a resting place for Protestants and lies under the control of the municipal authorities. These days the City cemetery witnesses the burial of more Catholics than Protestants, but even within the cemetery they continue to inhabit quite distinct and separate parts of the graveyard. Nowadays most of the city's Protestant dead are either buried or cremated at the vast and fashionably named Roselawn on the edge of the city boundary, whilst Catholics are, for the most part, either buried in Milltown, the City, or in one of the many smaller plots of consecrated ground which are scattered across the greater Belfast area. Sectarianism, however, does not always nestle in the

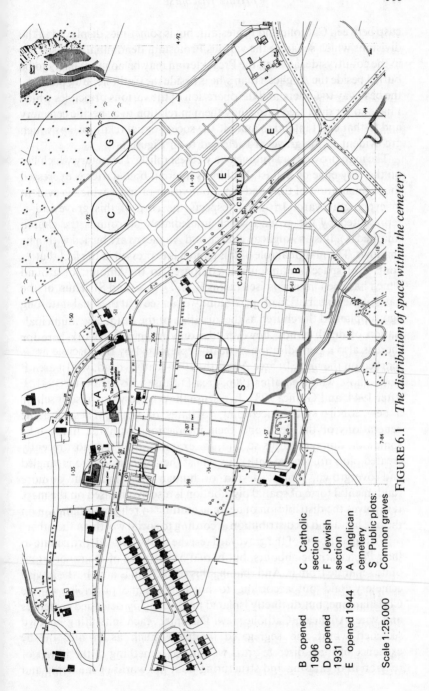

FIGURE 6.1   *The distribution of space within the cemetery*

B opened 1906
D opened 1931
E opened 1944

C Catholic section
F Jewish section
A Anglican cemetery
S Public plots: Common graves

Scale 1:25,000

cusp between Catholic and Protestant, but is sometimes displayed in the divisions which separate the various Protestant denominations, so that in the countryside, at least, the Presbyterian may be no more likely to be buried beside the Anglican than s/he is beside the Catholic. But, perhaps, the best way to understand the operation of the various principles which I have so far discussed is to study them in relation to a specific cemetery and to that end I intend to analyse the socio-spatial relationships which are evident in the graveyard referred to in Figure 6.1.

The map provides an outline of a well-established cemetery which lies on the very edge of Belfast. Within its internal boundaries is expressed the segmentation of time and the sub-division of space which is evident in every graveyard. In many respects the core of this graveyard is represented by the ground which immediately surrounds the church (marked A). It is an Anglican church and Anglicans are buried within its shadows. The marginal role of this church is expressed in the fact that its control of space is miniscule as compared to the amount of ground which has been municipalised (areas B, C, D, E, G and S). Thus, on the basis of the distribution of space alone we can see that the local state long ago supplanted the church as the guardian of the dead. The municipal-isation of death is not, however, the only principle at work here for there is also a periodisation of death represented by the discrete areas marked on the map. In area A rest the 19th-century dead, whilst area B holds those who died after 1906, area D those who died after 1931, E after 1944, and G since 1983. In a sense the cemetery organises itself on a new cohort system according to dates of death. These are the generations of the dead and their interactions with the living take somewhat different forms so that, for example, only the most recently created plots are tended with care, whilst the older graveyard is tangled and overgrown, almost devoid of human attention. But a more fundamental form of spatial distribution is also symbolised on the map. It involves the distribution of death according to religious affiliation on the one hand and its distribution according to social worth on the other.

Within section C of the graveyard rest the Catholic dead, proximate to their Protestant neighbours, but buried on the edge of their world and quite separate from it. And echoing this separation is area F, the Jewish cemetery, laid out according to much the same principles as the Christian one, but distinctly isolated and staunchly defended by fences and wire. Anglican, Catholic, Jew, Dissenter; each inhabiting his own secluded world and segregated in death much as in life. In the existence of these discrete areas we can see something of the power of religion in organising and structuring both the world of the living and the world of the dead. Though it is a political religion which rules here as much as any eschatology of the soul. What is more, this division of territory according to confessional boundaries is not unrelated to the second principle of which I wish to speak: the distribution of space according to social worth. This latter is manifested by the presence of area S, which, in the words of one informant, 'is on the bad ground near the dump'. This is the public plot, where once the poor were buried. The last interment of an adult occurred here in 1969, but it is still used for the burial of the stillborn, and in their unmarked graves is symbolised their social value. 'No monument, headstone, plinth, railing . . . shall be erected or placed on or around the graves, nor shall the graves be permitted to be planted (sic)'.[5] And these anonymous and communal graves which, figuratively speaking, were once regarded as the resting place of all-comers, are here preserved for the poor and the stillborn. Thus, the cemetery inscribes in spatial terms the social cleavages which afflict the living and the distinctions which order the latter are very often evident in the minute details of the gravestone inscriptions. The use of the cross on the Catholic headstones, or the use of occupational titles (Dr, Rev., Capt.) on other headstones, for example, further serve to underline the demarcations which structured the past lives of those who lay beneath them. But the most basic distinction of all has yet to be mentioned.

The arrangement of the cemetery into grids and blocks of space of roughly equal areas, is homologous to the arrangement of the dead in the interment books held by the municipal authorities. The most important form of spatial segregation, however, exists within each of these broad territorial areas and it is represented by the separation of the dead from each other—the myriad private plots which make up the mosaic of the cemetery. The private plot is in many ways the prime monument to the modern way of death. It is the final expression of that individualisation whose origins Tocqueville and Durkheim had traced to a modern 'disposition to isolation', and which Foucault traced to the operation of disciplinary power. In both accounts individualisation is seen as the brand of the modern world. And in the graveyard the individual is sacred in his isolation. The private plot, however, is usually erected within the social networks created by the conjugal family so that husband, wife and unmarried children are the usual occupants of the grave, and the family name invariably dominates the space which the grave occupies. But the processes of individualisation and isolation do not just occur in physical space, for on these earthen plots are erected administrative and legal spaces—each grave is numbered, measured and recorded, so that the legal ownership of the grave constitutes part of that contractual world which dominates the living. And the bureaucratic records which relate to the possession and occupancy of the grave mirror the disciplinary records to be found in the school, the factory, the hospital and the welfare agencies through which the living pass. By announcing the individuality of those who lie beneath, the single granite headstones express more than mere sentiment; they express disciplinary order itself. It is a disciplinary order which is evident in the procedure which is followed by the municipal authorities on opening up a grave— whereupon they demand of an informant:

> Surname and other names, time of death, cause of death, religious persuasion, occupation or rank in life, place of residence, place of death, condition (married or single, widow or widower) of the person to be buried; the name and address of the persons having the management of the interment, the date on which the funeral is to take place and the number and section of the grave to be opened.[6]

Built on this disciplinary segmentation of bodies is yet a further sub-division. It is a sub-division of grief and sentiment, such that the individual dead are lamented and remembered singly. Indeed, apart from some specially designed war graves, or those erected after collective tragedies such as that at Aberfan in South Wales, it is hard to find cemeteries in which there are collective expressions of sentiment and loss and only a common tragedy seems likely to generate the impetus to construct a common mortuary. Yet, there is much more than mere isolation written into these markers of the dead, for in the epitaph we are able to discover a great deal about the socially structured world of the living and above all a great deal about the social structuring of sentiments. And as an entry into this world it will prove useful to consider a few simple inscriptions.[7]

> CASE 1. Erected by Richard Bell in memory of his six children who died young.

> CASE 2. The family burial ground of Hugh Allen.

> CASE 3. Here lieth the body of John Carson.

From the content of headstones it is possible to deduce much about the distribution of both power and sentiment within the family as well as the ways in which such phenomena change and alter over the decades.

119

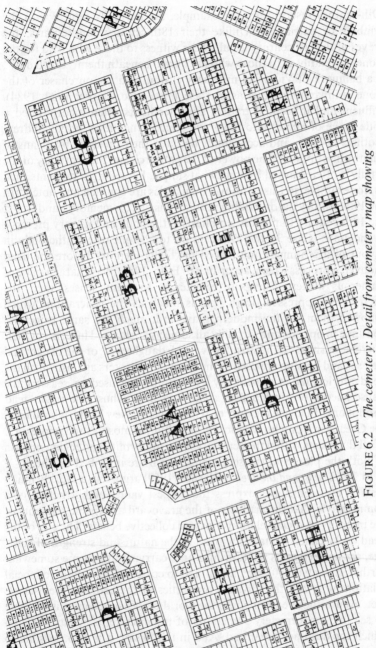

FIGURE 6.2 The cemetery: Detail from cemetery map showing distribution of land (lettered areas) and individual graves (numbered)

19th-century inscriptions, for example, are normally replete with the symbols of patriarchy. Unlike their 18th-century counterparts, the graves of the last century usually bear witness to those who paid for the stones as readily as to those who are buried beneath them. 'Erected by', is a hallmark of Victorian mortuary custom and the purchaser of the stone is invariably male, as in Case 1 (see also Clarke, 1982, 1984). Affluent and influential traders and merchants often incorporated a wide range of affines into the grave – nieces, nephews, grandchildren, mothers-in-law – and accordingly declared their presence by means of lengthy inscriptions. The power of the patriarch and the centrality of the family is often marked by somewhat simple, but telling statements such as, for example, in Case 2 above; only males are counted and noted.[8] In the 19th century the overriding sentiment is one of 'memory', and whilst the 18th-century tombstone emphasised the body and its very presence in the grave (Case 3), the 19th-century tombstone deleted the body in favour of a sentiment and placed the living memory before the dead cadaver, a process which, according to Etlin (1984), was characteristic of numerous western European cemeteries. In many senses, then, the Victorians suppressed death just as much as the generations which followed them. In the modern graveyard, much the same principles continue to operate and virtually all subjects are located in terms of their kin relationships – as husband of, wife of, daughter of, or son of ego; and age, sex and kinship are used as the dominant markers against which the dead are located. Occasionally gravestones are used to reassert the transcendence of kinship over spaçe and time. Thus, one might read inscriptions, 'In loving memory of JH who died in New York', who 'died in the Great war', or who 'was lost at sea', but the most lasting impression of all that exists within the cemetery is the uniformity and regimentation of both the plots and the sentiments which are inscribed on them.

In *The Living and the Dead*, Warner (1959) argued in a Durkheimian fashion that cemeteries express the deepest values and structure of a community – that the artifacts of the graveyard are visible referents of the intensity of social relationships and collective beliefs. The city of the dead, as he called it, stands witness to the nature and strength of class, age, sex and religious relationships and, carrying this theme somewhat further, Young (1960) even attempted to correlate the solidity of social relationships with the physical properties of the artifacts themselves. Yet, even without entering into the world of measurement it is possible to see in every cemetery something of the discrete principles through which the dead are organised. And in that vision it is also possible to grasp something of the principles which order the social relationships of the living. For, according to Zonabend (1973) and on the basis of her study of the cemetery of Minot, 'the geography of the dead reflects the social morphology of the living' (1973:15), though to subsume the intricate mechanisms which order and structure the cemetery under the concept of segregation is, perhaps, to do an injustice to the principles involved. But segregation in its many and varied forms is a hallmark of the cemetery. Protestant from Catholic, Catholic from Jew; still-born from live-born; stranger from kinsman and most telling of all, individual from individual. Both the architecture of the cemetery and the carefully inscribed epitaphs on the solitary tombstones stand witness to the overarching principle of segmentation.

THE DISTRIBUTION OF DEATH WITHIN THE CITY

The brand of death is its individuality. The policing process which individualises and normalises life; which registers it at birth, marriage and death, and tracks and traces human identity from the cradle to the grave, bequeaths to death its dominant feature. Death is an isolated affair which, in most cases, has been monopolised by the affective bonds of the family and expelled from the consciousness of the community. To write, therefore, of the distribution of death is to write of its distribution throughout the city individually and singly. But death's arbitrary empire, as McManners calls it, nevertheless has a social order. Patterns are created and revealed, sub-divisions are constructed and analysed, and the dead are seen to coalesce into larger units. These patterns and these sub-divisions can take many and varied forms; the dead can be grouped according to their diseases, their causes of death, their ages, their consanguinity, their sex, their social classes, or their occupations, and each regrouping will redistribute death into a different pattern. In the western world this kaleidoscope of death has tended to be refracted through medical discourse and medical practice and it is that discourse and that practice which best reflect the changing images of death which we have at our disposal. It was the medicine of social spaces which first sought data on deaths' distribution within the city, and it was the medicine of social spaces which developed the techniques and tools of analysis through which the distribution could be known. The segregation of the dead within the cemetery and their segregation according to their diseases and therapeutic régimes is echoed in the segregation of the dead within the official reports of death which proliferate within the western world. The medicine of social spaces sub-divides the world of the dead into ever finer detail and ever more specific grids. New categories are devised and new rates of mortality are invented in the incessant search for truth; that persistent attempt to edge nearer reality with greater and greater accuracy which characterises western science. So that absolute numbers are transformed into rates, rates are standardised and made age-specific, and diseases are cross-tabulated with class, occupation, residence, marital status and other features of social life. Our vision of human mortality is shaped and patterned by these artifactual features of the reporting. More important, perhaps, is the fact that the conceptual framework through which mortality is analysed and reported itself reflects theories concerning the causes of death and disease. Thus, the undue emphasis which 19th-century analysts placed on the recording of mortality by weeks and months and districts or localities, makes sense only within an anti-contagionist theory of disease which was especially anxious to mark out the arbitrary points at which epidemics started and stopped. Here, however, I intend to concentrate on just a few of these distinctions and in order to illustrate the powerful impact which conceptual frameworks have on our vision of deaths' distribution I propose to analyse two dimensions of mortality and one population. The dimensions are those of geographical and social space on the one hand, and age on the other; and the population is the stillborn of Belfast in 1981.

Geographical and Social Space

In 1981 there were some 4048 deaths registered in the city of Belfast, whilst in 1881 there were 5436 deaths, but the ways in which the deaths were analysed, described and sub-divided in each of those years was entirely different and had very little in common except a reference to a common geographical area – the city. Even the concept and significance of geographical space failed to remain stable during the period, whilst the differentiation of the dead in terms of age, social class and disease, underwent even more fundamental alterations. Traditional analyses of the differences involved usually take an evolutionary stance and trace the victory of scientific medicine over epidemic diseases and the consequent influence of the so-called diseases of affluence and longevity on the 20th century mortality rate. The epidemic diseases of the 19th century are seen to give way to circulatory and degenerative diseases of the 20th. Condran and Cheney (1982), for example, in their analysis of mortality rates in Philadelphia 1870–1930, relate just such a story, but they fail to recognise that the tale which they tell and the mortality which they see is a product of the concepts and frameworks which they use. The mortality, of course, exists independently, but the way in which it is subdivided, categorised and explained, is variable. What is seen is a product of the discourse which produced it.

The distribution of death in geographical and social space was, as I suggested in Chapter 2, first mapped out by the adherents of the 19th-century public health movement: Grimshaw in Ireland, Farr in England, Villermé in France.[9] And it was the spread of death within geographical space which first drew their attention. The main impetus for this focus came from the anti-contagionists, anxious to prove that disease, far from spreading contagiously, operated within discrete geographical areas. (Their concern to trace the path of disease through the seasons was inspired by the same concern.) Villermé's report on the distribution of mortality in Paris 1828, and Grimshaw's analysis of the healthy districts of Dublin 1872, mark in many ways the limits of the process. For it did not take much to realise that superimposed on geographical space was a social space – a space between rich and poor (see Delaporte, 1986). It was not long, therefore, before the language of geography was overlaid and eventually supplanted by the language of social class. This concern with tracing the distribution of mortality across space, class and time was, between 1828 and 1872, to give way to a concern with tracing the distribution of disease within the same terrain and whilst the social was superimposed on the geographical, disease was superimposed on mortality. Medical geography thereby came to constitute a small part of that medicine of social spaces which I have discussed previously.

This attempt to correlate the social with the geographical and the pathological with mortality persists even today (see Pringle, 1983), though it now makes sense to do so only if the geography of disease is reduced in its entirety to the disease of social class. Nevertheless, the attempt to correlate mortality with district continues to demonstrate the variability in mortality experiences of different sectors of the city's population. Death, it seems, does hide in pockets within the city boundaries and it is unevenly spread. In my own sample of 1981 deaths, for example, 40 per cent of deaths were concentrated into just 14 of the city's 51 wards and in Pringle's study of 1971 deaths, age-sex standardised mortality rates were seen to vary from 49.1 to 201.6 in the Belfast urban area. But these observations have entirely different implications for the 20th-century observer than they would have had for the 19th-century counterpart. Of course, the Annual Reports of the Registrar General still organise mortality by geo-political areas, but the logic for so doing is an administrative one rather than a medical one and the fine division of mortality by city district has long disappeared (somewhere in the 1880s, with the rise of the germ theory of disease). [10] Social class analysis on the other hand (devised by Grimshaw during the 1880s) has moved from strength to strength. Originally confined to the analysis of mortality during the census years, appearing regularly after 1913, it has now become routine. [11] It figures in both the 1981 Annual Report of the Registrar General (1984), as well as in a specially designed report on Northern Ireland's infant mortality (Baird 1980) and, needless to say, it demonstrates the existence of a gradient for infants such that the rates among the 'unskilled' are between two to three-and-a-half times greater than for the 'professional' class.

Age and Mortality

The mapping of mortality by age which seems so natural to a 20th-century observer occurred through a rather slow and long drawn out process which commenced in the 19th and terminates in the 20th century. In England, it was not until the publication of the 25th Annual Report in 1865, that the influence of age on mortality was truly attended to and it was in the supplement to that report that the technique of life table analysis—from which age specific mortality rates could be deduced—was first introduced. [12] Thus, by the time that the first Irish report was published in 1869, [13] age had become a standard against which disease and mortality could be measured. The commonly used death rate, however, was until 1877 a rate applicable to all and only in that year were age-specific rates introduced in the general report. Of the numerous sub-divisions which were produced at that stage the most interesting was, perhaps, that for infants. [14] The publication of a new Infant Mortality Rate (IMR) suggests the emergence of a new focus for medical discourse and, to a certain extent, correlates with the emergence of childhood and the medicalisation of the family in general. This focus on infancy is particularly interesting because of the complex alterations which it underwent during the 1877–1984 period (see Armstrong, 1986), and because of what that complexity signifies about the attitudes of the living towards the dead. In Belfast in 1881, for example, the IMR was 132 per thousand, whilst in 1981 it was 13.2 per thousand, having travelled through a high point of 156 per thousand during 1891, but we cannot compare on a similar basis the neonatal or perinatal rates, or that for stillbirths. Stillbirths, for example, were not compulsorily registered until 1927 and in that sense 1927 represents the time from which the stillborn were given a social and legal existence. The fact that they were so registered signifies not only an underlying point of medical interest, but also a point at which attitudes towards the foetus altered in social discourse in general, though as I have already hinted, the social rights of the stillborn to formal burial remain ambiguous. And as social identity was awarded to the infant and the foetus, it became possible to construct their biographies and to recognise their individuality. Neonatal mortality enters the record a little earlier, in 1905, but official recognition of the neonatal mortality rate occurs only in 1938, whilst the demand for a perinatal rate was not satisfied until 1954 and the demands for a special certificate on which to record perinatal deaths surfaced only in the ninth (1977) revision of the *International Statistical Classification of Diseases, Injuries and Causes of Death*. These shifts, changes and introductions represent, of course, far more than mere technical rearrangements of data. They reflect a social concern with age in general and with infancy in particular, and in that reflection we can see the emergence of new social and medical objects of interest and new points of focus for mortality.[15] These interests were, of course, also reflected in other features of medical discourse, not least of which was hospital architecture which, through a series of important shifts in the 20th century, came to mark out in ever finer detail our image of the infant, the child and their respective qualities (see Prior, 1988).

Stillbirths

The manner in which these conceptual and theoretical distinctions impinge on our image of mortality can, in many ways, best be studied through an analysis of a particular sub-group of the dead and the group which I propose to study is the stillborn. By analysing the distribution of stillbirths throughout Belfast in 1981 I hope to relate not just 'facts' about mortality, but also the mesh within which those facts are discovered and reported on.

I have already indicated that the stillborn foetus as a social and medical object received its formal status only in 1927 when the registration of the stillborn child was made compulsory. The formal link between the foetus and the child was, however, delayed until the establishment of a perinatal mortality rate in 1954 and the further standardisation of the perinatal category through the use of a special certificate, was, as I have just stated, demanded only in 1977. In a sense, then, the foetus as an object of mortality was dragged into the 20th century slowly and deliberately, and one can only discuss the distribution of foetal mortality within the context which conferred social recognition on it, though, as Scott *et al.* (1981) has indicated, this recognition is still somewhat ambiguous.

As with every other mortal group, the stillborn are not merely analysed according to their simple and absolute numbers, but are further differentiated along a series of axes through which it is assumed their demise can be measured and understood. On recording a stillbirth a whole set of associated facts are required and it will be as well to make a simple list of what is included in, and inferred from these data. It incorporates: employment of father (or mother where fathers' employment is unknown), the age of the mother, the age of the father, the marital status of the parents, the social class of the father, the place of residence of the mother, the parity of the mother, the period of gestation, the sex of the foetus, the weight of the foetus, the place and date of birth of the foetus and the medical cause of death. This information once collected and tabulated can then be used to plot the occurrence of these deaths in time, place, social and diagnostic space. Thus, of the 66 occurrences of stillbirth in Belfast in 1981, it is possible to state that 31 were female; that their deaths were distributed unevenly throughout the year (the peak month being June); that the majority of them (39) were born of fathers in skilled, or semi-skilled manual occupations; that the median age of mothers was 25, and of fathers 28; that the mean period of gestation was 34 weeks; that 17 of the foetuses were illegitimately conceived; that the modal category of cause of death was 799.900 (that is 'unknown'); and that a significant percentage of mothers (41 per cent) were ordinarily resident outside of Belfast and had been drawn into the city by virtue of its hospital facilities. Now this jumble of empirical detail can be used to tell us about death in two ways. First, it can be used in a statistical mesh so as to enable us to plot the occurrence of these deaths on a social and clinical map. And secondly, by analysing the categories of information collected, it can be used to clarify the logic of death which operates in the late 20th century (and it is the latter distribution which determines the former). Thus, from the categories which are listed above, it is clear that the logic of stillbirths is to be sought in the social and economic circumstances of the mother; her employment, her social class, her place of residence, age and marital status. The distribution of stillbirths can only be described in terms of the world which is bounded by these categories, for if the causes of foetal death were to be sought in some other region of social or economic behaviour, then the categories of inquiry would reflect that change of thought and analysis. And with the alteration of categories would follow a changed picture of deaths' distribution.

In 1881, of the 5436 deaths which occurred within the city, 1776 of them were of infants aged under five years. In 1981 the comparable figure for infants was just 79. In 1881 one in every seven children died before reaching their first birthday, whilst four out of every ten burials were for children aged less than 14 years. It is their nameless corpses which populate the graveyards of Victorian Belfast. Their social status is, in part, reflected in their namelessness, whilst their gradual identification on the cemetery stones seems to march hand in hand with the medical process which differentiated and thereby produced infant mortality. By contrast with 1881, most of the deaths in contemporary Belfast are of people aged more than 55. In fact, approximately 75 per cent of all deaths belong to the over-55 group and 50 per cent of deaths occur to people aged over 70 years. But this shift in mortality from childhood to old age is not the factual basis from which we can deduce other truths about the organisation of death. (Though attempts to do just this are made by Chaunu, 1976; Stannard, 1977; and Stone 1979.[16]) On the contrary, the recognition and description of this shift is dependent on the discourse which developed a meticulous chronology of death and which placed age into ever sharper focus within the official reports. Similarly, the recognition of social class and race differentials in mortality can only be recognised within the context of the discourse which produces them. And the same principle applies to shifts in disease. People, of course, live and die independently of discourse, but the way in which they recognise, organise and interpret their lives and deaths is not so independent. The reflection of age, class and disease in the official reports of mortality is itself part and parcel of the intricate processes which constitute the social world. And the segregation of the dead on the pages of government publications both reflects on, and is reflected in the numerous social practices which impinge on death in the world at large. In Belfast the dominant sources of division are age, sex, disease and social class, though there are in addition many lesser sources of division such as marital status and illegitimacy. Paradoxically, the study of the geographical distribution of death within the city which had played such a dominant part in 19th-century epidemiology and which this sub-section takes as a starting point, is now of only minor and esoteric interest. Nevertheless, within the terms in which we are forced to speak, it is clear that death is differentially distributed, and that it is hidden by the features of age and district, so that rather than being in the midst of life, death is more often to be found at the margins. At the margins of the city, on the edges of normal life span and in the marginality of the hospital and nursing home.

RÉGIMES OF THERAPY

The emergence of pathology with its emphasis on the somatic basis of disease created a vision of death as itself pathological, as an abnormal transition of being. And with the introduction of this equation which balanced death with pathology, came the processes whereby death was both explained via disease and then managed and hidden under the veils of clinical expertise and bureaucratisation. Consequently, belief in the virtue of preparing for one's own death, which according to both Ariès (1983), and McManners (1981a) had persisted up to the very end of the 18th century, disappeared, and so too did the image of death as a religious rather than a mundane experience. From that stage onward death was regarded as a condition to be treated, a condition amenable to medical therapy. It was no longer the priest, but the doctor who was summoned at the hour of death.

Hospitalisation and bureaucratisation are powerful processes and, as we have already seen, the bureaucratisation of death contains a key to the understanding of the contemporary organisation of death. But hand in hand with the emergence of disciplinary power in the state bureaucracies has marched the processes which have generated the medicalisation of death, and the institutional basis of that medicalisation has been represented by the hospital. The hospital and the nursing home function in part to structure the modern way of death and fewer and fewer of deaths' victims manage to escape the medics' realm. I have already recorded that in Belfast only a minority of individuals died 'at home' (just 22 per cent of the 1981 sample), whilst the majority died either in hospital (58 per cent of the sample), or nursing homes (13 per cent). And this percentage of hospital based deaths appears rather low when compared with the patterns displayed in other European and North American countries. Death in the modern world is, therefore, not merely structured by the hospital, it is also hidden by that very same mechanism.

In the modern world death is a disease. It is explained in terms of disease and it is frequently understood and justified in terms of disease. Divided according to the elements of the current nosology, the majority of the dead fall into three large categories: those who die from circulatory conditions come first (Category VII of the nosology), followed by those who die from neoplasms (Category II), and finally those who die from respiratory causes (Category VIII). Now, because disease is seen as the most important feature of the process of dying, death tends to be contained and ordered in terms of therapeutic structures, and to a certain extent the distribution of death throughout the nosology reflects its distribution throughout therapeutic régimes. Thus, those whose principal pathology is seen to be in terms of neoplasia are far more likely to die in nursing homes than most other groups (about 30 per cent of those whose deaths were attributed to the occurrence of neoplasia in the 1981 sample died in nursing homes), and a high percentage also die in hospitals. For these individuals there are specially designed homes and mission centres. Even the last named group has its own therapeutic base and a startling 83 per cent of them died in hospital or nursing homes. But in their case it is perhaps not so much that their diseases determined their therapies, but that their therapies determined their diseases. These are the old, the senile, the geriatric population, whose primary 'pathology' is age itself, and whose clinical conditions are many and various. Only those who are said to die from circulatory conditions seem to spread themselves across a range of therapeutic settings—perhaps because their deaths, being unexpected, do not lend themselves to therapeutic intervention. Yet these 4048 deaths are not merely distributed throughout different régimes, they are also subdivided within the régimes themselves so that, for example, by examining the clinical profile of the hospital we can discover a new distribution of death; a distribution which is drawn and redrawn with each change of profile.

Table 6.1, lists the mortality in a Belfast hospital during 1982 and from this simple listing we can discern a number of important characteristics about the organisation of death. First, and as one would expect, death is distributed according to forms of therapy rather than forms of disease. Surgery, medicine, neurology, oncology, and obstetrics are forms of specialist practice which, although fastened to certain forms of disease, are nevertheless independent of them. And second, behind the forms of therapy lurk other principles of therapeutic organisation, the most important of which is age. The 188 deaths from the geriatric wards and the 132 in the neo-natal unit are proof of the significance of age in therapeutic régimes. Hospitals, of course, are not designed for death; on the contrary they are supposedly structured towards cure, but, in so far as death does occur in them we can see that it is organised and structured according to many of those principles which are evident in the cemetery and the city. This is not to say that the dying are in any way aggregated, or combined into a single group whose only denominator is their imminent demise. In fact, their segregation occurs in a much finer mesh than the term 'hospital' suggests. In the hospital one's dying is not the focus of a therapy and so it is both strange and significant that in one of the most modern expressions of terminal care—the hospice movement—one of the primary aims is to remove the dying from 'the hurly-burly of a busy ward [which] is not conducive to coming to terms with death',[17] and to segregate the dying from the ill as well as from the healthy and to place them within a régime which is purposely designed for death. In many respects, this desire to segregate the dead within the therapeutic spaces is echoed in the nursing texts of the age, for it is only in the 1970s that such texts began to carry a special section on the treatment of the dying patient (see, for example, Burns *et al.* 1973). In other words, something which had previously passed as merely a technical problem of procedure (Britten 1979), was now seen as a phenomenon which demanded special skills and special attention.[18] And this segregation of death and the dead within the wards is further emphasised by the nature of the procedures which are supposed to be followed. Thus, and according to the 'Nursing Procedures Book' of a Belfast Hospital, the dying patient should be separated from his/her neighbours and nursed 'in a side ward or in a quiet corner of the ward'. Nursing staff are informed that 'It is important to ensure privacy for the patient' and that the patient's condition should not be discussed within his or her hearing. Solemnity and solitude are the watchwords of terminal care and, when death has been confirmed, the nurse should 'ensure that the curtains are drawn closely round the bed'. This is the very epitome of the modern mode of dying: hidden and clinicalised to the very end.[19]

The vision of death as a pathology and the segregation of the dying into various régimes of medical therapy constitutes the basic framework within which all other clinical reactions to and organisations of death occur. And the structures through which the dead are segregated and hidden from the living find their resonance in the minutiae of interactions which occur within the hospital wards. The details of these interactions have been extensively studied by Glaser and Strauss (1965, 1968) in relation to North American hospital practices and procedures, but it is important to recognise that those interactive episodes are themselves patterned and shaped not just by the institutional context in which they occur, but more importantly by the discourse which makes of death a pathology. After all, death only finds itself in hospital because we have a vision of it as an untimely event brought on by disease. And even our definition of death, sub-divided as it is into brain, biological and cellular death owes its origins to modern pathology. At other times, and in other cultures such intepretations would be incomprehensible.[20]

TABLE 6.1 *The distribution of deaths by wards/clinical specialism in a Belfast hospital, 1982*

Ward Type	Number of Deaths
Surgery 1	36
Surgery 2	24
Surgery 3	40
Surgery 4	45
Medical 1	47
Medical 2	60
General Medicine	66
Genito-Urinary	25
Coronary Care	34
Neurology	25
Haematology	35
Geriatric Unit 1	20
2	31
3	40
4	25
5	18
6	22
7	40
Obstetrics	0
Gynaecology	14
Neo-Natal Unit	132

THE SEGREGATION OF THE LIVING

On the basis of his work for *The Gold Coast And The Slum*, Zorbaugh (1929) claimed that 'There is no phenomenon more characteristic of city life, as contrasted with the life of the rural community or the village, than that of segregation' (1929:232), and such segregation takes social, economic and what Park had called 'moral' forms. The business district was segregated from Towertown; Little Hell was differentiated from the Gold Coast; and the Rialto of the half world stood isolated from all of these. The processes of differentiation at work within the city established a social and moral segregation between geographical areas and served to make the city 'a mosaic of little worlds which touch but do not interpenetrate'. It is unlikely, however, that Chicago ever exhibited the stark and somewhat bizarre implements of segregation which have in recent years cut through the geography of Belfast – a city in which social segregation has been reinforced by political, economic and physical processes, the most brute expression of which is undoubtedly the concrete wall – the so called 'peace line' – which separates Catholic from Protestant, Republican from Loyalist West Belfast.

The physical segregation in Belfast of the living from each other has been extensively studied and extensively documented (Boal and Douglas 1982), and it is important to note that the physical segregation is part symptom and part creator of the social, political and economic differentiation in which it is embedded. From our point of view, these facts are of significance only in so far as they form the network of social relationships in which death occurs and in which death is organised and to which it is related. Yet these same processes and practices not only serve to reflect the differences, but also serve in a small way to sustain and regenerate them. In many respects religion is one of the most significant sources for the segregation of the dead and, as we shall see in later chapters, it pervades many fundamental aspects of the organisation of death, but it is only the most highly visible manifestation of a set of processes which are endemic within the city. And there are many other forms of segregation which have a non-sectarian origin and a non-sectarian structure, and which also assist in the processes by which death is distributed within the city. Of the latter the most important are those forces which generate individualisation. But in addition to that basic and elemental force, death is also segregated according to other dimensions and so one's age, one's place in the socio-economic hierarchy and one's diseases also serve to structure the final hours and one's manner and place of disposal. I have tried to demonstrate the importance of these latter factors in organising the dead and the dying of Belfast and I have argued that the significance of such factors in everyday interaction is reflected in the importance which they have been awarded in official descriptions and explanations of death. Death in the modern world is seen basically as an abnormality, not just as a product of disease, but as a disease in its own right. Death and disease are equated in the hospital and the nursing home, as well as in the reports and analyses of mortality which the medicine of social spaces instigated and developed during the past century and a half. In the chapters which follow I shall further argue that the individualisation of the dead also results in an individualisation of grief and bereavement. That the same medicalisation process which has converted death into a pathology – a break and a rupture from normality – has further extended its influence to the mourner in such a way that grief and bereavement are also capable of being viewed as pathogenic processes. In fact the capacity to pathologise human behaviour has no end.

7 The Social Distribution of Sentiments

MOURNING AND MELANCHOLIA

> Mourning is not the spontaneous expression of individual emotions.
> (Durkheim, 1968:567)

In 1915 Freud wrote an essay on mourning and melancholia in which he attempted, among other things, to draw distinctions between normal and pathological grief.[1] Three years earlier Durkheim had published his Elementary Forms of the Religious Life in which, by way of illustrating the nature of 'piacular' rites, he described a violent, bloody and altogether intemperate scene of grief which was drawn from the world of the Warramunga. Durkheim disarmingly described the latter as 'guided by etiquette', though it is clear that its propriety was solely premised on the social context in which it occurred. In other words, the way in which 'normal' grief was expressed was variable and as far as Durkheim was concerned, 'Mourning is not a natural movement of private feelings wounded by a cruel loss; it is a duty imposed by the group. One weeps, not simply because one is sad, but because one is forced to weep' (1968:568).[2] Consequently, both the intensity and the substantive detail of publicly expressed grief was subject to social pressure. This argument of Durkheim's, that grief and mourning are socially patterned, had itself been preceded some six years earlier by Hertz's claim that grief is distributed and redistributed according to social principles.[3] And whilst both of these claims were preserved and developed within social anthropology during the 20th century, they were absolutely and entirely ignored by those who studied the manifestations of grief in western cultures – a study which, incidentally, fell under the control of a normalising psychology. It is in the light of these discussions that I wish to analyse the nature of social loss in Belfast and in this chapter I intend to do three things. The first is to trace the routes by which grief and sorrow were normalised and medicalised during the 20th century. The second is to examine the evidence for the claim that human grief is socially patterned and socially channelled. And the third is to analyse some of the ways in which sentiments of grief and sorrow were distributed across the dead of Belfast during 1981. The core of this chapter is concerned with an analysis of the responses which were made to the deaths of 415 people. But I have not analysed the private expressions of sentiment which no doubt accompanied most, if not all of the deaths. Instead I have analysed the very public expressions of loss which were made by the bereaved through the use of obituary notices placed in the various Belfast newspapers. These notices, which are listed in the newspaper 'deaths columns', provide a unique but detailed record of the beliefs, sentiments and social relationships which surround death and the dead, and taken together they go some way to providing a sociological portrait of human loss and sadness as it manifests itself in the modern world. In Belfast, the practice of making such public declarations is so common that it was possible to trace entries for all but 39 of the 415 subjects and, what is more, the missing cases proved themselves to be a very instructive group. But before embarking on the study of those public declarations I would like to place the analysis of funerary sentiments in a wider sociological context. Firstly by glancing at the processes which have sought to normalise and medicalise grief in the 20th century and secondly by examining the evidence for the claim that human grief is socially structured and socially patterned.

THE NORMALISATION OF GRIEF

The body, as we have seen, is invariably used as a site in which explanations for death can be discovered. It is also a point on which a whole array of medical, legal and bureaucratic practices are concatenated, to say nothing of the social and ritualistic practices which routinely focus on the human frame. The latter are nowhere more evident than in cases of death. People cry over corpses, they wash corpses, they coffin corpses and carry them and bury them and erect gravestones over them, and they do so in a framework of emotional turmoil. Such turmoil is what is normally referred to as grief and one of the questions which arises in the study of such grief is the extent to which it is, or can be socially patterned.

Grief in the 20th century is primarily understood and 'managed' on the basis of principles which were first elaborated within the context of a normalising psychology. The starting point of normalisation rests in Freud's 1917 essay on mourning and melancholia in which he drew distinctions between normal and pathological responses to loss. This theme of pathology was extended in 1940 by Klein who asserted that all grief is in a sense pathological in so far as it apes the manic-depressive state—though for most people the phase is transitory. Now, these ideas contrast quite markedly with those of the 19th century in which grief, although it was sometimes viewed as a cause of insanity,[4] was never interpreted as itself pathological. Grief, if anything, was a condition of the human spirit or soul rather than of the body and in that sense it could neither be normalised nor medicalised. The work of the psycho-analysts, however, was only the first in a series of processes which sought to medicalise grief. The second stage was represented in the work of Lindemann (1944).

Lindemann's work was the first to place the study of grief on an empirical footing and the first to establish a 'symptomatology of grief'. His work was based on the reactions of 101 bereaved 'patients' and included a number of subjects involved with the notorious Cocoanut Grove fire. His primary aim was to establish the symptomatology of grief and the secondary aim was to discuss the management of grief. The symptomatology was drawn in terms of five or six factors and the general conclusion which Lindemann arrived at was:

> Acute grief is a definite syndrome with psychological and somatic symptomatology. (Lindemann, 1944:141)

Furthermore, and in addition to reducing grief to a somatic state, Lindemann sought to measure it, and he did so by dividing his patients into those who suffered from normal and those who suffered from morbid grief. The two variables along which such normalisation was assessed were those of intensity and duration, and he further argued that the management of grief should be related to these forms and factors. Needless to say, grief management was discussed in terms of the principles of clinical medicine alone.[5]

The 'pathological' features of grief were also emphasised in a somewhat disturbing article by Anderson (1949), entitled, 'Aspects of Pathological Grief and Mourning', but the most forceful attempt to reduce grief to a somatically sited disease was that proposed by Engel (1961) in his paper 'Is Grief a Disease?', in which he directly compares grief to pathogenic bacteria. Further developments in the attempt to characterise grief as a (double-edged) disease occurred with the publication of Parkes' work in the 1960s and 1970s though, as the following quotations illustrate, the symptomatology of the proposed disease remains somewhat ambiguous:

> Of all the functional mental disorders almost the only one whose cause

is known, whose symptomatology is stereotyped and whose outcome is usually predictable is grief. That grief is a mental disorder there can be no doubt, since it is associated with all the discomfort and loss of function which characterises such disorders. (Parkes, 1965:1)

By 1972, however, the blanket assessment that grief is a mental disorder was somewhat modified and now only the abnormal forms took this symptomatology.

On the whole, grief resembles a physical injury more closely than any other type of illness . . . But occasionally . . . abnormal forms arise, which may even be complicated by the onset of other types of illness. (Parkes, 1975:19)

For all of these authors and investigators, then, grief was something in the body which could be measured and assessed. The intensity and duration of grief were factors whose origins could be located in the biochemistry of the body or in the infantile history of the subject, and the context in which grief was analysed was viewed in medical terms, or at best in psycho-therapeutic terms. Furthermore, the medicalisation and normalisation of grief took place within a theory of developmental stages which incorporated a somewhat Hegelian view of personal and behavioural processes. In this view, human behaviour is seen to involve an unfolding of human potential towards an ultimate stage of stability or 'reintegration' This theme has dominated the study of many and varied facets of death. Kubler-Ross (1970), for example, analyses the responses of the dying in terms of five stages: denial and isolation, anger, bargaining, depression and acceptance. And Backer *et al.* (1982) invoke the concept of stages in order to account for attitudes to death among children and therapeutic responses of hospital staff, as well as the responses of the terminally ill. In like manner, most of those who discuss grief also use the developmental metaphor. Thus Parkes (1975) talks of phases of yearning and phases of despair. Backer *et al.* (1982) list three stages: yearning, anger and guilt, and disorganisation. Kavanaugh (1972) lists seven stages: shock, disorganisation, volatile emotions, loss, loneliness, relief and re-establishment. Attempts to categorise grief as it occurs in specific age groups and populations have also been made and probably the most notable of these was that of Bowlby (1961) in his study of bereaved children. Broadly speaking, however, it is in terms of stages and timescales that the normal is assessed and it is within this context that grief is seen to unfold within the human psyche.

Despite the fact that both Lindemann and Bowlby gave a hesitant nod in the direction of social factors when they were assessing the impact of grief on the bereaved individual, most authors seem to have remained quite ignorant of the work of Durkheim, and Hertz. The Durkheimians, of course, had sought, very early on in the 20th century, to discuss and explore the fact that the intensity of grief was not the product of some inner unfolding, but of social processes which tended to channel grief in some directions whilst deflecting it away from others. This structural distribution of grief seems to have been more or less ignored until the publication of Peter Marris's work on Widows (1958) and Gorer's work on the bereaved (1965), and though both of the latter authors continued to assess grief in terms of the 'normal', 'stages' and timetables, they did supplement the study of grief with the missing link of social structure.

Broadly speaking, however, it is clear that psychology and anthropology adopted incommensurable standpoints on the study of grief, so that whilst the first concentrated on the subjective experience of grief in different populations, the second concentrated on the outward expression of grief and utilised that outward expression as an indicator of inner sentiment. In western culture, it was psychology which therefore dominated the study of grief and bereavement during the 20th century and, overall, the problem of grief, like death before it, became medicalised and individualised and subsequently fell under the control of medical personnel. Thus, the priest was ousted from the aftermath of death in favour of the doctor and grief was treated (in all senses of that word) as a private and segmented emotion. It was this segmentation and individualisation of grief which prompted Gorer to carry out his study of the phenomenon, and it was on the basis of that study that he theorised about the denial of death in western culture. It is to this private distribution of grief that we will eventually turn, but before doing so it is essential that we examine something of the Durkheimian theory of sentiments and, in consequence, say something about the social context of bereavement.

SENTIMENTS AND SOCIAL STRUCTURE

The attempts to normalise grief in terms of the assumptions and theories of psychology, took a new turn, as we have seen, in the analysis undertaken by Lindemann. And this concern to trace out the nature and limits of grief in empirical populations was further developed in the work of Marris (1958) and Gorer (1965). Marris's work was based on a

study of 72 London widows, whilst Gorer's work encompassed a far
wider range of bereaved individuals drawn from a number of age, sex,
class and regional groupings. In both cases the intensity and duration of
grief were studied empirically and some estimate of the normal and the
abnormal was made. Neither study, however, explored the Durkheimian hypothesis that grief is socially distributed and socially
controlled. In fact, Gorer, an avowed anthropologist, reached the
somewhat curious conclusion that contemporary mourning practices
are marked by a total lack of ritual—the consequence of which is
'maladaptive behaviour'. In the England of the 1960s, he concluded,
'The most typical reaction [to death] is . . . the denial of mourning'
(1965:113). Marris's work also rested on many of the prevailing
assumptions of psychological theory, though he did recognise that
sociological factors impinged on the intensity and duration of grief.
Thus, in his 1974 work he asserted that:

> The severity of grief depends, then, on the degree of [social]
> disruption: and it can be at least crudely predicted from the emphasis
> which a society places upon different relationships. (Marris, 1974:38)

In that sense, the loss of infants and of the old is, for example, less
disruptive than the loss of those in the economically active age-groups,
or of the married.

The claim that grief is controlled and distributed in terms of social
ritual, as I have suggested, can be traced back to the work of Durkheim
and Hertz. Both men argued that the intensity of grief expended by any
individual or group was dependent on a socially constructed formula,
rather than on innate or natural feeling. Thus, the mourning of infants
or strangers was always cursory, whilst the mourning of healthy and
active adults was not. In many respects it would seem that both of these
authors adopted a curiously strong version of sociological determinism
with regard to this issue, though their relevance to this chapter rests
solely in their suggestions concerning the social variability of mourning.
Nevertheless, it is perhaps useful to note that they saw an equivalence
between the experience of sorrow and the expression of sorrow in a
manner which today would be regarded as unacceptable. And in order to
underline the virtues and importance of this line of thinking, it will prove
useful to glance at some of the studies which have touched on this
problem.

One of the strongest adaptations of the Durkheimian thesis was that
advanced by Monica Wilson in her (1957) study of the Nyakyusa. This

study had its precursor in Godfrey Wilson's (1939) analysis of Nyakyusa burial rites which emphasised a number of issues which are worth noting here. Most important from our point of view was his claim that a 'normal' emotional response could not be assessed in purely statistical terms but only in terms of what is regarded as obligatory by any given group. To obey the constraints of the group is normal, to ignore them is abnormal. Normality was, therefore, socially imposed.

Secondly, the emotions which were so imposed were often socially differentiated. Thus, whilst Nyakyusa burial 'is a lively event',[6] there were still marked differences between the reactions of males and females. Broadly speaking 'the women wail and the men dance', and the funerary ritual emphasised male strength and courage as against female fear and trembling. The women wept all of the time; the chief mourners wept only once or twice and, according to Wilson, the latter were *obliged* to show grief. Finally, he noted that the length of the mourning period depended on the status of the deceased: high status, extended mourning; low status, truncated mourning. The clearest expression of such sociologism, however, was that given by Monica Wilson in her discussion of Nyakyusa *rites de passage*:

> The rituals heighten the emotions and canalize them. They both teach men to feel, and teach them what it is proper to feel. (Wilson, 1957:232)

Other observations on this funerary theme have been provided by Goody (1962) in his study of the LoDagaa. Goody claimed two things in this connection. First, that different social relationships demanded different expressions of grief and second, that the amount of grief displayed varied according to the social status of the deceased. Thus, he noted that among the LoDagaa physical restraint was used on the bereaved (either symbolically, or physically), and that the differences in standardised restraints indicated a diminution of the grief expected in the three classes of kinsfolk affected by bereavement. Hence, conjugal and parental roles demanded the sharpest display, followed by siblings, followed in turn by those who fulfilled filial roles. Furthermore, he often implied that the elaborateness of the funerary ritual was a direct function of the amount of wealth to be redistributed at death, though that was not the only source of differentiation, and it was equally clear from the study that this was also dependent on the existence of a social personality. Thus, 'The LoDagaa display no public grief at the death of an unweaned child, for it is not yet accorded human status' (1962:149).

Some parallel observations of the differentiation of grief were also given by Huntingdon and Metcalf (1979) concerning the Bara of Madagascar. The latter, it would seem, engage in on-cue crying only at funerals and on only two occasions: while the body is lying in the womens' hut before burial and just before the secondary burial of the exhumed bones, though 'only the women are expected to cry' (1979:27); whilst, according to Hopkins (1983), Roman funeral rights demanded open and dramatic expression of grief, especially from women (1983:226). And Douglass (1969) observed that in Murelega, public displays of grief were expected from a wider group than that encompassed by the immediate family of the deceased. Thus, the *auzoa*, or neighbourhood, and the kin group, as well as the *echekoak*, or domestic group were activated at times of death and expected to manifest sorrow. In similar fashion, Geertz (1960) observed that Javanese funerals involved everyone who lived near the deceased, but that 'tears are not approved of, and certainly not encouraged' (1960:72). Whilst Danforth (1982) informs us that in rural Greece 'crying over the graves of her relatives is an obligation imposed upon a woman by virtue of her participation in a network of human social relationships' (1982:115). The most adventurous claims of social anthropology on this theme of public displays of sorrow, however, are undoubtedly those made by Radcliffe-Brown in his study of the Andaman Islanders (1922).

In that work Radcliffe-Brown offered a theory of weeping. He noted that in Andamanese society there were seven occasions for ceremonial weeping, three of which involved reciprocal (interactive) weeping and four of which involved one-sided weeping (as, for example, in weeping for a dead person). In keeping with his broad functionalist position he sought to discover the purposes of such weeping both for the individuals involved and for the social structure as a whole. He concluded that for individuals, ceremonial weeping served to release emotional tension, but its wider, social purpose was more interesting and more fundamental. Thus, of weeping, he stated:

> The purpose of the rite is to affirm the existence of a social bond between two or more persons. (Radcliffe-Brown, 1922:240)

Social bonds were therefore asserted and emphasised in public declarations. Consequently, without the bond there could be no weeping. Thus, in Andamanese society children, who had not yet been awarded a social personality were 'little mourned' and, 'a stranger who dies or is killed is buried unceremoniously or is cast into the sea' (1922:109).

My purpose in citing these various cases of anthropological and historical investigation is solely to illustrate the point that grief, at least in its public manifestations, is socially variable and that the social location of a deceased person has much to do with the manner in which grief is expressed. It is not my intention to enter into a debate as to whether sentiments are truly 'within' individuals, or whether they are imposed from some other source.[7] Nor is it my intention to assess the theoretical implications of the findings of Radcliffe-Brown as against, say, Durkheim. It is enough to show that grief is distributed according to social principles and to suggest that the experience of grief is, in some part, reflected in its public expression. Hopkins (1983) asserts that 'rites are the cultural mirror in which feelings are reflected', and that seems a very useful line of enquiry to follow, but in the next section of this chapter I intend to broaden this principle somewhat and claim that all public expressions of grief act as a mirror in which private feelings are reflected, and as the public expressions wax and wane so does the social base of the sentiments behind them.

THE SOCIAL DISTRIBUTION OF SENTIMENTS[8]

No last farewells were spoken,
No time to say goodbye,
You were gone before we knew,
And only God knows why;
Our hearts ache with sadness,
And secret tears flow,
For what it means to lose you darling,
No one will ever know.

We sat beside your bedside our
hearts were crushed and sore.
We did our duty to the end till we
could do no more,
In tears we watched you sinking, we
watched you fade away
And though our hearts were breaking
we knew you could not stay.
You left behind some aching hearts
that loved you most sincere,
We never shall forget you Jimmy
Dear.

Page two of the *Belfast Telegraph* contains up to two hundred such notices on most evenings of the week together with some additional Birthday Memories and In Memoriam notices. The sentences are expressed through the clichéd style of the medium and the same words and phrases can be picked out with monotonous regularity.[9] 'Deeply regretted by the sorrowing family circle'. 'At rest'. 'A smile for all', a heart of gold, one of the best this world could hold'. 'A silent thought, a little prayer, knowing you are in God's care'. The prose and the verse tap out a weary sadness across the full width of the page.

> Three little hearts still love you,
> three little hearts still care,
> three little hearts all wonder why
> Daddy isn't there.

The phrases evoke something of the sorrow and the grief which their donors experienced, and through the clumsy style one can sense a little of the human loss and suffering which lies behind these printed and preselected words. Such standardised sentiments as these also appear (with lesser frequency), in the *Liverpool Echo*, the *Yorkshire Post*, the *Dundee Courier* and a whole range of other papers which criss-cross the British Isles. Yet page two stands as one of the more lasting records of bereavement which relatives and friends can leave behind, for when the graveside flowers have faded and the headstones have been lost in the overgrowth of indifference, the printed word will remain to be read.

In its own way page two exists as a massive, but relatively unexplored human document on the funerary customs of a whole society and it can be used in much the same way as Gaby and Michel Vovelle (1970) used iconography to signify changing patterns of belief about death and the hereafter in Provence; or, indeed, in the way in which Vovelle (1973), and Chaunu (1976), have used wills and testaments to measure changing attitudes towards death in France during the 17th and 18th centuries. For the modern death notice not only documents sentiments of grief, it also serves as an explicit statement on the beliefs and practices which envelop human mortality. Analysis of these notices can yield data on the prevailing images of death, on the extent and nature of dechristianisation, on the privatisation of death and on the extent to which death is or is not monopolised by kinship networks. Careful analysis of course has to be tempered with cautious interpretation. The greatest single problem in the use of death notices as a source of sociological data is in relating them to the social characteristics of the population to which they refer, for the verse and the prose alone are strangely lacking in personal detail. They tell us almost nothing about the contexts of the deaths, or of the occupations, class membership, marital status, or age characteristics of the persons whose names appear on the newspaper page.

By tracing the 415 subjects of the 1981 death register sample through the Belfast newspapers, however, it was possible to tabulate sentiment against social characteristics. And the emerging patterns were further elaborated by examining the newspapers in which the notices were placed. The latter proved possible because Belfast newspapers have markedly different readerships, the *Belfast Telegraph* and the *Newsletter* being read by a predominantly Unionist and Protestant population, whilst the *Irish News* is read by a predominantly Nationalist and Catholic population. The contrasts in style of the obituary notices within the three newspapers are instructive and highlight marked differences in the beliefs and funeral practices of different segments of the city's population.

Of course, not everyone has a death notice inserted in a newspaper and in the existing sample there were some 39 subjects who merited no mention at all, but the missing 39 were not randomly distributed and tended to fall into quite distinct groupings. In so far as the extent and nature of a person's death notices can be utilised to tell us something about the social evaluation of the deceased, then, the absence of these individuals from the newspaper pages is particularly enlightening. But I wish to leave aside the excluded dead for the moment and concentrate on the included dead.

Unlike most parts of Britain, where one death notice per deceased is deemed sufficient to announce death, it is fashionable in Belfast to insert as many citations as possible in the appropriate paper. Only one of the citations is intended to perform an informative function—stating the place and time of burial or cremation; the remainder are expressions of sorrow or support, and acknowledgements of a social bond. The highest number of citations recorded in this sample was 90—for a murder victim. The Rev. Robert Bradford MP, however, was cited in 132 notices on the occasion of his murder and the hunger striker Bobby Sands MP had notices which covered four full pages of the Irish News on 7 March 1981 alone (but not a single one in the 'Unionist' newspapers).

Including murder victims, the average number of notices per person was seven, but a sizeable minority within the sample (20 per cent) received more than ten notices, though many (14 per cent) had just one informative notice in the English style. The latter was normally the response characteristic of families of professional workers. The bank manager's death announced on the day of his cremation and the accountant's death announced somewhat abruptly and without embellishment both fit into this pattern. The usual style of the notices emphasised the privacy of the event and the undesirability of any ceremony.

OTHER, Alan Norman—Oct 27th 1981.
Dearly loved husband of Kathleen.
House and funeral strictly private.
Family flowers only.

TABLE 7.1 *Mean number of obituary notices in a 10 per cent sample of deaths in Belfast in 1981, according to occupational grouping, sex, age and marital status of deceased*

Variable	N	Mean number of notices
Occupation:		
1 Non-manual	106	4.03
2 Manual	270	8.59
Sex:		
1 Male	176	8.29
2 Female	200	6.44
Age:		
1 Aged 1–59	65	12.37
2 Aged 60 +	311	6.25
Marital status:		
1 Married	159	9.16
2 Unmarried	190	5.97

The starkest of these solitary notices simply announced 'house closed'. This desire for lack of ceremony together with an emphasis on privacy and restriction of the grieving process to the immediate family was distinctive of professional workers and occurred irrespective of religious affiliations—even though the privatisation of the mourning period would be regarded as particularly unusual in Irish Catholic culture. The dead of the professional class were also the most likely to be found 'resting' in a funeral parlour or, in the case of the Catholic dead, in the local chapel, and they were the least likely to be returned to their homes to await burial. This dearth of publicly expressed sentiment was, moreover, a feature of the deaths of non-manual workers in general and it is possible to get some estimate of the distribution of public sentiment for the various groups involved by glancing at Table 7.1.

In fact, one can see that the association between manual workers and public declarations of grief is extremely strong. Indeed, the table expresses in yet another form the dominance of the ethos of privacy among the non-manual group. And although one cannot measure sorrow or sadness on the basis of this kind of evidence it is possible to gain an estimate of the extent to which publicity and privacy pervade the middle and working classes respectively. Thus, among the latter, grief is frequently placed on public display and one can readily find such responses as the following: 22 citations for the 72-year-old widow of a labourer; 24 for the road sweeper's wife; 37 for the wife of a bricklayer, all dutifully placed by sorrowing daughters (four notices), sons (five), grandchildren (nine), sisters (four), nieces and nephews (five), cousins (six) and friends (four); each citation carrying a special verse and the occasional homily:

> So if you have a mother
> love her while you may
> for we wish with all our hearts
> that we had ours today.

As the example of the bricklayer's wife demonstrates, the public expression of sentiment is dominated by the kinship group. Relatively few non-kin notices are ever donated other than for murder victims. In fact the notices seem to be frequently used in order to mark out the limits of the kinship network including, where appropriate, citations from emigrants in Australia, the USA, South Africa and Canada. However, for the working class at least, there were occasional citations donated by friends rather than relatives and in the more traditional working class areas of the city the immediate neighbours sometimes donated a notice to 'their esteemed neighbour'. Occasionally one could find evidence of second order relationships apparent in the notices—these were notices placed by friends of the bereaved rather than by friends of the deceased. These might express sympathy—'To Billy on the death of his mother', or might simply note a regret—'for the mother of Billy'. The average number of such notices was, however, very small except in the case of victims of violence, in which event the non-kin notices outnumbered those from kin members. The latter, in fact, suggests two things about the distribution of grief. First, that grief is overwhelmingly regarded as the preserve of the immediate family (the 'sorrowing family circle', as it is frequently referred to). And, second, that where a death is perceived as holding implications for the members of a wider community, it is regarded as appropriate and necessary to express some kind of a relationship to the deceased person. But if one excludes murder victims, then what strikes one most about these notices is the manner in which they underline the trend towards the monopolisation of death by the family. And it is of interest to read Ariès (1983) on this point:

> In our former, traditional societies, affectivity was distributed among a greater number of individuals rather than limited to the members of the conjugal family. It was extended to ever widening circles, and diluted . . . Beginning in the eighteenth century, however, affectivity was, from childhood, entirely concentrated on a few individuals, who became exceptional, irreplaceable, and inseparable . . . The sense of the other now takes on a new primacy. (Ariès, 1983:472)

Thus, most deaths are taken out of the social networks in which they occur and are subsequently privatised within the kinship group. The deaths of Protestants seem to be particularly vulnerable to the processes of privatisation and they express most vividly that movement towards hidden death (*La mort inversée*) of which Ariès has spoken. Only within Irish Catholic culture does death seem to exist within a public field. In the *Irish News* notices, for example, the terms private and closed are demonstrably absent from most of the citations. Indeed, in many of the citations the community is urged to participate in the grieving process and there are frequent notices from clubs and societies which 'urge all members to attend the funeral' at the appointed hour.

The importance of the conjugal family in declaring the presence of death and in making some public declaration of death is to a certain extent illustrated in Table 7.1. The table illustrates the marked differences in the mean number of death notices allocated to the married as against the widowed and single. And we can also see within that table some further patterns concerning the distribution of obituary notices. It is noticeable, for example, that the extensive repertoire of sentiments available for these citations is more readily called on for the use of male decedents than for females and we can also see within the table the effects of age patterns on public declarations. Thus, and excluding infants, (whose position I shall discuss shortly), the under-60s are cited in a markedly greater number of notices than are the over-60s, though it is also the case that within the 1–59 group there are marked variations in the number of notices awarded.

The distribution of the notices, then, is clearly uneven. The factors of sex, occupational grouping, marital status, age and mode of death make a significant impact on the number of citations which any one person will receive. In addition to simple distributions, however, we must also consider the nature of the sentiments which are distributed. I have already pointed out that some notices are merely informative – they announce the name of the deceased, the date of death and the place and time at which the funeral will take place – but it will be clear by now that there is much more than procedural and biographical detail contained in these contemporary bills of mortality. In fact, they can be utilised in two major respects. First, to estimate the extent to which funeral procedures have been subject to the process of dechristianisation and second to inquire into the images of death which prevail in contemporary Irish society.

By enumerating the number of notices which contain some reference to Christian culture and by separating them from those which do not, it is possible to gain some measure of the degree to which Christianity continues to impinge on the death process. English death notices, for example, are strikingly secular in their tone and content as compared to those of Ireland. But there are dangers in assuming the centrality or marginality of Christian belief in the death process on the basis of these notices alone. None of the clerics and nuns who fell within the sample, for instance, had citations which made any reference at all to religious belief and this in itself should serve as a warning about the validity of inferences on such a matter. Moreover, it is frequently very awkward to distinguish between those citations which contain elements of Christian belief and those which do not, as many of the notices imply belief in resurrection and the like without stating so clearly, or without encompassing such a belief within Christian symbolism. What, for example, is one to make of such phrases as; 'It's only goodnight', 'Only sleeping, we shall meet again in the morning', or 'You deserve the rest'?

Nevertheless, by counting the number of notices which make some explicit reference to some aspect of Christian culture, marked differences appear between Protestant and Catholic attitudes towards death (see Table 7.2). In the *Irish News*, for example, the number of notices which contain religious references outnumber those which do not by five to one, whilst in the predominantly Protestant papers there is a virtual equivalence in the number of secular to religious notices. Protestant references range from the simple 'Redeemed', through biblical references—'The Lord Is My Shepherd'—to the most popular of all which involves the incorporation of religious belief into inelegant verse:

> Just like a tiny snowflake a tear fell from his eye,
> and as I wiped the tear away my heart cried 'Why oh why?'
> But God has His own reasons. He knew you needed rest
> so in God's hands I leave you because he only picks the best.

In general, a number of deductions concerning Protestant eschatology can be made from these notices. For example, there is a broadly based belief that most of those who die are 'with the Lord' and hell is obviously something reserved for others, or for strangers and Catholics. Futhermore, and combined with this belief in personal salvation, there is a notion such that the body and soul are conceived of as distinct and separate entities, 'Absent from the body, present with the Lord', is a favourite for the newspaper obituary. And, finally, one can see within the sentiments a vision of the afterlife as a state of peace, rest or tranquillity and as a place where reunions are made. Moreover, the language in which these notices are couched is often deliberately theocentric, rather than Christocentric. It is God the Father rather than God the Son who dominates here.

TABLE 7.2 *Mean number of 'religious' obituary notices in a 10 per cent sample of deaths in Belfast 1981, according to occupational grouping, denomination, sex, age and marital status of deceased*

Variable	N	Mean number of notices
Occupation:		
1 Non-manual	106	1.00
2 Manual	270	4.31
Denomination:		
1 Protestant	259	1.95
2 Catholic	115	6.63
Sex:		
1 Female	200	2.97
2 Male	176	3.84
Age:		
1 Aged 1–59	65	6.62
2 Age 60+	311	2.70
Marital status:		
1 Married	159	4.38
2 Single	190	2.67

Catholic references, on the other hand, take a noticeably different form. Gone are the biblical references, so too the notions of salvation, of being select or chosen. Instead we can read a language which is reminiscent of pre-Reformation Europe.[10] St Theresa, St Martin, Michael the Archangel and even Padre Pio are requested to pray for or intercede on behalf of the deceased. 'Mary Queen of the Gael pray for him', 'Sacred Heart of Jesus have mercy on his soul'. The emphasis on the soul is, of course, held in common with Protestant eschatology, but here the vision is predicated on the existence of an ante-chamber to Heaven in which intercessions and prayers can make all the difference between entry and exclusion. Moreover, the theocentric visions of Protestantism have given way to a Christocentric eschatology, where Christ is both saviour and judge of the dead. A judge whose decisions can be swayed by the intercession of the God Mother. In the cases of members of the Republican movement who have died, or who have been killed, these pleas for intercession are mingled with political sentiments (something which is entirely absent from comparable Protestant notices). 'To break the connection with England the never failing source of all our political evils, and to assert the independence of my country – these were my aims', reads one notice of an old Republican. And needless to say, those who are killed 'on active service' have citations swathed in politico-religious references.

Though the sentiments which are expressed through these notices and the language of such expression is immensely varied, the predominant images of death which are held within a community emerge clearly through the opaque style.[11] Sometimes the notices serve as a message to the deceased themselves (as with the two citations which opened this section), sometimes they serve as a means of urging others to stay loyal to their families, or to love their mother. Many of them simply underline the enigma of death:

Not till the loom is silent
and the shuttles cease to fly
will God unfold the canvas and
explain the reason why

Though that particular enigma related to the death of a 93-year-old man. Very often, however, the death notice is used to signify what is considered to be the mode of death: suddenly, at hospital, as a result of an accident, or murdered. Side by side with such comments the donor might express belief in the virtues of death: 'peace after suffering', 'peace after pain'. Comments of the latter type were especially prevalent among the notices of cancer victims, but once again it was the working class bereaved who were the most forthcoming with such statements.

Aside from sentiment and belief it is evident that patterns of behaviour can also be inferred from the content of these notices. One does not need to count citations in order to discover that cremation is as rare in Ireland as it is common in South Wales or London, but there are features of funeral practice which a study of death notices can reveal with exceptional clarity. I have already remarked how it is possible to gain an insight into the extent to which the privatisation of grief emerges as a feature of bereavement among the professional sector in particular and the Protestant community in general. Similarly one can discover the obverse of such behaviour as it is manifested in the public death of Catholic culture. With the exception of notices for Catholics from social class I, all of the *Irish News* notices made plain the fact that the corpse, or 'remains', was awaiting burial from the home address, whilst in the *Newsletter* and the *Telegraph* the most frequent references were to the presence of the deceased in the funeral home or funeral parlour. But perhaps most impressive of all is the way in which these notices manifest the sectarian social arrangements within which the living live. From death bed to graveside sectarianism declares its victory and not only are the deaths of Catholics and Protestants announced in different newspapers (only two members of the entire sample had notices in the *Telegraph* as well as the *Irish News*), and not only do such notices draw on distinctive cultural traditions to express sentiments of loss and sadness, but they announce the segregation of the very tombs in which the dead will rest: the Catholic cadavers are despatched to Milltown, or the City cemetery, and the Protestant cadavers to Roselawn or Carnmoney.

The analysis so far suggests, then, that the publication of death notices serves, at least in part, as a mechanism whereby kinship, community and political groups can reaffirm and reassert their solidarity. The topography of kin and community relationships can be marked out and thereby sustained and solidified by means of these notices. Such acts of delineation are never clearer than in the announcements of murder victims, and those who are killed as a direct result of political activity. I have already remarked that murder victims have an immense number of citations in the Belfast papers: 127 for an assassinated Ulster Defence Association official, 132 for the Rev. Robert Bradford, MP; 67 for an Irish National Liberation Army member who was killed whilst priming a bomb and the highest number of notices in my sample for an ambulanceman murdered by the Irish Republican Army. Naturally, many of these notices contain nothing more than the aforementioned religious and secular sentiments (in fact, one of the citations of an alleged, though notorious, Belfast murderer queried: 'Why does God always pick the roses and leave the thorns behind?'), but it is evident that the placing of a notice for those who die violently also functions as an expression of political solidarity. Apart from notices placed by kin members, the murdered are also cited by friends, neighbours, political and social groupings and on occasion by groups who had no contact at all with the deceased. Such notices usually make plain the cause of death and in so doing reaffirm common sentiments. 'Murdered', 'Murdered by the enemies of Ulster', 'Murdered by terrorists', 'Murdered by the enemies of Christ'. In the *Irish News* the agents of murder are different. 'Killed by Irish renegades', 'Murdered by pro-British opportunists', 'Murdered by British thugs', 'Murdered by Thatcher's gunmen'. But in addition to the sentiments of loss, shock and tragedy one can also witness the rejuvenation of political and moral sentiments which are further attested to by attendance at the massive funeral cortège which a murder victim usually receives. Indeed, Durkheim's claim that a society going through circumstances which sadden, anger, perplex or irritate it 'exercises a power over its members, to make them bear witness by significant acts, to their sorrow, perplexity or anger', could just as well apply to urban Belfast as it did to the social life of the Australian outback.

There is one further bonus which arises from a matching of obituary notices to death certificates. It is the possibility of discovering the social characteristics of the unmentioned—of the excluded dead. The excluded dead are not a homogenous group and they are themselves liable to subdivision, but what is intriguing about them is the ease with which they can be slotted into the expected Durkheimian categories. Into the first of the three sub-groups which compose the excluded dead fall those who, the Durkheimians would have claimed, were never admitted into the full flux of social life in the first place. Here belong the stillborn and the handicapped infant. The six-month-old hydrocephalic baby, the three-month-old baby with congenital heart disease, the seven-month-old boy afflicted by Down's syndrome, all belong here. In addition, not one of the 66 stillborn babies (the subject of a separate survey), were regarded as worthy of a citation. The death of the new born child is, as Hertz would have said, an infra-social event, and since society has not given anything of itself to the child it is not affected by its disappearance and remains indifferent to its loss. It is a theme which is taken up by Hopkins (1983) in relation to ancient Rome: '. . . dead babies and infants, especially if they were girls, did not have a social personality which justified individual commemoration. In strict law they received no formal mourning' (1983:225).

Into the second category it is possible to place those whose physical disabilities, or social behaviour precluded their full participation in social life. The 49-year-old man suffering from mental handicap, the 73-year-old suffering from senile dementia, the two suicides in the sample, the old, single women of 'no previous occupation', and the single men whose occupations had extracted them from city life—the merchant seaman and the lighthouse keeper. These are the individuals who are discovered dead many days (or months) after death and to whom only the Coroner will pay any attention. And it is here that one finds echoes of Marris's (1974) claim that the severity of grief depends on the degree of disruption and can be predicted from the emphasis which a society places on social relationships. In that sense, these are the individuals whose lives are little emphasised and therefore little remembered.

Finally there are the outsiders, the strangers, who are admitted to society, but never into it. Here we must place the Dubliner killed in a bomb explosion, the 23-year-old British Army Corporal shot through the head and the 19-year-old soldier who died similarly. Outside and unmourned perhaps, but unlike the other two sub-groups, this last will, one assumes, be mourned elsewhere.

8 The Disposal of Dead Persons

THE CATEGORY OF THE PERSON

> For the Tallensi, personhood is finally validated at the death of the individual. (La Fontaine, 1985:132)

Discourse creates its own object. Death is, in this sense, a product of the forms of knowledge and practice which surround it. And so too with the dead person. Indeed, our very notion of a person is, as Mauss suggested in his 1938 paper, nothing but a product of social organisation.

> From a simple masquerade to the mask, from a 'role' to a 'person', to a name, to an individual; from the latter to a being possessing metaphysical and moral value; from a moral consciousness to a sacred being; from the latter to a fundamental form of thought and action – the course is accomplished. (Mauss, 1985:22)

In other words and ignoring the evolutionary dogma contained in this assertion, concepts of 'self', 'individual', 'person', 'role' and 'identity' are both socially organised and socially created. They are organised and created out of the legal, moral, religious, social and political practices which surround them. Thus, the Christian individual is different from the Hindu counterpart, the European (a person before birth) contrasts with the Tallensi (who gains personhood only at death) and the slave of ancient Rome (who had no *persona*) stands empty in the shadow of the modern American (whose rights to personhood are enshrined in constitutional law).

It follows from this, then, that if we wish to know what a person is we have to analyse and examine the very social practices which surround personhood – a task which is far beyond the scope of this study. Death, however, is at least one point in human existence where a few of the numerous practices concerned with personhood, identity and individuality tend to converge. In fact, I have already demonstrated how the individuality and uniqueness of human beings is persistently underlined in many of the investigative processes which are contingent on the discovery of a human death. And I have also sought to show how

153

acts of segregation and mourning dovetail into these processes. But there is more to the creation of persons than this and in this chapter it is my intention to examine the nature of personhood at death.

Funerary practices in Ireland tend to circulate around at least three modes of personhood – each one of which is articulated, to a greater or lesser degree, on the human frame. The first of these three is the corpse itself – human flesh and bone. The second is the soul which (during life at least) is assumed to reside in the human body. And the third is the persona or social being which was shaped and fashioned through the multitude of social contacts which the deceased made during life. And in the three days which normally intervene between the announcement of physical death and the moment of disposal, these three modes of being have to be attended to in their distinctive ways.

The centrality of the physical body to funerary procedures is beyond question; without a body there can be no funeral.[1] It is the existence of the soul, however, which provides the *raison d'être* of the funeral service. And the hypothesised duality of body and soul means that there are at least two problems which confront the living. The first is to prepare for the disposal of the corpse and the second is to prepare for the disposal of the soul.

Belief in the existence of the human soul constitutes an integral component of funerary ritual in Europe in general and Ireland in particular. It is not a belief which is unique to the West, but questions concerning the survival of the individual soul have been encompassed in a peculiarly Western eschatology (see Brandon, 1967). In Ireland the interconnection of soul and body is not a problem which is ordinarily considered in everyday affairs, but at death the position is quite different. Then, issues which have possibly lain dormant for the entire length of a human existence are awarded singular attention, for death is commonly regarded as the point at which body and soul are divorced. It has not always been so and, according to Ariès, it is a belief which arose only in the 13th century. Subsequently, at the hour of death:

> The *homo totus* and the body . . . retreated into indifference, while the soul . . . invaded every dimension of the individual; the soul has become the whole man. (Ariès, 1983:286)

In Belfast, matters concerning the departure of the soul are mainly regarded as the preserve of clerics. The clericalisation of the funeral is again something which Ariès traces to the 13th century, but it is still clearly evident in the modern funeral. It is the priest or 'minister' who accepts the coffins into the sacred areas of chapel and graveyard and it is they who officiate over the acts of disposal. The centrality of the clerics to funeral procedure is emphasised in this study by the fact that just over 80 per cent of the subjects in my 1981 sample had some kind of a religious ritual performed on the day of their disposal (though such ritual did not normally seem to be extended to stillborn babies).[2] And the funeral directors whom I interviewed could only recall having ever attended a few disposals where there was an entire absence of religious intervention and those were mainly cases of cremation rather than burial. But whilst matters relating to the soul are regarded as the preserve of clerics, those relating to the treatment of the corpse are held to be the preserve of professional body handlers, or undertakers. Again, it was not always so and it would seem that, even within living memory, it was common for the kin group to prepare its own dead for disposal, but this is no longer the case and today all funerals are managed by one of the eight or nine firms of undertakers in the city. To describe the latter as a group of body handlers is, in some ways, to underestimate their role, for they are in many respects the directors of a complex social drama in which the body is the most important prop. Indeed, those undertakers who constantly underplay their ritual role are often disparagingly described by other undertakers as 'mere body snatchers', though the extent to which undertakers in general get involved in the processes of grief and mourning seems to be variable. In any event it is clear that in analysing the disposal of body and soul, we must of necessity consider the work of both the funeral director and the cleric, for both the professionalisation and the clericalisation of the funeral are central processes in the acts of disposal which impinge on death.

Yet body and soul do not exhaust the elements of being which are present at the funeral, for there is usually a third element present and this *tertius gaudens* is the social being of whom Hertz spoke:

> Death does not confine itself to ending the visible bodily life of an individual; it also destroys *the social being grafted upon the physical individual*, and to whom the collective conscience attributed great dignity and importance. (Hertz, 1960:77.) [Emphasis added.]

Thus the dead 'person' is present in three dimensions: as a corpse, as a soul and as a social being. The funeral is organised around each of these and it is this superimposition of being which, in part, accounts for the intensity of feeling which is aroused at funerals. Here, however, I shall be focusing in the main on the ways in which these entities are organised and managed, rather than on the sentiments which the funeral generates.

THE BODY

According to Van Gennep, the body is frequently used as a base on which social transitions are traced. The truth of such a claim is nowhere more evident than in funerary ritual and the treatment of the body during the various stages of mortuary procedure almost directly reflects its volatile social status. Indeed, throughout the process of disposal the body acts, rather as Van Gennep suggested (1960:70), like a piece of wood on which social symbols are carved. Van Gennep, of course, was not only interested in the nuances of body symbolism; he also forwarded a theory concerning the structural framework of the great social rituals. It seems to me that both lines of Van Gennep's thinking are worth pursuing here, and so I intend to adopt both the assumption that the process of disposal has an underlying structure and the notion that images and perceptions of death are fashioned on the corpse.

According to Van Gennep, all *rites de passage* have a tripartite structure. The trilogy can be expressed in three words: separation, transition, incorporation. The subject of a rite is first dismissed from the existing state of affairs, then stands in a liminal phase of disorder and is finally reintegrated into a new society. This commonality of structure was also, to some extent, discussed by Hertz (1960) and consequently had a very powerful impact on the writings of social anthropologists in general (see Vizedom, 1976), and more especially on the work of Goody 1962), Huntingdon and Metcalfe (1979), Turner (1969), Douglas (1973) and Danforth (1982). And this thesis of tripartism can be profitably applied to the funerary rituals of Ireland. This is particularly the case when we consider the manner in which the corpse is treated; but before I examine the ways in which this is so, I would like to say a few words about those who are responsible for actually managing the corpse between the time of death and the moment of burial.[3]

Following death, the body is handled by a number of individuals. The nursing staff of the hospitals have to perform the 'last offices' for the corpse, the hospital porters have to transport the body to the mortuary and mortuary attendants must prepare bodies for autopsy or discharge from the hospital. Here, however, I intend to concentrate on the work of the professional body handlers of whom I spoke earlier. It is they who collect, prepare and encoffin the cadavers before burial or cremation and it is they who, in carrying out their work, reflect most fully the attitudes concerning death and the dead which appear in contemporary Belfast. In describing the treatment of the body I shall therefore concentrate on the role and the work of the professional undertaker and refer to the work of other groups only in passing. There are, of course, significant differences among undertakers in their treatment of the cadaver and one of the most important of these is contingent on the fact that, in the main, there exist two groups of undertakers—Catholic undertakers for Catholic corpses and Protestant undertakers for Protestant corpses.

Dismissal

Once a death has been certified, dismissal is an all pervasive theme in the treatment of the body. Few people actually demand to take charge of the body and it is repeatedly dismissed from one site to another. Thus, it is dismissed from the hospital ward to the mortuary, from the home of the deceased to the undertakers, or from the hospital mortuary to the funeral parlour. If a death occurs on the street, an ambulance crew will refuse to transport the corpse and so the local authority is obliged to tender a contract for the collection of corpses, the so-called mortuary contract (which at the height of political conflict in the early 1970s involved the collection of hundreds of bodies in a year). At this stage the status of the body is at its lowest. It is regarded as a repository of disease. It is a source of danger, and dealing with bodies is regarded as low status work (Pine, 1975). Any initial work that needs to be done, whether it is in the hospital or the mortuary, is normally relegated to juniors and subordinates. It is very rare for higher status individuals to come in physical contact with the dead, though the polluting nature of the corpse cannot, of course, be attributed simply to its perceived physical properties. We must assume that, as many anthropological studies have demonstrated, it is death as a social category rather than as a physical phenomenon that is truly the pollutant. Thus, Douglas (1966) argues that death is polluting because the corpse is one of those many entities which falls between distinct classificatory boundaries, and that things which are anomalous are always regarded as dangerous or polluting. Turner (1969) argues that states of liminality stand opposed to the organisational features of structure and are therefore invariably regarded as dangerous.

Whatever the source of such pollution, it is noticeable that the collection of bodies is normally carried out surreptitiously, and at this stage there is a great deal of emphasis on hiding the face of death. Curtains are drawn around the death bed, the face of the corpse is covered with a sheet, bodies are enclosed in coffin 'shells', the shells are carried in closed vans. In hospitals and nursing homes there are frequently designated times when bodies may and may not be collected. The bodies themselves are moved down back stairs, leave by back doors, are transported out of side entrances and are left in back rooms. Even in the funeral directors premises themselves, it is noticeable that bodies are brought in by the goods entrance and only leave by the front entrance (Figure 8.1). According to the *Manual of Funeral Directing* (MFD), 'Of first importance for funeral premises is a building with two entirely separate entrances' (MFD, 1981:18:3)—so that the ugliness of death can be reserved for the rear of the premises (see also Unruh, 1979).

During these preliminary stages the body takes on a 'thing-like' quality. It is constantly referred to as 'it' or sometimes in more abrasive terms. Occasionally there is reference to the 'remains', but never to him or her, still less to Mr, Mrs or Miss. A body, whether it be in a hospital mortuary, a funeral home or in transit is a mere thing to be disposed of. It is transported like any other thing and is very often stored in rooms along with other stored things. On arrival at the undertaker's premises it is usually dumped in a rather disorderly preparation room, and the disorder of the body is often reflected in the general disorder of the room. At such times as these the corpse takes on the characteristics of a commodity; to be value added in a process of production. The body becomes a mere object to be cleaned, beautified and presented appropriately. The *Manual of Funeral Directing* (1981) emphasises this commodification of the body in a number of ways. 'Note', states the Manual, 'vehicles used for the conveyance of bodies must be taxed "Goods" (1981:5:3). Such 'objectivation' is often apparent in the treatment of children. To the funeral director infants are different from adults only because of their size. They are difficult to embalm or require special coffins. Neither the child nor the adult is perceived as having peculiarly human qualities at this stage and it is only when the corpse re-emerges on the day of disposal that it will once again be awarded some of its personal characteristics.

Transition

These caretakers of the dead, as Pine (1975) has called them, are also responsible for managing the body during the transitional phase and they do so on special premises. It is immediately apparent to any visitor that undertakers (in common with mortuary technicians), are often very conscious of their uneasy status in the eyes of the living and seem to be aware of the polluting nature which death has in the eyes of the latter. They are keen to be perceived as professionals and often pin certificates

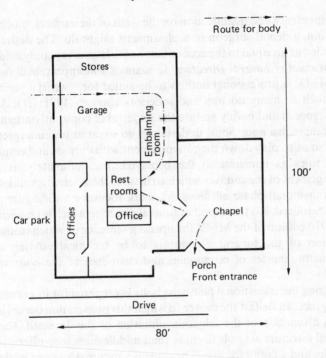

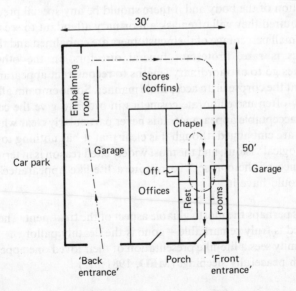

FIGURE 8.1 *Sketch plans of two funeral directors' premises*

of competence and qualification on the walls of their offices, much as an optician, a dental surgeon or a pharmacist might do. The desire to be regarded as an equal to the accountant or the lawyer is plainly evident in the *Manual of Funeral Directing*. In manner and appearance, suggests the MFD, 'a professional note' is to be aimed for, '[wear] a plain dark suit such as many doctors and solicitors choose' (1981:1:1). And in dress, speech and bodily gesture the undertaker constantly attempts to generate such a note. Some undertakers go so far as to reinterpret their roles so as to play down their involvement with corpses and emphasise their roles as ministers to the bereaved. But, ultimately, it is the management of the cadaver which structures their activities and during the transitional phase all necessary work focuses on the figure of the corpse. Indeed, it is this aspect of funeral directing which is underlined in the 1970 edition of the MFD, the opening sentence of which reads: 'The function of the funeral director is to be technical adviser, agent, contractor, master of ceremonies and custodian of the body for his client.'

During the transitional phase the body is prepared for its eventual re-emergence. In Belfast the degree to which this preparation occurs is very much a function of the religious affiliation of the deceased. Catholic funeral directors act as little more than middle men, who offer a hearse for hire and a coffin for sale. They spend a minimal amount of time on preparation of the body and if there should be any special preparatory tasks required they will often ask a mortuary attendant to see to them. Only a small percentage of their customers are embalmed and the use of cosmetics is rare. Protestant funeral directors on the other hand sometimes go to extraordinary lengths to reconstruct appearances and to present the corpse in an acceptable manner. Some embalm all corpses and very often use elaborate cosmetics in order to give the cadaver a socially acceptable appearance. It is never particularly clear why bodies actually are embalmed, though it is clear that it has nothing to do with eschatological visions, and the most widely cited reason is in terms of the appearance of the corpse. 'To restore a life-like appearance', as the MFD would have it:

> This is perhaps the most valuable aspect of the treatment. The change effected is truly remarkable—gone is the deathly pallor . . . Instead the family sees a life-like presentation of their loved one appearing as though peacefully sleeping. (MFD, 1981:5:7)

The appearance of the body at death is, in fact, a subject of some precise and specific ideas. All of the funeral directors to whom I spoke insisted that the corpse should look 'peaceful' and 'restful' (see also Barley, 1983). The MFD underlines the point:

> The aim of the funeral director or his assistant should be to attain a natural posture [for the corpse] . . . The lips smoothed into a natural relaxed position . . . the lids should be set as in natural sleep . . . The posing of the arms and hands is also worthy of careful attention for hands can be most expressive . . . How often one sees them left with fingers stiff and straight! The fingers should be bent to a natural pose. (MFD, 1981:5:6)

Needless to say, a myriad of other details are also required to be attended to in this quest for naturalness, and embalmers in particular take great pride in their ability to capture a 'natural' pose (even working from photographic records of the deceased if necessary). It is, however, normally the head more than any other part of the body which is taken to represent the distinguishing features of death and the individual. But whether it be the head or the torso, an ability to 'restore', 'reconstruct' or 'fix' the remains is, among embalmers, regarded as an indispensable and highly valued art. The arbitrariness of the naturalness, however, is plainly evident in both conversation with undertakers and in the written documents of the MFD. Thus, it is not natural to leave the corpse with its arms straight down beside it. It is natural to have the nose 'centered and pointing to the ceiling.' It is not natural to leave the hair untidy. It is natural to close the eyelids. And one is reminded here of Mauss' (1979) comments on the techniques of the body and their cultural variability. For, according to Mauss, physical stance and the performance of physiological functions are socially fashioned and thus alter from one social group to another. The study of natural stances, of physical gait, therefore, tells us much more about prevailing social beliefs than about human physiology. And, in the case of the present issue, it also says a great deal about some of the prevailing images of death which are present in contemporary Irish culture, for here, death is seen as equivalent to sleep, rest, peace and tranquillity.

Some bodies, of course, cannot be sculptured into restful and peaceful poses and, for various reasons, it is sometimes impossible to present the body without the signs of death monopolising attention. These are the 'bad remains' which undertakers normally dislike dealing with[4] and, needless to say, when the signs of death are visibly present on the corpse, the coffins are closed. Death, therefore, is only put on display when it is in accord with an acceptable image. Ugly, brutal death is still very much hidden from view and, unlike some other cultures, such as those mentioned by Huizinga (1924), this is not one which dwells on the processes of physical decay and putrefaction which death inevitably brings in its train.

Re-emergence

The re-emergence of the body for 'viewing' is the third step in the trilogy. In accordance with its modified status, the corpse eventually reappears in new clothes. The old clothes and the old order is discarded and in its place is a new form of dress. As Hertz observed, 'the dead are put into a new wrapping which is sometimes precious' (1960:55). Not only is the corpse dressed (usually in a modified shroud, with the face left uncovered), but it is also coffined. The container is in many ways the central prop of the drama which is to unfold and it is a *sine qua non* of the drama that an appearance of grandness be asserted. The container must look both solid and expensive, and coffin styles are frequently given names which fit with this desired image such as 'The Monarch' or 'The Ambassador'. But most significant of all is the fact that the coffin marks out a personal private space within which the body rests and which serves to ensure that the bones of the dead will not be inter-mingled.

In line with the modified alteration of status, the corpse is often moved so as to occupy another space. It may be moved to another part of the funeral directors' premises, or may be returned home or may be taken to a chapel overnight.[5] In any event the slight change of social status is accompanied by a spatial transition. In the case of the Protestant funeral directors the corpse is more often than not moved to the 'rest room' (Figure 8.1). The very title of the room is intended to accord with that prevailing image of death which I have already mentioned. These rooms are sometimes decorated in the style of a bedroom, with table lamps and curtains surrounding the cadaver. They are often carpeted and furnished and designed so as to look 'warm'. The cadaver itself is laid out in accordance with the image of serenity which is regarded as so desirable. In the case of Catholics, the hands may clasp a rosary or a crucifix and the subject may be dressed in the robes of a confraternity. Sometimes the corpse is dressed in a uniform, or in expensive everyday clothes, but the most common forms of dress are those which are suggestive of sleep and rest. At this stage the bereaved are occasionally given 'visiting cards' listing the times at which they may visit the cadaver. The MFD is quite liberal in its applause for such idiosyncracies as long as the central message of death is conveyed. Thus:

Whatever the style of the interior, whether casket or coffin, the acid test is—does it finally present the deceased in a restful and natural manner. (MFD, 1981:5:9)

In Ireland, at least, the viewing of the body is usual and, apart from some exceptional circumstances, the coffin remains open until the third day after death when disposal normally occurs. On the day of disposal the elements of grandness come into their own. The coffin will first be carried through the streets by relatives and friends of the deceased (a practice which predominates among the working class of Belfast), and at an appropriate point, placed in a limousine and transported to the cemetery. At all stages the coffin is visible—even whilst it is within the hearse, and its public display stands in marked contrast to the concealment which characterises the previous stages.[6] The body is present, but hidden. It will not reappear again and the living can henceforth only relate themselves to the soul and the social persona of the deceased. Throughout the burial trilogy, then, the human body is used and manipulated by the living to convey an image of death and the hereafter. Indeed, both the nature of the corpse and of death are defined through the range of social practices which surround them.

THE SOUL

It is, perhaps, a reflection on the secularisation of Western culture that most 20th-century analyses of the funeral have concentrated more on the expression of social than of religious function. Thus, Mandelbaum (1976) opens his analysis with the claim that 'Rites performed for the dead generally have important effects for the living. A funeral ceremony is personal in focus and is societal in its consequences'. Firth (1951) states:

> A funeral rite, is a social rite *par excellence*. Its ostensible object is the dead person, but it benefits not the dead, but the living. (Firth, 1951:63)

This focus on social function stands in clear contrast to, say, the work of Tylor (1871). And the emphasis placed on the profane aspects of funerary ritual is apparent in almost every other 20th-century anthropological work on the subject. It forms a dominant theme of, for example, the works of Bloch (1971), Douglass (1969) and, to a lesser extent, Goody (1962). Moreover, in concentrating on the social effects of the funeral, the essential religious message of these rites is often lost. It is a point which Bowker (1973) makes when he claims that what mortuary rituals have in common is not their social function, but their religious purpose. And in making that point his work effectively serves to draw our attention to the religious meanings of funerary ritual and to the religious context in which disposal occurs.

The significance of religious ritual for the dead of Belfast is partly expressed in the fact that the overwhelming majority of dead in my 1981 sample of deaths had some kind of religious service associated with them, though there were some 83 people whom I could not trace or for whom the position was unclear. What is more, the ritual was also (except in one or two cases) a clericalised ritual in which a priest or minister had exclusive control over the proceedings. It was the cleric who accepted the body into the chapel (though there were few Protestants who were actually buried from a place of worship), and it was the cleric who led the funeral cortège into the graveyard. It was the cleric who decided whether the ritual was to be performed for any given person and it was normally only he who spoke at the religious service. But it is more the nature of the service than the structure of the proceedings which I wish to examine here for, as I hope to demonstrate, it is that more than anything else which determines the relationship between the living and the dead.

It is in fact to a 19th-century rather than a 20th-century writer that we have to turn in order to gain an insight into the religious meaning of funerary ritual. The writer is Bachofen and the insight is contained in his claim that the most important feature of funeral symbolism is its emphasis on rebirth. To the latter, the theme of rebirth constitutes an 'inner truth' of human culture.[7] Thus:

> The funeral rite glorifies nature as a whole, with its two fold life- and death- giving principle. Death is represented as bound up with life, and even as its foundation. (Bachofen, 1967:39)

It is therefore the spiritual or physical rebirth of the individual which constitutes the focal point of the service. And it is, once more, a point which Hertz emphasised in his 1905 essay:

> Each promotion of the individual implies the passage from one group to another: an exclusion, i.e., a death, and a new integration, i.e., a rebirth. (Hertz, 1960:81)[8]

In Ireland this question of rebirth is usually encapsulated within

Christian eschatology, and in all three types of service which I am about to discuss the issue of rebirth forms the central hinge around which other activities pivot. But the ways in which the regeneration of the dead supposedly occurs is differently interpreted in the various strands of Christianity and in this section I intend to discuss the impact of Anglicanism, Presbyterianism and Catholicism on the departure of the dead.

The disposal of the soul is a process which occurs quite abruptly in Irish Protestant culture. It occurs on the day of the funeral alone. After disposal there will be no prayers for the dead and no further ritualistic concern with the repose of the soul. Even in Irish Anglicanism this is the case. The disposal of the Catholic soul, however, is more of a process than an event, and the possibilities for the living to intercede on behalf of the dead are always present. In fact it is the eschatology of these two forms of Christianity which determines the nature of their funeral services, each of which take a markedly different form from the other.

Protestant Eschatology

So also is the resurrection of the dead: It is sown in corruption; it is raised in incorruption: It is sown in dishonour; it is raised in glory: It is sown in weakness; it is raised in power: *It is sown a natural body; it is raised a spiritual body*. There is a natural body and there is a spiritual body.

(Quoted in: *The Order for the Burial of the Dead According to the Church of Ireland* and *The Book of Public Worship* of the Presbyterian Church in Ireland). [Emphasis added.]

The features of Christian belief which impinge on funerary ritual are primarily those which concern the resurrection and the judgement of the dead. The resurrection lies at the base of the quotation which opens this section. Christ is the 'first fruits' and then 'every man in his own order'. But belief in the resurrection is also linked with belief in a judgement. There are a number of possibilities concerning the judgement of the dead. There is scope for belief in only one judgement and scope for belief in two judgements. There is scope for belief in an immediate judgement and there is scope for belief in a final judgement. There is scope for belief in a personal judgement and there is scope for belief in a collective judgement. And it is not easy to correlate the various permutations with specific social groups or, even, with specific denominations.

The basis for belief in a final judgement is alluded to in the Anglican funeral service. Thus:

> We shall not all sleep, but we shall all be changed, in a moment, in the twinkling of an eye, at the last trump (for the trumpet shall sound), and the dead shall be raised incorruptible, and we shall be changed.

The implication of such a belief is that there exists something of a hiatus between physical death and spiritual rebirth. But according to Chaunu (1976) this belief jars against the belief in an immediate judgement which is implied by a number of Biblical passages and, in particular, that in which Jesus is reputed to have stated to those on the cross at Calvary, 'Today you shall be with me in paradise' (Luke 23, 43). It is a statement which was closely considered by both Calvin and Luther (see Chaunu, 1976), and which, if accepted at face value, has important implications for the relationship between deceased and survivor.

Many, if not all, Irish Anglicans hold that there are two judgements of the dead, one immediate and one final. But there is no equivalent belief that the living can assist the dead during the period of the hiatus—nor that the dead can assist the living. There are, therefore, no prayers for the souls of the dead. Evangelical Protestantism, on the other hand, tends to adopt the view that there is only one, immediate, judgement and in that event, of course, there is no point in indulging in prayers for the dead since they cannot in any way influence an outcome. But it is not easy to discover what the empirical distribution of these different beliefs actually is. Yet it is clear that it is these kinds of considerations which determine the relationships between the living and the dead, and the way in which Anglicans and Presbyterians, in particular, relate to the dead is quite different from relationships which exist within Irish Catholic culture.

In the funeral service itself, however, there is very little emphasis placed on the question of judgement and the texts are more readily geared towards consoling the living and emphasising the rebirth of the dead. In fact, the Presbyterian order of service is particularly conscious of the mourners, and comparatively little is said concerning the state of the soul. In that respect it seems to reflect its 'this-worldly' orientation in general and this point was further emphasised by one of my clergymen informants who claimed that 'the service doesn't emphasise body or soul, but the grief of those left behind'. Indeed, a contrast is evident in the opening sentences of the Presbyterian and Anglican services. The former opens with the sentence 'Blessed are they that mourn', whilst the latter begins 'I am the resurrection and the life'. The emphasis on resurrection, however, occurs in both churches and in both parts of the funeral service, the first part of which is held either at the home of the deceased, the funeral home or the church, and the second part of which occurs at the graveside. It is, however, the latter which constitutes the final dismissal and as the coffin is lowered into the grave both Anglican and Presbyterian will verbally reaffirm their belief in the 'sure and certain hope of the resurrection to eternal life'.

In Anglican and Presbyterian Ireland, therefore, all ritualistic preparations for the dead are finalised on the day of disposal. The tombstones of those who are buried will be erected to 'the memory of the dead', rather than to their souls or their bodies. In the same manner, the Memorial Book in the crematorium in which the names of the dead are written (and which few ever return to read), will also mark the memory of the dead rather than the repose of the soul. Such is the dismissal of the dead—an event achieved in a double act, first a physical dismissal, on to which is added a spiritual dismissal. The links between living and dead are therefore severed and although visits to the graveside will be made long after death they can have only a private, inner significance to the bereaved. It is a situation which contrasts markedly with the visit to the Catholic cemetery.

Catholic Eschatology

The relationships between the living and the dead in Catholic culture are quite different from those which we have discussed so far, though much the same kinds of problems concerning the resurrection and judgement of the dead are faced by Catholic and Protestant eschatology.

In Irish Catholicism the *homo totus* still lives and the distinction between the body and soul, which is so clearly marked in Protestant culture, is absent. Both body and soul are believed to be resurrected and so, in a curious kind of way, there is a heavy emphasis on the presence of the body, despite the fact that this is in no way evident from the work of the Catholic funeral directors. It is this belief which also accounts for the long-standing opposition of the Catholic hierarchy to cremation (an opposition which only began to crumble in the 1980s). It is therefore the *homo totus* who is resurrected after death and not simply the soul.[9]

Broadly speaking, Catholic doctrine seems to hold to two judgements of the dead, the first being an immediate judgement and the second a deferred one on which resurrection depends. Furthermore, the first is viewed as an individual or a particular judgement, whilst the second is a collective judgement comparable to that which figures in Judaic eschatology. And there is no doubt that Catholic eschatology provides for a tripartite vision of the hereafter so that heaven, hell and purgatory all figure in the Catholic geography of the afterlife.

It is the belief in a prolonged period of purgation which acts as a foundation for distinct social practices in Catholic culture. For during the period of purgation it is possible for living and dead to interact. Prayers for the soul of the dead are frequently offered and so are requests for intercessions from the Saints. Equally, it is possible for the dead to serve the living, though requests for assistance are usually directed to the Saints and especially to 'Our Lady'. In many ways, the organisational structure of the world of the dead is believed to reflect that of the living and so a hierarchy of authority and saintliness is envisaged. These interactions between living and dead are diffused throughout the entire breadth of Catholic ritual. Thus, they are evident in the funeral service itself, which is forcefully directed to the passage of the soul, the obituary notices which are placed in the newspapers, as well as on the tombstone inscriptions.

The theme of resurrection is emphasised on a number of occasions in Catholic ritual. At the graveside, in the funeral mass and in the prayers said in the home of the deceased before burial occurs (see Christian Burial, 1983). But the overriding concern of Catholic ritual is with the passage of the deceased through the hereafter. The introduction to the funeral mass sums up this concern:

> The Church offers the Paschal Sacrifice for the dead so that, through the union of all with one another in Christ, the dead may be helped by prayers and the living may be consoled by hope. (Christian Burial, 1983:23)

Furthermore, and as distinct from the activities of the Protestant churches, there are prayers for the dead on the seventh and thirtieth days after death, as well as on the anniversary of death (at which point there will be a number of notices placed in the *Irish News*). And in this manner the relationship between living and dead exhibits an active rather than a passive structure, which thus contrasts decisively with important elements of Protestant culture.

It may be objected, of course, that organised religion has very little hold over modern populations, or, that the finer points of theology rarely enter into the daily considerations of the majority of the laity. And it does seem fair to assume that the range of private accommodations of the living towards the dead is much richer than can be expressed within, or assumed from the official doctrines of the various churches. Nevertheless, whatever the nature of the private accommodations are, they tend to exist within the broad framework of Christian eschatology. Thus, belief in a resurrection is widespread (as is evident from the newspaper notices), and so is belief in a judgement or reward system. It is also clear that in Irish Catholic culture there is a firm belief that the living can intercede for the dead (as is evident from the tombstone inscriptions), and that it is possible to form a tenuous relationship between life and death. Moreover, whatever private visions of the hereafter people might hold, it is clear that they are based on a belief in a radical discontinuity between life and death, for, in this culture, there is neither a role for ritual offerings to the dead, nor for the provision of grave goods (cf. Gnoli and Vernant, 1982). And thus it seems fair to conclude that Christian eschatology both structures the interrelations between the living and the dead and gives to the funeral service its most fundamental and basic rationale. For, although the body is and must always be present at the funeral service, it is truly the spiritual being who constitutes the corner stone of the events which unfold on the day of disposal. The funeral is, as 19th-century writers were keen to emphasise, first and foremost a religious event and only secondarily a social phenomenon.

SOCIAL BEING AND SOCIETY

The disposal of the body and the ritual farewell to the soul neither completes death nor, in all societies, does it necessarily mark the point of death. For example, Goody (1962), Lydall (1982) and Mandelbaum (1976), all cite instances of cases where, to paraphrase Mandelbaum, it is society rather than nature which is endowed with the last word on whether a person has really died. And that, of course, is the true lesson of Hertz's teaching and the primary implication of his statement that death is more than just a physical event. In many ways, therefore, it is the demise of the social rather than the physical being which finalises death in many cultures. And Goody (1962), for example, discusses the ways in which, among the LoDagaa, death is not finalised until the social roles of the deceased have been redistributed among the living. Thus, for the LoDagaa, the role of lover and spouse, as well as the physical artifacts which constitute 'property', have to be reallocated before a corpse is truly ready for disposal.

The realignment of the social relationships which are disrupted by death, however, is of necessity a lengthy process and as such, its analysis lies beyond the scope of this study. But the very fact that the majority of the dead once lived in a mesh of social networks has implications for funerary ritual and it seems not unreasonable to expect that the social worlds to which the deceased once belonged are reflected in part within the funeral rite. Here, then, I intend to examine those aspects of the funeral which reflect and reinforce the social order and examine the ways in which the social links forged in life are carried over into death.

Whenever a person is pronounced dead, the nearest relatives of the deceased will seek out an undertaker to take charge of the body and prepare it for viewing and disposal. Broadly speaking, Catholics will seek out Catholic undertakers, and Protestants Protestant undertakers. It is a situation which was underlined for me on a number of occasions, but never so clearly as by the Protestant undertaker who cheerfully told me, 'We employ only Protestants and we bury only Protestants'.

A relative who inadvertently contacts the 'wrong side', will have his/her business 'passed on' to the appropriate side, though this is not always so and a small number of firms will, under certain circumstances, poach business from their opponents across the sectarian divide. It is clear, however, that such behaviour is often regarded as unfair and illegitimate and whenever such poaching occurs undertakers will be keen to tell you that a given body 'was really ours'. From the very first steps in the arrangement of the funeral, therefore, the preservation of social boundaries exists, at least as an unintended consequence of the management of death. This crystallisation of sectarian social arrangements is further underlined by examining the deviant cases, for, apart from 'poaching', a small number of Catholics or Protestants are always dealt with by funeral directors who are not their religious affiliates. The deviant cases are not, however, randomly selected. The most common source of Catholic dead for Protestant undertakers and of Protestant dead for Catholic undertakers are the partners of 'mixed marriages', (Catholic/Protestant marriages), that is, people who have in a sense crossed over the invisible line which segregates the city. It is therefore only when boundaries have been crossed during life that it is regarded as legitimate to cross them during death. And this sectarian theme is, as I have already shown, further reinforced by the religious service which is conducted in the presence of the corpse, as well as by the place of burial and the symbolism represented on the tombstone.

In the engagement of an undertaker and the registration of the death, other social links are forged. The most important of these are the links which are drawn out between the deceased and the members of the conjugal family. It is the spouse, brother, or eldest son who formally registers death, and it is he or she (but usually he) who will seek out an appropriate undertaker. From the very first, therefore, the primacy of the family in arranging matters of death is asserted. A grave will be purchased, arrangements for the religious service will be made, and distant kin will be notified all from within the kinship network. The grave itself will exist as a monument to the conjugal pair (plus any unmarried children who have previously died or who will die unmarried at some future date). But, generally speaking, the grave is of only marginal significance to social life in Ireland. It does not, for example, constitute a foundation of the social order in the ways in which Bloch (1971) and Douglass (1969) discovered to be the case in Merina or Basque society. This reaffirmation of family and kinship links is also evident, as I have already shown, in the placing of obituary notices, but it is often at its clearest in the socio-spatial arrangements which are manifest in the procession which occurs on the day of the funeral.

On the day of physical disposal, the undertaker will first seek out the principal mourner. This is usually the spouse or son, but may be a brother or brother-in-law, for males predominate among those who organise the funeral. The principal mourner will be given a central place in the funeral cortège following immediately behind the coffin. Where a coffin is carried, these socio-spatial arrangements are even more evident, for social distance is expressed through physical distance of the mourner from the coffin as can be seen from the simple sketch plan of the cortège which is outlined in Figure 8.2.

This arrangement has a certain fluidity in practice so that, for example, whenever the coffin is carried through the streets the carriers

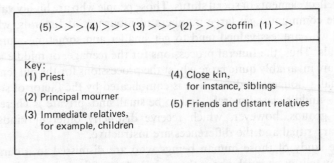

Key:
(1) Priest
(2) Principal mourner
(3) Immediate relatives, for example, children
(4) Close kin, for instance, siblings
(5) Friends and distant relatives

FIGURE 8.2 *The order of the funeral cortège into the graveyard*

are circulated from the back to the front, but they are always drawn in a temporal order which reflects the spatial distribution outlined above. In the earlier stages of the funeral the position of priest is filled by the 'conductor', who is usually the funeral director and it is the latter who normally determines the timing and pace of the funeral. Moreover, the procession can also serve to underline gender roles. Thus, only men carry the coffin and, generally speaking, only women weep.[10] It is men who conduct the ritual and women who organise (where appropriate) the funeral meals. In the words of one informant, 'men make the arrangements and women make the tea'. These acts of reflection, and reinforcement are, however, displayed most sharply at military funerals.

In military funerals it is the military rather than the social order which is immediately reinforced. The pall bearers, for example, must be drawn from the same rank as the deceased and are placed in order of seniority whilst, 'officers attending as mourners, march in seniority from front to rear, and other ranks march in a similar order at the rear of the funeral' (MFD, 1981:12). Space and social order are therefore appropriately distributed and thereby act to reinforce the elements of the social world from which the deceased was drawn. And it is in military funerals that the use of symbolism is most evident. Thus the use of flags and military emblems is constantly used to reaffirm and reassert faith in nationhood, comradeship, the regiment, the battalion, or the political worlds which are associated with the deceased. In Belfast, however, almost any funeral can become a political funeral and thus become incorporated into the political culture of either of the two communities which populate the city. The social significance of such political funerals is, however, to be dealt with in the next chapter.

As well as reflecting and reinforcing aspects of kinship, military or political organisation, it is also true to say that the funerals in a broad way reflect elements of social status. Those people who are highly valued by the community get large numbers of mourners at funerals, whilst those who are less valued tend to get smaller and sometimes cursory funerals. Thus, the funeral processions for the teenage, or middle aged dead are invariably quite large whilst the processions for the old tend to be small (though this distinction is complicated by the factor of social class—middle class funerals tend to be small and 'private'). There are some groups, however, which receive distinctly different kinds of funerary ritual and the differences are instructive.

The study of those human beings who are dismissed in a cursory fashion tells us as much about the social values of the living as does the study of those who are dismissed with elaborate ritual. In that sense, the excluded dead constitute a sociologically significant category, even when their numbers are comparatively small. In Belfast, there are a number of groups whose funerary ritual is strikingly sparse, and the spartan nature of their disposal is a direct reflection of their position in the social structure. The largest of these groups is the stillborn. Some stillborn babies are buried in individual plots and according to Christian ritual, but such formal burials are rare. Usually, their burials are 'contracted out', that is, a firm of undertakers is awarded a contract to dispose of the unwanted infants who populate the hospitals. They are subsequently buried in common plots and without religious ritual. One assumes with Hertz that 'The death of a new-born child is, at most, an infra-social event; since society has not yet given anything of itself to the child, it is not affected by its disappearance and remains indifferent' (1960:84; see also Goody, 1962). In those cases where parents make their own arrangements for burial they are still likely to encounter resistance to formal ritual. This is especially the case in Catholic culture. Thus, one undertaker reported that if he was requested to organise a funeral for a stillborn child he would 'Give the father a box and tell him to do it himself', and 'certainly wouldn't encourage a hearse'.

The burial of an infant under one year of age is not as devoid of ritual as that of a stillborn baby, but there is a distinct privacy about the event. The burial is not announced, the wider kinship group is not involved, and the participation of the wider community is never considered. But infants are not the only group to suffer abject burial, for other deaths are also subject to contract. Disposals are 'contracted out' to cater for those deceased who have no kinship network, or whose kin are likely to be indifferent to the death. So the existence of a contract is itself an index of social antipathy towards a corpse. It is therefore interesting to find a contract for the burial of inmates of the old lunatic asylum in existence. This, of course, covered the deaths of the geriatric patients within the existing hospital. It was not possible to discover the proportion of such deaths which fell within the terms of the arrangement, but the fact that a contract exists is notable. The subjects of these burials are disposed of in publicly owned plots and with a minimum amount of ritual—only the undertakers attending the burial. The lack of a social network in life seems, therefore, to be reflected in a lack of a network in death. In that respect these deceased are to be twinned with the stillborn and they stand in marked contrast to the disposals of those whose deaths have a political significance and who are the subject of the next chapter.

THE DISPOSAL OF DEAD PERSONS

> The ideas and practices occasioned by death can be classified under three headings, according to whether they concern the body of the deceased, his soul, or the survivors. (Hertz, 1960:29)

The social practices which circulate around each of these entities serve to fabricate the objects of their attention. Essentially, the body is used as a symbol on which the modern image of death is inscribed, but it is also used as a point at which to articulate concepts of personhood. For, at death, personhood is defined through the overlap of body, soul and social being. The peaceful, restful and cosmeticised corpse acts to signal both a vision of the hereafter and a vision of the civilised self—washed, dressed and publicly presentable. And attached to this cosmetically prepared corpse is a soul. The soul, of course, is a nebulous, imponderable entity. But, in so far as we come to be aware of it, it is through religious ritual. The religious service of the funeral both structures the soul and its journey through the hereafter, and I have tried to demonstrate how the image of the journey alters between one set of religious doctrines and another. Moreover, it is possible to see how the social worlds to which the deceased once belonged are immediately represented in the organisation of disposal, and how, in the act of disposal, are buried the social, political and cultural symbols which served to define the social persona of the deceased. It is to the study of political symbols, and in particular to the political appropriation of the dead, that I now wish to turn.

9 Death, Politics and the Body

THE POLITICS OF DEATH

The relationships between death, politics and the body are multiple, though not all aspects of death are politicised (except in the broad Foucaultian sense). In fact, and in everyday consciousness, the politicisation of death is normally associated with violence on the body. And despite the fact that (statistically speaking) politicised deaths are a minor sub-group in the population of the dead, there can be little doubt that they have the largest impact of all on the living. Indeed, the few deaths which are politicised tell us an enormous amount about both the organisation of death in general and the nature of political debate in particular and it is to these politicised deaths that I wish to turn in this chapter.

There are a number of themes which I shall pursue in the pages which follow, all of which relate to the politicisation of the dead. Firstly, and paradoxically, I intend to examine the context in which death and its associated diseases have been depoliticised. Secondly, I shall examine the social distribution of violent death in Belfast during 1981, and having done so, I shall examine the role of the dead in the expression of political action and ideology (as well as some typical patterns of reaction to violent death). And, finally, I shall discuss some of the relationships which hold between the body politic and the politics of the body.

THE DEPOLITICISATION OF DEATH

In the earlier part of this book I argued that our 20th-century image of death is very much a product of 19th-century medical discourse and that pathology, in particular, has been responsible for imposing a physicalist schema of causation on death, as well as for promoting a definition of death which is couched solely in somatic terms. Pathology, sited within the bastion of the hospital, consistently and successfully sought to define and explain death in terms of disease categories; to delete human agency from explanations and accounts of death; to erase socio-economic factors from our analysis of human mortality; and, above all, to design and organise an investigative system which examined death primarily in a framework of physicalism. Indeed, this triumph of pathology is so long standing and the assumptions of pathology are so deeply embedded in western culture that their impact on our vision of death is mostly hidden. What is more, pathology has achieved its goals at the expense of an epidemiology which was once sensitive to the role of socio-economic factors in promoting health, illness and mortality, and has thereby obscured our understanding of the relationships which exist between death and social life. In short, it has been the success of the medicine of species over the medicine of social spaces which has resulted in our modern vision of mortality.

Broadly speaking and, as I have already noted, the medicine of social spaces attempted to understand and explain death and disease in terms of the socio-economic conditions of production and reproduction, and tried to align socio-medical investigation with the principles of political economy (see Coleman, 1982). In that respect, issues relating to health, illness and mortality were seen, in part, as political issues and, in the words of Coleman, death was viewed as a social disease. This politicisation of mortality was, nevertheless, supplanted by the principles of clinical pathology which, in opposition to social medicine, tended to locate the causes of ill-health and human mortality in the isolated individual and his or her personal shortcomings. In other words, whereas social medicine promoted a vision of death as a social disease, pathology developed a vision of death as a personal misfortune and thus detached human mortality from socio-political issues. Moreover, and as we are now aware, the forces which underpinned the development of social medicine suffered serious setbacks in the late 19th century with the rise of the 'germ theory' of disease. Henceforth, explanations of mortality adopted a thoroughly physicalist form.

Within the terms of this physicalist ideology, the body plays a major role. For the whole nature of the discourse and discursive practices which surround the dead are pinioned on the physical bodies of deceased individuals. Thus, the cadaver forms the basis and foundation of the system, and the cadaver is the unit which is policed and on which medical, legal and administrative power is activated. In that sense the corpse is undoubtedly shrouded in distinct political practices. Yet, paradoxically, the essential thrust of clinical pathology was to lead to the depoliticisation of death.

Of the 4048 deaths which were registered in Belfast during 1981, few would have been regarded by the inhabitants as in any way related to political processes. Indeed, most of them would have been interpreted by kin, medic and priest alike as normal, natural, deaths. Moreover, and as I have demonstrated in Chapter 3, the very fact that the explanations of these deaths were medicalised would have been sufficient to secure their normalisation. Consequently, there was very little scope, and even less motivation, for any of the deaths to be appropriated by political organisations for specific political ends.

In the 1980s the only deaths which are seen as being overtly related to political processes are those which are classified as violent deaths, though not all violent deaths are politicised. Nevertheless, there is a politics of violence where there is no politics of heart ailments or cancers, and only a violent death is likely to be appropriated by a political movement for political ends. What is more, the 20th-century concept of violence is very specific and excludes much of what would have been regarded as violence by, say, 19th-century Europeans. In that sense, the scope for the politicisation of death is exceptionally narrow and an examination of the changing concept of violence can tell us much about current visions of death.

In 1981 there were 244 deaths certified in Belfast as due to violence.[1] They were classified according to their external 'cause of injury' and subdivided into three large groups: Accidental deaths, Suicides and Homicides. In 1881 there were 153 such deaths (a rate of 1.5 per thousand). The way in which these earlier deaths were subdivided was similar, but what is interesting about them is not so much the sub-categorisations of violent death, but the various phenomena which were regarded as forms of violence.

It is not easy to discern a coherent picture through the mass of changing detail which characterises the nosological treatment of violence, but I would argue that previous to the rearrangement of the Registrar General's nosology in 1881 there existed a nascent theory of structural violence in which deaths from such things as 'starvation', 'neglect' and industrial poisoning were regarded (and indeed, classified) as violent deaths. And I would further argue that this nascent theory persisted in a less well defined form until the 1940s, after which time violence tended to be understood solely in terms of direct personal injury mainly stemming from human agency. After that point any form of violence which was mediated through social and political structures, and which resulted in death, was reclassified as a disease or as an ill-defined condition. Consequently, deaths from privation, neglect and environmental sources were no longer regarded as violent deaths.

The evidence for these arguments is, in part, contained in the Annual Reports of the Registrars General for Ireland, England, and Scotland

and it is those reports to which I will now refer. Prior to 1881 there was a vast range of deaths which were considered as 'violent deaths'. As well as recognisable forms of accidents, homicides and suicides (categories which are themselves somewhat problematic), deaths attributable to the following causes were also classified as violent: starvation, neglect, want of breast milk, intemperance, poisoning, industrial poisoning, injury at birth, opium and morphia habit and lack of care at birth. With the nosological restructuring of 1881,[2] deaths due to starvation, want of breast milk and intemperance, were reclassified as diseases and thus removed from the category of violence. It was an alteration which clearly stands witness to an obsessive 19th-century desire to medicalise every aspect of the human condition. In Ireland the above named conditions were subsumed under the heading of dietetic diseases, in Scotland under local diseases, in England under dietetic diseases or ill-defined conditions. In 1901,[3] further alterations were made: deaths from food poisoning, industrial poisoning, injury at birth and opium or morphia habit were also removed from the list of violent causes and starvation was reclassified as a 'General Disease'. Yet, by 1911,[4] there was a slight reverse and starvation and poisoning from industrial processes were placed back into the list of violent causes, and lack of care at birth was deleted, though in 1931[5] the latter was again transferred into violent causes. These classifications and reclassifications were finally reorganised in the late 1940s with the introduction of N codes and E codes in the WHO nosology.[6] And from that point onward it was the concept of injury which dominated the classification. In fact, there was introduced a subtle equation which balanced violence with direct personal injury so that any violence which was mediated through socio-structural processes was, by that very fact, excluded from the class of violent events. N codes covered the nature of injury, and the E codes covered the external source of injury and with the ninth revision[7] N codes were dispensed with so that all deaths were now coded in terms of the major classification (a nosology of diseases) and only classified to an E code as a supplementary classification. That is to say, violent deaths are now coded and classified first and foremost in terms of the anatomical site of injury and only secondarily in terms of sources of violence. Thus, deaths from neglect and industrial poisoning still figure in the table of violent deaths, but the nature of their external source is obscured and their point of origin displaced.

These sporadic redefinitions and reclassifications of violence and violent deaths tend to demonstrate a movement away from a structural theory of violence (which admittedly took a somewhat shadowy form after 1881), and towards an image of violence which is highly personalised. Indeed, not only did all vestiges of the structural theory of violence disappear between 1881 and 1947, but all violence was eventually reduced to categories of injury stemming from direct human sources alone. And, as I have already stated in Chapter 2, the 'E code' assumed the form of a supplementary and voluntary classification so that even active human agents assumed a peripheral position in explanatory accounts of death. Moreover, this concept of violence, which has so successfully invaded medicine during the current century, has also wormed its way into the social sciences in general. Thus, Oberschall (1973), for example, is able to define violence as 'the use of force with the intent of inflicting damage or injury upon one's opponent in order to coerce him against his will'. And, as far as I can determine, most of those who discuss the nature of violent death in Northern Ireland adopt this narrow concept of violence (see Murray, 1982; Poole, 1983) and thus ignore that tradition of social thought which recognised forms of structural violence whose source can not be located in individual human beings.[8]

The official treatment of violent deaths therefore echoes the treatment of death in general—a medicalisation of causes resulting in a depoliticisation of explanations. The current vision of death reflects this general position, and mortality as a human experience is not considered a subject for incorporation in political manifestos. In modern Ireland it is not death which is politicised, but the dead. And the political organisation of death circulates around the appropriation of bodies, rather than theorisations of health and illness. It is the body which is the focus of politics more than any specific image of death and it is the corpse, rather than any specific ideology of human welfare, which serves as the hub of political activity.

THE SOCIAL DISTRIBUTION OF VIOLENCE

On January 5th, 1976, a minibus containing employees of John Compton Ltd., travelled towards Bessbrook, Co. Armagh. At about 5.30 pm it was stopped by 10 or 12 armed men, who surrounded the bus. They ordered the occupants to get out, and asked if any of them were 'Catholic'. The one man who answered that he was a Catholic was told to get clear of the bus. The gunmen then murdered the remaining (Protestant) occupants systematically. The victims were: James Lemmon (aged 50), Kenneth Wharton (late 20's), Walter

Chapman (mid 30's), and his brother, Reggie Chapman (mid 20's), John McConville (19), Robert Chambers (mid 20's), Robert Freeburn (mid 50's), Robert Walker (about 40), James McWhirter (mid 50's), and John Bryans (in his 40's). (Details from *Irish Times*, 6 January 1976).

I have argued that in the modern world violence is defined solely in terms of immediate personal injury. It is certainly the case that all of the studies on the nature and distribution of violence in Northern Ireland adopt such a view, and do so somewhat uncritically. In terms of this concept it is possible to say that there were some 244 deaths in Belfast during 1981 which were directly attributable to 'violence'. Among these 244 there were, of course, some deaths which were classified as homicides, some as suicides and many which were categorised as accidents, and the problem as to how any given death is classified into one of these three great orders is a subject for investigation in itself. Most sociological research on the issue has concentrated on the problem of suicide and analysed the ways in which sudden violent death is promoted to the status of suicide through the interpretative acts of coroners' officers, pathologists and coroners themselves (see Atkinson, 1978; Douglas, 1967; Taylor, 1982). The same interpretative problems arise, however, in the establishment of accidents, homicides and industrial diseases. Indeed, the determination of the last three categories is a subject of complex legal debates and practice, the study of which lies far beyond the scope of this book. Before examining the social distribution of violence, however, it would be useful to demonstrate the nature of some of the complexities involved in the assessment of violent death in general and political deaths in particular. In this respect it is important to realise at the outset that to accept the classificatory decisions of the GRO, the Coroner, the Royal Ulster Constabulary (RUC), or even the courts on such matters could lead one to ignore many instructive cases. And, as I hope to show in both this and further sections, it is just not possible to establish a register of, say, homicides from which we can draw unambiguous conclusions about political deaths. Indeed, as the following case studies will illustrate, the categories of homicide and 'political murder' are highly problematic. The summary descriptions of the deaths are those of the Belfast Coroner.

CASE 0133
Cause of Death I (a) Multiple Injuries

At about 11.20 pm., on date D, a police Hotspur Landrover was travelling countrywards on Y street. As it approached N street it was attacked by a mob throwing stones and other missiles. The deceased went from its nearside in front of the vehicle raising his arms as if to stop it. The vehicle swerved to its offside, but struck him causing injuries which resulted in his rapid death. The alcohol concentration in his blood was 327 mg per 100 ml.

The death was classified for GRO purposes as an accident, and seems to have been accepted by relatives as such, but a Republican spokesman described it as a murder of an innocent protestor. Indeed, this death was overlaid with political implications for two reasons. First, because the deceased had been protesting in favour of the republican hunger strikers, one of whom had died that day. And secondly because, in the past, there had been accusations of homicide involving the use of police vehicles (and a few weeks after this death, the issue surfaced once more). In fact, it is a death which throws into high relief the two issues which I mentioned above: the determination of what is and what is not a homicide, and what is and what is not a political death.

The following death also contained political ambiguities:

CASE 4004
Cause of Death:

I (a) Laceration, bruising and oedema of the brain associated with fractures of the skull.
The deceased was a schoolboy son of a milk roundsman. At about 6.10 am. on date D, he was a passenger in his father's milk lorry travelling countrywards up the X Road. When near Avenue A they were attacked by a mob who threw stones smashing the windscreen, and causing the lorry to crash into a lamp standard. The deceased died three days later in the N Hospital.

The 'mob', in fact, were protesting about the death of the first hunger striker and were violently enforcing a closedown of shops and businesses. This death was both categorised as a homicide and widely regarded and publicised as such. The funeral of the victim and his father took on a distinct emotional and political tone, and newspaper obituary notices expressed regret for this and the deaths of 'all other innocent victims murdered by the IRA'.

In short, then, similar deaths in similar circumstances can have widely differing interpretations placed on them and, as I shall indicate later on, they can also encourage widely different reactions among different sections of the population. Yet, in forwarding these case studies it is not my intention to cast doubt on any of the classificatory decisions which were made about them, but rather to illustrate the precariousness of such social categorisations. And, on the basis of these two cases, I would claim that if we are to study homicides and 'political' deaths, we have to treat them, at the very least, as components of a wider class of violent deaths. For to do otherwise would be to accept uncritically the official political view of what constitutes homicide (see, for example, Murray's 1982 treatment of this issue) and, consequently, to restrict unnecessarily the investigation of politicised death.

Who is it, then, who dies from violence and how does the wider population respond to such deaths? The answer to both questions is in some senses relatively easy to provide in so far as it is possible to offer a crude quantitative analysis of patterns of violence in Belfast. Indeed, what follows is a brief examination of 25 per cent of the violent deaths which were registered in Belfast during 1981.[9] For ease of analysis I have decided to compare them with the characteristics of 'normal' non-violent deaths which occurred in Belfast during the same year. We shall see that the patterns which emerge from an analysis of a sample population are relatively clear and provide a plain and unencumbered view of the directions in which violence flowed in Belfast during the early 1980s.

As one might expect, and as is evident from Table 9.1, age is the most powerful and striking factor with which violent deaths are associated. The numbers in the 0–19 age-group are rather too small to encourage firm conclusions, but it is nevertheless clear that violence is predominantly a scourge of those in the younger age-groups and especially of those

TABLE 9.1   *The distribution of violent deaths by sex and age of deceased in a sample of 453 deaths, Belfast 1981*

| | | | Violent deaths | | |
| | Male | | | Female | |
Age	%	N	Age	%	N
0–19	42	12	0–19	29	7
20–59	56	48	20–59	25	32
60+	7	160	60+	5	194

in the 'economically active' sectors of the population. The other dominant characteristic of this sub-group of the dead is an over-representation of males. Table 9.1. again illustrates the distribution, and this connection between violence and males is even stronger when the deaths from poisoning are withdrawn from the group. In that sense the deaths of the ten men cited at the opening of this section are particularly characteristic of those who die violent deaths.

This pattern of age, and sex relationships is far more strongly marked for those deaths which were officially classified as homicides, than for violent deaths as a whole.[10] In fact, it is quite a distinct pattern, and contrasts vividly with, say, the pattern of homicide in late 19th- and early 20th-century Belfast. Then, females appeared in much larger numbers and, most significant of all, the majority of homicides were committed on children. Thus, in 1881, for example, 45 out of 131 homicides were committed on children aged under five years. (In similar fashion, of the 71 males and 93 females 'murdered' in England and Wales during 1880, 51 of the males, and 61 of the females were aged less than five years.)

On other social characteristics, however, no clear patterns emerge. Thus, if we analyse violent deaths by occupational class there appear to be no distinct relationships between violence and class. Table 9.2

TABLE 9.2   *The distribution of violent deaths by denomination and occupational class of deceased in a sample of 453 deaths, Belfast 1981*

		Violent deaths			
'Protestant' Occupational class	%	N	'Catholic' Occupational Class	%	N
Non-manual	10	87	Non-manual	13	23
Manual	16	198	Manual	16	104

illustrates the lack of difference in the distribution of violence among these two groups. In a similar fashion there appears to be little relationship between religious denomination and violence. In this respect the finding is quite different from that of Murray (1982), though, there can be little doubt that during some years (as, for example, 1972 and 1973) there would have been a marked overrepresentation of Catholics among the population of the 'political dead'. Nevertheless, on the basis of this sample, there are no grounds for believing that violence is monopolised by one group for use against the other, nor for believing that either community has a privileged protection from violence. What is more, this equality in the distribution of misery is also evident in the characteristics of the homicide group.

In sum, then, the only clear conclusion which we can draw from the tables is that violence is primarily directed against men in the working age groups. Men are therefore more prone to such things as being killed in road and industrial accidents, to self-poisoning and to homicide. And this age and sex pattern is even stronger for the homicide group than it is for the 'violent death' group at large (only two of the homicides in my sample were female). In terms of the homicide group the fact that such a pattern emerges encourages one to draw two conclusions. First, that there are, at least, some rules to the political conflicts which engulf the city, and that these rules serve to limit the target population for violence. Thus, children, women and the old, are more or less exempt from the population which is subject to politicised violence (though not, of course, immune). Second, that the 'target' populations for violence must be selected, at least in part, on the basis of the groups or ideologies which they symbolise. That is to say that men in the active age groups are the subjects of 'random' sectarian attacks only in a personal sense.[11] In other words, they are killed because they represent the State, or Republican–Nationalism, or Protestant–Unionism (as in the case of the subjects killed at Bessbrook).

The official government report from the GRO allocates violent deaths in Northern Ireland during 1981 as follows: 601 as a result of accidents, 90 as a result of suicides, 117 as a result of homicides and 48 whose categorisations are undetermined. (By the standards of the 1970s this level of violence was somewhat low.) But from a study of the 62 case histories in my sample (which are naturally too detailed to reproduce here), a further set of distinctions could be drawn; namely, a distinction between those who were the subjects of a private, almost hidden violence: a product of suicidal and accidental actions mostly in the home. And a group which was subject to a public and well publicised violence, most of which were either road accident victims or homicides. In the sections which follow I intend to examine the political implications of the homicides in particular. Firstly, by analysing the general functions which political deaths have for the various communities which make up Belfast, and secondly by examining in some detail the responses which were made to the particular deaths which were included in my sample.

THE POLITICAL USES OF THE DEAD

Modern Belfast is, in many respects, dominated by political instability. In fact, such instability is an integral component of the political culture and has been so since the birth of the city in the early 19th century (see Budge and O'Leary, 1973). Most contemporary commentators would, however, place the origins of the modern phase of political violence somewhere in the late 1960s, so that the period between 1968 and the present day is generally seen as constituting a distinct and discrete historical phase (albeit, one with a long pedigree). During this period it is estimated that more than 2500 individuals have lost their lives as a direct result of political violence, though the basis on which one could arrive at such an estimate is, as we have seen, somewhat problematic.[12] But whatever the figures which any given analyst might arrive at, there is no doubt that during this period the impact of political violence has been keenly felt by almost the entire population, and most residents of Belfast would have a friend, relative or associate who has been killed, injured or otherwise affected by the 'Troubles'. Relationships with the political dead are often cited as descriptive aids in everyday conversations. Thus it may be said of someone that his or her father was killed in such and such an event, or that his/her brother was assassinated in such and such a year. And remarks of this kind often serve to place the individual concerned in the wider collective tragedy. But most political deaths are little mentioned, and with time one atrocity tends to merge all too easily into the next. Some deaths, however, are regarded as being especially significant. This is usually the case because they mark in some kind of perverse way the introduction of a new phase in the intensity of violence. Thus, during the early phase of the present 'troubles' the murder of three 17-year-old British soldiers in Belfast in 1971, the murder of 15 people in McGurk's Bar during the same year and the murder of 13 people in Derry on 'Bloody Sunday', January 1972, constituted three examples of this process (see Flackes, 1980). In 1976 it was the deaths of three children aged eight years, two years and six weeks respectively, which prompted the largest known peace movement in Northern Ireland into action. And in 1981, the year on which this study is centred, it was the deaths of the Republican hunger strikers which monopolised the headlines and the political territory, though the murder of a Westminster MP, of two Unionist politicians in Co. Down and the death of a young milk delivery boy, also made a distinct impact on the Protestant population. As the last sentence suggests, responses to violent death are variable and the variability is related to the segmented character of the Belfast population. But at this stage I wish to illustrate some general principles concerning the role of the dead in Republican and Unionist political culture, before going on to discuss the ways in which specific cases have been absorbed into the political process.

In his *Elementary Forms of the Religious Life*, Durkheim discusses at length the social consequences of religious ritual. In that discussion he emphasised two things in particular. First, that collective ritual brought individuals together in common purpose, thus contributing to social solidarity at the level of interaction. And, second, that collective participation in ritual served to sustain and revive commonly held sentiments, thus contributing to social solidarity at the level of social values. I would like to argue that these integrative and cohesive consequences of religious ritual are, in some ways, equally evident in the political organisation of the dead, and that the appropriation and celebration of the dead can, in certain contexts, both serve to integrate political communities and to underline and revive commonly held political beliefs.

The role of the dead in Republican and Unionist culture is complex, but there can be little doubt that the dead have a pivotal position in the expression of both political action and ideology. The worship of the political dead in particular, involving as it does marches and assemblies of large numbers of people, comes close to forming the elements of a civil religion. Most important, perhaps, is the fact that the political dead are regarded as symbolising the strongest and most vibrant elements of the political culture. Special emphasis is placed on their apparent sacrifice of self for political principles, their political foresight and their unflinching valour (see, for example, NGA, 1976). In that sense, the dead are used to symbolise opposition to an antagonistic political culture and to embody hope for the future. To remember the dead is to approve of the dead, and to approve of the dead is to condone the elements of the ideology with which they are now associated. In Republican culture the heroes of the 1798 rebellion, (and Wolfe Tone in particular), together with the dead of the 1916 rising, are awarded pride of place. The pilgrimage to the grave of Tone, at Bodenstown, and the veneration of dead republican heroes is an important part of the culture. The Easter commemorations of such dead, which always centre on graves and graveyards, and which involve public assemblies of the kind which Durkheim had in mind, tend therefore to serve the socio-political functions which I outlined above. Equally, in Protestant culture, the dead of the two World Wars and especially the dead of the Somme (a significant group in Unionist folklore), are believed to epitomise the sacrifice for 'Crown and Country', for 'Freedom and Liberty', which is seen as so necessary to the continuance of Protestant Ulster. And, in like manner, the memory of such dead is revived and underlined with marches and ceremonies during July and November. This use of the dead to symbolise and emphasise essential elements of political culture pivots not just on the ancient dead, but also on the modern dead. Thus, the January memorials for the victims of 'Bloody Sunday' (Catholic and Nationalist), are matched by the November memorials (Protestant and Unionist), for the victims of 'Republican Terrorism'. Each society in a sense incorporates its dead in terms of, and into, its own political culture and thereby uses them to reassert and reinforce basic themes of political ideology and political action.

The manipulation of the dead as political symbols also occurs in other ways and for other purposes. And overlapping with the function of integration is another, which this time serves to differentiate rather than integrate the living, that is, to mark out and preserve the boundaries between the two parties which live and exist in the sectarian world of the North of Ireland. In fact, implicit within the above discussion is the assertion that the dead are often used as symbols for the differentiation and ethnogenesis of social groups (see also Bell, 1987). Thus, as the paragraph above suggests, the dead which any given group reveres are a reliable index of its political sympathies. The veneration of Wolfe Tone in Republican circles is matched by the veneration of William of Orange in Loyalist circles. The veneration of the Easter 1916 dead has its counterpart in the veneration of those who died in the British armed forces during the two World Wars, and so on. Such acts of remembrance are actively associated with the manipulation of various symbols, all of which can be used to mark out one's political allegiance. The wearing of an Easter Lily or an Autumn Poppy is not, therefore, merely a symbol of remembrance, but is also a sign of political allegiance.

In addition, of course, the political dead can also be used in acts of political mobilisation. The clearest case of the role of the dead in such mobilisation is probably that on which the 1976 Peace Movement was based, when, following the deaths of two infants and an eight-year-old child on 10 and 11 August, a spontaneous and euphoric movement for peace emerged in Belfast. Some 20 000 people attended the first rally and the movement was to last with some force for a further two years (McKeown, 1984). The use of the dead for mobilising the living is, however, a widespread activity in Belfast. The Democratic Unionist Party (DUP), for example, frequently launches politico-military rallies on the basis of political murders. Thus, in 1981 it promoted its 'Third Force', (vigilante), campaign following the murder of the Rev. Bradford MP. In a similar fashion, militant Republicans are quite open about the use of their 'Fenian Dead'[13] for political recruitment. And in 1981, the year with which we are primarily concerned, the Republican movement both engineered and exploited the deaths of ten hunger strikers for purposes of political mobilisation and were consequently able to make significant electoral gains on both sides of the Irish border on the basis of the strikes (see Beresford, 1987). Indeed, in many respects, political ideologies in Ireland are frequently articulated on the (dead) bodies of past heroes. That is to say, the elements of a political ideology are structured in terms of both the behaviour and the symbolic force of certain key individuals. And the dead are thus used to symbolise complex ideological issues. This is, perhaps, because ideologies are more easily explicable when they are fastened on to personal characteristics and, it is partly, if not wholly, why political rallies in Belfast often centre on graveyards and other memorials for the dead.

Cohesion, differentiation and mobilisation do not, however, exhaust the potential uses of the political dead to the living. For the dead can be, and are, also used for purposes of political legitimation. They can be used either to legitimise a political movement, or to defend a particular strategy. The use of Wolfe Tone, James Connolly and Patrick Pearse by the Republican movement, and such people as Carson, by the Loyalists is indicative of such treatment.[14] And there are many other figures from Irish history who are similarly used for the legitimation of political movements. But the most sinister manner in which the dead are used for the justification of the activities of the living involves appeal to the concept of vengeance, that is, the appeal to crude concepts of retribution as, for example, are called on by para-military murder groups. In Belfast during the early 1970s such appeals were frequently immersed beneath a vicious campaign of sectarian assassinations in which hundreds were killed, though revenge and retribution were not the only motives for such killings (see Dillon and Lehane, 1973; McKeown, 1984).

Integration, differentiation, mobilisation and legitimation are, then, four of the dynamic political processes which revolve around the dead. Whilst death has been depoliticised, therefore, the same is not true of the dead and in Ireland, as in other political cultures (see Kearl and Rinaldi, 1983) the dead are used for the manipulation of live political issues. I would argue that in many respects the pivotal feature of this kind of treatment lies in the use of the body. It is in relation to the dead individual that ideologies are articulated and that organisations are activated. And it is frequently the body and its disposal which acts as the focal point for the use of political symbols. It is over the body that political speeches are made and it is often in the presence of the body that political sentiments are regenerated. But, unfortunately, the human body has a further political function; a function at which I have so far only hinted; that is, as an object of attack. In this context the body is used as a political symbol ripe for destruction and, in Belfast, opposition to a political ideology is all too frequently expressed on the frail bodies of human beings.

RESPONSES TO VIOLENT DEATH

It would be misleading to consider those who die from violent causes as a homogeneous group. It would be equally misleading to think of the political dead in such terms. In both cases there are important and consequential differences between the individuals who make up these populations. And the differences express themselves most clearly in the responses which are made to their deaths.

In somewhat broad and general terms it is possible to draw a distinction between those who die from public and those who die from private violence. For the first there are public responses; very often on a grand scale. For the second, there are sparse responses and occasionally no public response at all. Thus, we can often look in vain for any public recognition of the deaths of the old, the clinically insane, the lonely and isolated individuals whose lives pass unnoticed within the city. For the political dead, however, there are usually many public forms of recognition, the most visible of which is the massive funeral cortège which follows the deceased to the graveside. It is these forms of recognition together with the political interpretations which are placed on such dead that I wish to examine here.

For the politicised dead there are a number of significant responses which are worthy of examination. The funerals of the political dead have their political significance underlined in a series of ways and usually they form the occasion for the public display of sympathy and political affinity. Political funerals can, on occasion, be massive. For example, the *Belfast Telegraph* reported the presence of 60 000 people for the funeral of Bobby Sands MP, whilst, during the funeral of Robert Bradford MP in the same year, in addition to a massive funeral cortège, offices and factories closed for one hour and some 15 000 people congregated outside the City War Memorial as a 'mark of respect'. On a much smaller, but still impressive scale there were a number of cases in my sample where political victims had quite large funerals. Seven hundred people attended the funeral of a Catholic civilian who was assassinated. 'Thousands' lined the streets for the funeral of a Protestant para-military group member, whilst six 'officers' carried the coffin. For the victim of a Provisional Irish Republican Army (PIRA) murder there was a guard of some 200 ambulancemen, whilst more than a thousand people gathered outside the victim's home. Moreover, and in addition to widespread participation, these occasions were often used as an opportunity to denounce political opponents and to voice political sentiments in a graveside oration.

The politicisation of the dead is sometimes so intense that the control of the dead body frequently becomes a live political issue. Thus, many republican burials in which the use of nationalist and military symbols is predominant have recently been subject to a process of political amplification. Such amplification has arisen as a result of attempts by the police to prevent the occurrence of Republican para-military funerals. The use of berets and gloves (the marks of IRA membership), and the Tricolor, together with the trappings of militarism have been forcefully suppressed in an attempt to prevent displays of 'terrorist' ritual. As a consequence, Republican funerals can often take the form of open and direct political struggle between the State and its opponents. In Protestant culture the manipulation of political symbols is visible in the use of such things as gloves, sashes and flags (on the coffins of Orangemen, for example). And the military funerals of the police and members of the armed forces are invariably saturated with political symbols. But unlike the former, these latter are not subject to political suppression.

The images of death which are associated with homicide, are also subject to varying hues of politicisation. Generally speaking, paramilitary organisations like to present an image of their dead as active agents rather than passive victims. It is an aspect of death which is strongly emphasised in republican culture. To be described as 'killed in action', or to die 'on active service', is something of an accolade awarded to the glorious dead (see NGA, 1976). In Protestant culture, on the other hand, there tends to be an emphasis on the dead as passive victims. And for members of the Royal Ulster Constabulary (RUC) and Ulster Defence Regiment (UDR) who are killed, this is combined with an emphasis on 'duty', and 'sacrifice'. On both sides of the sectarian divide, however, images of passivity and innocence are applied to almost all of those who are not involved in military or, para-military movements.

For the military and para-military dead the aforementioned concept of sacrifice looms large. Here, for example, is an extract from an In Memoriam notice placed in the *Belfast Telegraph* for some members of the UDR.

They *served* and *fought* and *died* so that we might be *safe* and *free*. Grant them O Lord eternal peace and give them the *victory* and in these days of unrest filled with grave uncertainty let's not forget the price they paid to keep our *country free*. [Emphasis in original].

The military dead in particular are viewed as having died for, 'God and Ulster', or for 'Ireland's freedom' or for 'Their Country's Freedom'. In many respects this concept of a violent sacrificial death is approved and encouraged within most strands of Republican and Loyalist ideology. It is extensively encouraged in Nationalist Republican literature and is, for example, an especially strong theme in the writings of Pearse, the sage of Irish Nationalism (Pearse, 1966). But, rather than examine these general principles it will perhaps be more instructive to examine the particular and detailed responses which were made to the deaths of the individuals in my sample of 62 violent deaths.

In Chapter 7 I discussed the use of newspaper obituary notices for the investigation of public responses towards death. Using the same principles of enquiry it is possible to draw up a profile of responses which are made in Belfast towards violent deaths in general, and political deaths in particular. By so doing we will be able to see how the politicisation of the dead activates a wide spectrum of sentiments which cover all shades of death.

The statistical detail is provided in Tables 9.3, and 9.4. As expected, it indicates that those who die from violence receive vastly more citations in the newspapers than their counterparts who die from non-violent causes. The average for the former is almost three times greater than the average number of notices received by the latter. And the average, naturally, hides a wealth of important detail. Of the largest, there were 133 for a member of the Irish National Liberation Army (INLA), who blew himself up; 137 for a murdered MP; 76 for a policeman who was murdered and 93 for a murdered ambulanceman. Of the lowest, there were none for a Marine Commando killed by a bomb; none for an alcoholic who died from hypothermia; one for an 81-year-old retired farmer who also died from hypothermia; and two for a suspected suicide.

This surfeit of citations obviously affects the averages of the other

TABLE 9.3   *Average number of newspaper citations for those who died by (1) non-violent and (2) violent causes in a sample of 453 deaths in Belfast, 1981*

Variable	Mean number of notices
Total number of notices	
1 Non-violent deaths	6.95
2 Violent deaths	19.87
Number of religious notices	
1 Non-violent deaths	2.90
2 Violent deaths	7.45
Number of non-kin notices	
1 Non-violent deaths	1.59
2 Violent deaths	10.61

TABLE 9.4   *Mean number of obituary notices for those who died by violence in a sample of 453 deaths in Belfast, 1981: according to sex, occupational class, denomination and age-group of deceased*

Variable	N	Mean number of notices
Sex:		
1 Female	19	9.00
2 Male	43	21.44
Class:		
1 Non-manual	12	17.16
2 Manual	49	17.35
Denomination:		
1 Protestant	40	16.70
2 Catholic	20	21.25
Age:		
1 15–59	39	23.52
2 0–14, 60 +	23	7.65

measures which I discussed in Chapter 7—far greater response from the community at large, a far greater number of religious notices and also a far greater number of secular notices, though within the world of the violent dead there are significant variations as well. Males have, on average, a greater number of citations than women and the young have more citations than the old. There is no significant difference in the number of citations for members of the two denominational camps nor, surprisingly, for occupational class, though the distribution of citations is rather volatile for each of these groups. In many ways, however, the distribution of public sentiment reflects the same patterns for the violent as for the non-violent dead. And the sentiments expressed in these notices mirror those of which I have already spoken. Thus, the notices for Catholics reflect Catholic eschatology and the notices for Protestants reflect Protestant eschatology, but in addition to such sentiments, the political dead bring forth other reactions which it is worthwhile to examine.

Notices for the political dead normally adopt an accusatory tone: 'Murdered by the British Army of Occupation'; 'Murdered by the IRA'; 'Murdered by a callous and cruel British government'; of a policeman, 'murdered by the people he tried to protect'. And occasionally there is an expression of vengeance; 'Vengeance is mine saith the Lord. I shall repay'. Often they emphasise that sense of sacrifice and duty of which I have already spoken: 'Laid down his life for his country'; 'Who sacrificed his freedom and his young life for the cause of Irish independence'; 'Greater love hath no man than this, that he lay down his life for his friends'; 'On active service. He who dies for Ireland, lives'; 'Murdered while serving his people'.

These responses are offered from a wide variety of individuals and organisations, but it is usually through the medium of an organisation that the sentiments are expressed. For the death of one RUC man, for example, there were citations from the following organisations: colleagues in the RUC, bowls clubs, darts club, Orange Lodge, accordion band, neighbours, former colleagues, football supporters clubs (3), and a social club. For the Rev. Robert Bradford the list included: Schools, darts club, Apprentice Boys, Community Associations, Bakery workers, Renewal association, Residents association, Shipyard workers, Presbyterian Congregations, Democratic Unionist Party, Electricity workers, World War Veterans, Unionist Constituency Parties, the Orange Order, 'The people of Donegall Rd area', 'The People of Sandy Row'. For the Hunger Strikers the net was spread just as wide and included the same range of community, residents and housing associations, plus dozens of notices from the various republican political organisations; Sinn Fein Belfast Comhairle Ceanntair, clubs of the Gaelic Athletic Association, prisoners' organisations, USA support groups, and social clubs (which 'will close as a mark of respect between 1.00 and 5.00'). But to any observer what would be most striking is the divisive effects which these political deaths have. There was not a single mention of any hunger striker in the Unionist newspapers and not a single mention of any policeman in the Nationalist paper. No mention of an assassinated Catholic civilian in the one and no mention of an assassinated Protestant civilian in the other. The mourning of the political dead is thus sharply split.

This selectivity of attention in the obituary notices is also reflected in the partisan treatment which these deaths receive in the various newspapers. The publicity of homicide is, as it were, subject to principles of political diorism.

CASE 0136

Shortly before 1am on date D, the deceased was walking home alone on the Ormeau Road. As he crossed the bridge he was shot 3 times by gunmen who escaped in a motor car. The UFF [a Loyalist paramilitary organisation] admitted responsibility in a message to the Press, but the deceased is not known to have been associated with any illegal organisation. No one has yet been made amenable.

This death was prominently displayed on the front page of the *Irish News* the following day. There were also associated articles covering the speeches made by various Nationalist politicians who condemned the death. The same death, however, received no mention in the *Newsletter* (Protestant and Unionist), and a relatively brief mention in the *Telegraph*. None of the Unionist politicians seem to have condemned or commented on the death in any way. An even greater degree of selectivity was evident in the responses to the death of a petrol bomber shot by the British Army, which received no mention at all in the Unionist papers. In a similar manner the death of a 12-year-old girl, as a result of a 'Plastic Bullet' wound and the death of an INLA 'officer', remained unmentioned by the one side, yet widely covered by the other. As a mirror image of this, the assassination of a 41-year-old Protestant man, killed as he was returning home from a pub, was front page news in the *Newsletter* and the *Telegraph*, and received no mention at all in the *Irish News*.

My purpose in citing these cases is not simply to record the selectivity of newspaper reporting, but to illustrate the fact that a death which is politically significant to one community, is of no interest to the other. In other words, the politicisation of death is not, as it were, a natural process, but rather manufactured through the interests and ideologies of various social groups. Indeed, as a final consideration, it will prove instructive to note the range of political issues which are covered by these deaths.

CASE 1939

The x school was to be used as a polling station on date D. On the previous day the Army took over the school to secure it. After doing so it was attacked by youths throwing stones and bottles, and two APC's [Armoured Personnel Carriers], and 2 Land Rovers were sent to quell the riot and make arrests. Before they arrived most rioters had moved towards A Drive. At about 9.50pm., the patrol entered X Rd and turned left. The 2 Land Rovers continued towards A Drive, and as they passed P Park, and G Gardens they were attacked by youths who threw stones and other missiles at them. One plastic bullet was fired from the second Land Rover, and one from the leading Land Rover, the windscreen of which was smashed by a missile, but no hits were observed by those firing them. The deceased then 12 years of age was returning home from a shop at A Park, and was struck on the head by the second of the two plastic bullets when she was passing No. 11 A Park. She was taken to hospital where she died three days later.[15]

This death was used by a number of different groups to condemn a series of different issues. Representatives of the Catholic Church and the Social Democratic and Labour party (SDLP) condemned the use of plastic bullets and requested their withdrawal. Sinn Fein, referring to the death as a murder, used it to condemn the British Government and 'injustice'. The residents of the area took the occasion to condemn the State and its police. The police, who referred to the death as an accident, used it to condemn the rioters, whilst Unionist politicians used it to condemn the hunger strikes and rioting in general. In a similar fashion, the death of a policeman was used by the DUP to attack the British Government, by the Official Unionists to attack the SDLP, and by the Republican Clubs and the SDLP to attack the Provisional IRA. And, as a final example, the following case of death of a 23-year-old man was used by the IRA to condemn the police, the SDLP to condemn the IRA, and by the Catholic Church to call for peace.

CASE 0606

At about 10.50 pm., on date D, a car was heard to stop outside No. 2., S Street, and keep its engine running. Seconds later 4 or 5 shots were heard, and the car was heard to drive off. About 10 minutes later the body of the deceased was found in an alley off S Street with 5 bullet wounds, and the eyes covered with tape. The PIRA [Provisional Irish Republican Army] later admitted responsibility, but as yet, no-one has been made amenable.

Each death, then, is woven into a complex web of political issues and always serves as an occasion for the elaboration of political principles and the furtherance of political struggles. As I have shown, the funerals of these victims further serve as occasions for the reaffirmation of social bonds and social values. In that manner, each death is fed into a spiral of violence and political instability which, in turn, forms the basis for further deaths.

Yet, whilst the funeral arrangements for the political dead are elaborate and detailed, those for the private dead are comparatively frugal. Thus, those who died from injuries and poisons at home received, on average, only 5.7 citations in the obituary columns of the various newspapers, as compared to an average of 23.87 for the group which died 'elsewhere' or in hospital. Moreover, the private dead received no mention at all in the general news coverage and seem to have had relatively small numbers of mourners at their funerals. There is reason to believe, therefore, that within this (numerically large) group of accident, suicide and homicide victims, there is a sub-group of social isolates whose deaths are marked by an almost complete and total absence of public recognition. Their isolated and private lives are thoroughly reflected in their cursory departure from the society of the living. The following case of death of a 40 year old unemployed man (classified as a suicide), typifies in many respects the social conditions in which this latter group finds itself.

CASE 0772

The deceased was separated from his wife, and lived alone, and suffered from alcoholism. He was to be prosecuted for drunken driving. At about 8 pm., on date D, there was an explosion in his bedroom in which he was badly burnt. He was taken to the H Hospital where he died seven days later. The rubber hose connecting the Kosangas heater to the gas cylinder had been deliberately severed, and after some gas had escaped, the deceased probably attempted to light a cigarette, and thus caused the explosion.

And so too the following case which brought just two citations in the evening paper.

CASE 3884

The deceased suffered from episodes of depression. On the morning of date D, she made her husband's breakfast as usual and he went to work at about 8.10 am. When he returned at about 5.10 pm, he found his wife lying dead on the bedroom floor with a plastic bag over her head held round her head by elastic. Her doctor was summoned and he confirmed death.

THE BODY POLITIC AND THE POLITICS OF THE BODY

Throughout this book I have argued that the human body acts as the hub of the organisational system which surrounds death and the dead. I have further argued that the administrative and investigative system through which the dead are monitored is both articulated on bodies and activated by them. And I have indicated how the explanatory logic of the system which attempts to account for death is similarly dependent on the presence of bodies. Indeed, it rests on the supposition that death is in the body, and that its causes can be located in specific anatomical sites. Moreover, and using the language of Foucault, it is possible to see that this search for somatic causes occurs within a complex web of political technology. In that sense, everything to do with death is endowed with a political significance. But this wider political context is almost universally ignored by political activists who choose to focus their political attention neither on the broader system in which death is organised, nor on death itself. Instead, they reserve their attention for those who have died violently and, more specifically, for those whose violent deaths can be easily and directly linked to the dominant ideological issues of Republicanism and Unionism.

In this chapter, therefore, I have attempted to demonstrate the ways in which the corpse can serve as a direct political symbol, or at least as an object on which political beliefs and activities can be focused and energised. As a consequence, I have argued that the political dead are frequently used as totems on which groups can strengthen ties of social solidarity, on which political movements can be mobilised, and which can be used as sources of legitimation for political actions.

In contemporary Belfast, then, the politicisation process focuses on the body rather than on any perceived diseases within it. But perhaps the most important role of all for the individual (from the point of view of the politicisation of the dead) is the fact that he or she is often regarded as a symbolic representative of an entire socio-political community. For many, this state of representation will be a welcome feature of their lives. For most, there will be little choice in the matter. But, whatever the advantages which may flow from this enforced sense of belonging, it will, at times of political instability, also contain inherent dangers. For, then, an attack on a physical body can be substituted for an attack on a political community. Then, the human body can be used as an alternative target for an assault on a political movement and its associated ideology, and in Belfast such targets are readily and easily chosen. The expression of such political violence has, of course, its limits and boundaries, and is aimed primarily at males in the 15–59 age-group. But among these males are several sub-groups: members of the police and military; members of para-military groups; and 'civilians'; and they serve as a target population for two closely interrelated wars. The first and most widespread is a sectarian war, a war between 'Catholics' and 'Protestants'. It was in this war that the victims of Bessbrook died. The second is a war of insurgence, involving elements of colonialism and imperialism, but the target population is, unfortunately, one and the same with the first. Thus, the pursuit of the one war will always have repercussions on the other. And in the burials of the victims, the virtues of both wars are continuously affirmed and reaffirmed.

10 Conclusion: Discourses on Death

The Consumers' Association currently publish a booklet entitled *What To Do When Someone Dies*. The book's contents accurately reflect the concerns of the culture in which it is produced. It contains no mention of the ritualistic procedures through which the corpse should journey, nor does it mention any ritualistic tasks which the living should perform for the dead. Instead, it contains details of the bureaucratic and other organisational procedures through which the living must journey in order to dispose of the dead. Indeed, the Foreword is quite explicit about the coverage of the book.

> No attempt is made to deal with the personal, spiritual or social aspects of death and bereavement, such as the psychology of grief and shock, the rituals and conventions of mourning, or attitudes to death. (Rudinger, 1986: Foreword)

And yet the book is a guide; a handbook for those whose friends and relatives are dead and states 'what needs to be done, [and] when and how to set about it.' It requires 131 pages to fulfill the tasks which are set forth in the brief Foreword and within those pages one can find an outline of the system which embraces death in the modern world. It is a system replete with formal rules for establishing death, registering death, disposing of the dead, acquiring documents, utilising documents and establishing legal rights to property, pensions and the like. In short, it is a booklet which guides the reader through the labyrinth of practices and procedures by means of which the dead are bureaucratically ordered and defined.

The bureaucratisation of the dead is a comparatively modern concern, and in the myriad acts of regulation which serve to make up the bureaucratic system, both the living and dead become embroiled in a network of state agents and agencies. The general practitioner, the registrar of deaths, the pathologist, the coroner and possibly the police, may, as we have seen, all be implicated in the preliminary arrangements, It is at this stage that the dead body is a public body and it is at this stage that the State asserts its investigative and explanatory rights over the corpse. The agents of state power can delve into the interior of the corpse, into its personal biography as well as its anatomy and physiology. Their inquisitorial rights have no bounds and no limits, and all aspects of human existence are potentially subject to their investigation. But these modes of investigation are not haphazard, or arbitrarily structured. On the contrary, they are tightly designed and well systematised. They are systematised and organised in two realms: a practical realm of activities and procedures, and a theoretical realm of concepts, ideas and principles about the nature of death, disease and the body.

In many respects, the world of practices and activities is visibly present in public bodies of another sort, namely, the registry office, the mortuary, the coroner's office and the hospital. And so this book has been concerned with such public bodies. What occurs in these organisational settings however, is patterned and, to a large extent, determined by the theoretical and conceptual frameworks which underpin them. What goes on in the registry office has no sense outside a theoretical framework which seeks to individualise death and to police its causes, and what goes on in the mortuary has no sense outside of a pathology which seeks to biologise death and normalise disease. Indeed, without analysing such frameworks it is impossible to comprehend the rationale for either the existence of the organisations or for the activities that occur within them.

To talk of the organisation of death is therefore to talk of the body of rules and practices through which human actors relate to death at both a physical and a theoretical level. The rules are contained and expressed in and through conversations, behaviour, manuals of procedure, textbooks, death certificates and the like, and they are composed and utilised in specific sites or settings. And, put together, one can see that these diverse and varied elements form a discourse on death, a discourse which defines the very nature and meaning of mortality in the modern world.

In terms of this discourse, death is first and foremost a physical fact located in human anatomy. And so the causes of death are located in that same anatomy, or at least, in the diseases which are made visible through it. Consequently, the human body comes to define both the space within which causation operates, and the space within which the origin and effects of disease are manifested. This emphasis on disease as a carrier of death, however, is in turn a component of a wider discourse which is effectively elaborated and refined in the annals of pathology. There disease is reduced to quantitative variations on the normal and its abnormalities are measured on the mortuary scales. Indeed, it is in such acts of measurement that pathology expresses its most fundamental assumptions about both death and the nature of disease, assumptions which effectively decontextualise them from the social, economic and political circumstances in which they arise.

The results of pathological examination are, of course, collated and summated in another realm. That realm is the GRO, and it is through its nosological categories and its tables of mortality that the aforementioned nosography finds its ultimate expression. For it is in the GRO that death, and the causes of death are made visible on the individual body. Such a focus on bodily anatomy serves, at the very least, a dual function. First defining a visible distribution of disease and, at the same time, reducing the (dead) body to nothing more nor less than the system of anatomy which it expresses.

Yet, as we have seen, discourses on death and the body are not confined solely to the theories and practices operated by state agents and agencies. Indeed, much that is to do with death occurs in what we can safely call a private realm, and 'the sorrowing family circle' constitutes the pivot of this realm. In fact, this appropriation of death by the immediate family grouping has been a source of much comment by many recent writers. Thus, in affairs of mortality, the modern family is said to have privatised death and monopolised sentiment. This, of course, is only partly true for, in Belfast at least, it is still possible for the death of a man or woman to evoke a deep and wide response among a much wider community, and it is as well worth examining the nature and distribution of these wider responses as it is to examine the nature and distribution of sentiment in the immediate family alone.

In the private realm, however, the body is still central to funeral processes. Sentiment is expressed over the body, religious ritual circulates around the body, images of death are imposed on the body and, above all, death is individualised through the body. Yet, in the private realm death also has a social, religious and political dimension which serves to structure features of human existence other than the physical. Thus, it is in the private realm that the soul and social persona of the deceased are structured and it is here that the social consequences of death are organised. But whilst the private world of the bereaved gives emphasis to the non-material features of social being, it is also true to say that the material presence of the corpse frequently provides a unique occasion on which social, religious and political practice can be effectively synchronised so as to refresh and rejuvenate the communal and cultural worlds of the living. Family relationships, religious beliefs and ritual, political interests and even sentiments themselves are, more often than not, reawakened in the presence of death, and nowhere more clearly so than in the funeral processes of the 'political dead'.

Death, disease and the body, each is defined by the practices which envelop it, and neither one is reducible to its physical or material manifestation alone. Death, a process rather than an event, evades imprisonment in the human frame. The multifaceted body, a social as much as a physical object, slips free of the limits set for it by the science of anatomy. And disease, a quantitative variation on the normal rather than an ontological reality, finds its facticity dissolved in the nosography of modern pathology.

Notes

1 Death, Disease and the Body

1. These deaths, to which I make frequent reference throughout the study, represent a 10 per cent random sample of all deaths which were registered in Belfast during 1981. The sample was drawn from the 4152 certificates which were processed in the Belfast GRO during that year. The Annual Report of the Registrar General, however, lists only 4048 deaths as having occurred during 1981. Some of the deaths in my sample, therefore, occurred during earlier years (the earliest being 1978), and were only processed during 1981.
2. I cite Foucault's 1970 and 1972 work merely as the starting points for the entire series of studies which were published in English between 1970 and 1985. The texts on which I have depended are listed among the references.
3. The only person who consistently argues against the 'denial of death' theme is Parsons, who claims that the modern approach to death dovetails perfectly into western scientific rationalism. See Parsons (1963), Parsons (1978) and Parsons and Lidz (1967).
4. On the history of scientific medicine Figlio (1977) and Jewson (1976) also contain instructive material and viewpoints.

2 Vocabularies of Causation

1. *Nursing Procedures Book*, Belfast College of Mental Nursing, 1982. A similar statement appears in the Procedure Book of the largest of these colleges, The South Belfast College of Nursing.
2. *What to do after a death*, DHSS, Belfast, Leaflet Number NIL.49A.
3. 18th Annual Report of the Registrar General, Ireland, *Parliamentary Papers*, 1882, 19, 891–1027.
4. 60th Annual Report of the Registrar General 1981, Belfast, HMSO, 1984.
5. 64th Annual Report of the Registrar General, England and Wales, *Parliamentary Papers*, 1902, 18, 1–500.
6. 1st Annual Report of the Registrar General, England and Wales, *Parliamentary Papers*, 1839, 16, p. 69.
7. 1st Annual Report of the Registrar General, England and Wales, *Parliamentary Papers*, 1839, 16, p. 65.
8. 4th Annual Report of the Registrar General, England and Wales, *Parliamentary Papers*, 1842:19:441–668.
9. 'Report upon the Table of Deaths', in The Census of Ireland 1841 (Dublin: HMSO, 1843).
10. Public Records Office of Northern Ireland (PRONI). *Crown and Peace Files* Ant I/25. See also, Coroners' Inquests Ireland, *Parliamentary Papers* 1842, 38, 185–223, and Blinderman (1976).

11.   PRONI. *Hospital Files*
     Hos 17/7/1/2   Hos 29/1/4/1
     Hos 27/6/1   Hos 28/1/4/1
     Hos 28/1/4/2   Hos 28/1/4/3

3   Categories of Death

1.   In both this and the other chapters of the book I have disguised some of the personal detail included in the brief case histories. Most of the alterations relate to such things as dates of death and initials of the deceased.
2.   See also Humphreys (1981) on the relationships between death and time.
3.   An interesting inversion of this principle is cited by Mauss: 'The Australians regard only the deaths we call violent as natural' (Mauss, 1979: 42).
4.   The material referred to in this section is drawn from a variety of sources including, of course, the 10 per cent sample mentioned in Chapter One, note 1. In addition, details were drawn from a 50 per cent random sample of 1982 Belfast Coroner's Inquests (N = 90), and the following Public Records:
    Crown and Peace Files: Ant I/24: Carrickfergus Coroner Inquests 1888– 89 (N = 90). Dow I/15: North Down Coroner Inquests, and Dow I/16: South Down Coroner Inquests (N = 74). Belf 100/59/A/B/C: Belfast Coroner Inquests 1941 (50 per cent sample N = 146). Belf 100/57/A/B, and Fer I/i.

4   The Pathology of Death

1.   For mortuary technicians death is, of course, routine. The only cases which my informants seemed to remember, and to some extent relish, were those in which the identification of the body posed a problem. Thus, severely burnt or severely damaged bodies were of interest because they necessitated the use of detailed and intricate testing procedures in order to establish identity. And one of my informants kept a somewhat grisly photographic file of his 'difficult ID cases'—which he offered to lend to me for closer scrutiny. The significance of identification and the profanity of daily routine in a Belfast mortuary is also mentioned (though in a somewhat different context) by Brian Moore in his, *The Emperor of Ice-Cream*.
2.   The sociological tool in question is a 25 per cent random sample of the Coroner's 1982 clients.
3.   On the issue of validation, see also Knowelden *et al.* (1985). According to my informants, post-mortems are indispensable for a number of reasons. One such informant summed up the need for them in the following manner:

To ensure that there have been no malpractices. To establish *the* cause of death. To allay suspicion. To establish liability, and to clear up clinical puzzles.

5 Accounting for Death

1. In Belfast, SIDS is not recognised as a valid cause of death by the State Pathologist's Office and so the apparent incidence of it is low.
2. *Manual of the International List of Causes of Death* (London: 1912) p. xxxvi.
3. Naturally, in the day-to-day practices of coders there are a number of illegitimate procedures in use, and this seemed to me to be one of the more important ones. It came to light when I asked why a given death was coded to Bronchopneumonia (which is regarded as a somewhat limited diagnosis), and the coder replied that she did not see how it mattered which item was selected for people aged 70 and over.
4. First and Second Reports from the Select Committee on Death Certification (London: HMSO, 1893) p.iv.
5. These issues are fully discussed in articles by Goldthorpe (1983), Stanworth (1984), and Heath and Britten (1984). See also McDowell (1983).
6. These problems naturally affect my own data, but I have tried to reduce the number of ambiguous cases by (1) using just two class categories that is 'manual' and 'non-manual') and (2) where possible and when appropriate, supplementing the single word occupational titles by other information.

   The group which I refer to as 'manual' (in Chapters 3, 4, 7 and 9) encompasses the members of OPCS classes III manual, IV, and V, whilst the group which I refer to as 'non-manual' encompasses OPCS classes III non-manual, II and I. In many cases the occupational descriptions of sample subjects was relatively unambiguous (for example, there were 62 'Labourers'). Moreover, occupational data was rather more reliable and informative for the 88 Coroners' cases in the 1981 sample than it was for the remainder. Nevertheless, there were frequent cases of ambiguity and wherever possible I attempted to gain further data on the subjects involved (from obituary notices and the like) before allocating them to the appropriate class.

6 Segregating the Dead

1. [1]. Ariès (1983) provides invaluable information, and innumerable detailed insights into church/cemetery relations, and almost every other issue which is raised in this sub-section. His analysis, however, often develops distinct Durkheimian themes. For example, he locates the origins of the modern tendency to ignore death in the fact that the community 'no longer has a sufficient sense of solidarity; it has actually abandoned responsibility for the organisation of collective life. The community in the traditional sense of the word no longer exists. It has been replaced by an enormous mass of atomized individuals' (1983:612–613). For a detailed discussion of cemetery architecture, see Etlin (1984).
2. The 19th-century fashion for fencing off graves is seen by French (1975) as an expression of a possessive individualism well suited to capitalist culture.
3. For a discussion of the theme of municipalisation in relation to Ancient Roman society, see Hopkins (1983).

4. Chadwick's Report also contains some interesting appendices on the burial rules devised by the municipal authorities for Frankfurt and Munich. See *Parliamentary Papers*, 1843, XII, 395–681. According to Ariès, however, the policing of the Paris cemeteries commenced in the 1760s (See ch. 11 of the 1983 work.)

5. Rules for the General Management of Cemeteries of the Newtownabbey Borough Council. And on the provision of separate burial grounds for children in the west of Ireland, see Aldridge (1969).

6. Ibid. Rules . . .

7. Taken from Clark (1982).

8. For some English examples see Rawnsley and Reynolds (1977), though the most instructive examples are, of course, provided by Ariès.

9. On Villermé's work see Coleman (1982). On Farr's work see Eyler (1979). Unfortunately, there is no comparable work available for Grimshaw, but Hayes (1970) provides a bibliography of his writings.

10. The Annual Reports continue to provide a breakdown of mortality by season, as well as meteorological reports, but there is no longer any rationale behind these. A good discussion of the implications of theories of disease for the collection of vital statistics is given in Eyler (1979).

11. Social space was further expanded during the 20th century by the collection and reporting of data on occupational mortality – a process which had commenced in the 1881 Census of England and Wales, but which was not refined until 1921.

12. *Parliamentary Papers*, 1865, XIII.

13. *Parliamentary Papers*, 1869, XVI.

14. A discussion of the nature and extent of infant mortality had, however, appeared in the Supplement to the Thirty Fifth Annual Report for England and Wales. See *Parliamentary Papers*, 1875, XVIII.

15. Two other divisions which occur in the Reports and which are worth mentioning are: the tabulation of mortality by marital status, first introduced in the 1875 Report for Scotland, and the tabulation of infant deaths against their legitimacy, first mentioned in the 1875 Report for England.

16. All three authors argue, with different degrees of complexity, that mortality rates constitute a material base on which attitudes to death are constructed. For example, Chaunu argues that high rates of mortality correlate with a preoccupation with death, and that it is only when rates decline that death denying attitudes predominate in any given society. Whilst Stannard and Stone argue that, during the 16th and 17th centuries, parents purposely restricted their emotional involvement with their children on account of the very high mortality rates to which the latter were subject, and that only when mortality declined could there be a growth of what Stone refers to as 'affective individualism'.

17. Northern Ireland Hospice, appeals literature.

18. The publication of the books of Glaser and Strauss in 1965 and 1968, of Brim *et. al.* in 1970, and Sudnow in 1967, on the plight of the dying patient stand as additional evidence for this point.

19. For a description of a truly hidden death see Simpson (1979-80).

20. A modern attempt to reinterpret death in positive terms, and as something other than a pathology is presented in Kubler-Ross (1975).

7 The Social Distribution of Sentiments

1. This essay was published in 1917 under the title of Mourning and Melancholia. See Standard Edition (1957) vol. XIV.
2. This is also the position adopted by Lévi-Strauss, as is evident from the following passage:

   > It is certain that social behaviour is not produced spontaneously by each individual, under the influence of emotions of the moment. Men do not act, as members of a group, in accordance with what each feels as an individual; each man feels as a function of the way in which he is permitted or obliged to act. Customs are given as external norms before giving rise to internal sentiments, and these non-sentient norms determine the sentiments of individuals as well as the circumstances in which they may, or must, be displayed. (C. Lévi-Strauss, 1969:141)

3. See, especially, the concluding section of Hertz (1960).
4. This is evident, for example, in the registers of 19th-century lunatic asylums, where grief is often cited as a cause of mania, or melancholia, but is never listed as an 'illness' in its own right. See Public Records Office of Northern Ireland, Hospital Files: Hos 28/1/4/1; Hos 29/1/4/1; Hos 27/6/1.
5. For a study of normal bereavement see Clayton *et al.* (1968).
6. The funerals of Catholic Ireland were, of course, also regarded as lively events, and were reputedly packed with activity and games. Mooney (1888) provides extensive examples of the games involved, and so too does Connolly (1982). Wakes are still quite common in Belfast (see, for example, Burton 1978:21), but they are far more sombre affairs than the ones cited by either Mooney or Connolly.
7. Gordon (1985), in fact, distinguishes between biologically based 'emotions' and socially mediated 'sentiments'.
8. This study is based upon a 10 per cent sample of the deaths which were registered in Belfast during 1981, and the subjects were traced through the Belfast newspapers of 1979, 1980 and 1981 (some deaths occurred before 1981, and were only registered much later).
9. One is reminded here of Hopkins' (1983) claim that in Ancient Rome 'Grief was expressed on tombstones from a limited stock of conventions' (1983:220).
10. Whilst reading Thomas (1971) I was struck by extensive similarities which were evident in the images of the world and the hereafter represented in the *Irish News* notices, and the images which Thomas claims were unique features of pre-Reformation European culture.
11. On visual images of death see Loftus (1986).

8 The Disposal of Dead Persons

1. A 'body', as in the case of the Coroner's court, is very much a theoretical object, and so parts of bodies, or even ashes can be used to stand in symbolic relation to the whole.

2. On the treatment of the stillborn see also, Peppers and Knapp (1980), and Lovell (1983).

3. I speak of burial mainly because cremation is not particularly widespread in Belfast. None of the Catholic dead in my 1981 sample seem to have been cremated, and only about 25 per cent of the Protestant dead were cremated. It was difficult, however, to get a precise figure for the latter.

4. Funeral directors, however, are always keen to point out that they are ready to 'work with anything'. A turn of phrase which further underlines the thing-like nature of the corpse.

5. The cadavers of Protestants are usually kept in the funeral directors' premises. The cadavers of Catholics are usually kept at home, except perhaps for the night before burial, when they may be transferred to a chapel.

6. The display of the coffin is not extended to the funerals of stillborn or live born infants. Or, indeed, to the funerals of the poor.

7. This is a theme which is taken up more fully by Bloch and Parry (1982).

8. Thomas (1968) seems to have been one of the few 20th-century anthropologists, apart from Hertz, to pick up and develop this theme.

9. The social distribution of belief concerning the resurrection of the body is far more complex than this paragraph would suggest. It is noticeable, for example, that there is an exceptionally heavy emphasis on the resurrection of the physical body in North Irish Biblical Protestantism, and thus contrasts between 'Protestantism' and 'Catholicism' cannot be easily drawn.

10. The connection between women and tears is brought out in the following, somewhat peculiar verse, which was inserted as a death notice for a member of an illegal Protestant para-military organisation.

> There our valiant brother lies,
> Wake him not with women's cries.
> Mourn the way that manhood ought—
> sit in silent trance of thought.

9 Death, Politics and the Body

1. 60th Annual Report of the Registrar General Northern Ireland (Belfast: HMSO, 1984).

2. 44th Annual Report of the Registrar General, England and Wales, *Parliamentary Papers*, 1883, 20, 1–380. 18th Annual Report of the Registrar General Ireland, *Parliamentary Papers*, 1882, 19, 891–1038.

3. 64th Annual Report of the Registrar General, England and Wales, *Parliamentary Papers*, 1902, 18, 1–500.

4. 74th Annual Report of the Registrar General, England and Wales, *Parliamentary Papers*, 1913, 13, 493–577.

5. 94th Annual report of the Registrar General, England and Wales (London: HMSO, 1933).

6. *Manual of the international statistical classification of diseases, injuries and causes of death.* Sixth revision (Geneva: WHO, 1948–49).

7. *Manual of the International Statistical Classification of Diseases, Injuries and Causes of Death.* Ninth revision; vols I and II (Geneva: WHO, 1977).

8. I am thinking here of the theories of violence discussed by Marx in volume 1 of *Capital*, and Sorel in his *Reflections on violence*. In this connection see also Galtung (1969).

9. This study uses as its basis the sample of 415 deaths described in Chapter 1 (note 1). Those deaths represented 10 per cent of all the deaths which were processed for the Belfast area by the Belfast GRO during 1981, and the sample contained 24 deaths attributed to violent causes (that is, coded 800–999). As the sub-sample of 24 deaths was too small for carrying out a worthwhile analysis, I supplemented the 24 deaths with a further 38, which were randomly chosen from the 251 deaths attributed to violence, and processed during 1981. The total number of deaths attributed to violence is therefore 62, which represents 25 per cent of all such deaths processed during 1981.

10. The social characteristics of officially classified 'Homicides' in a sample of 453 deaths, Belfast, 1981.

Characteristic	Number
Sex	
Male	16
Female	2
Age	
15–19	2
20–29	9
30–39	2
40–49	4
50–59	1
Denomination	
Catholic	7
Protestant	9
Unknown	2
Occupational Class	
Non-manual	3
Manual	15

11. In a strict sense it could be argued that very few people are killed as a result of random sectarian attacks, and that most are killed because they are policemen, members of the UDR, or, even, members of the PIRA. In using this phrase, it is not my intention to obscure the very important differences which exist among the victims of violence, but, as there is an element of sectarianism in almost all of these deaths, it seems to me to be justifiable to use the phrase to cover all political homicides.

12. Estimates of the number of people killed from political violence are available from a number of sources. For example, Murray (1982, 1983), Flackes (1980), and the *Annual Reports of the Chief Constable*, RUC, Belfast, HMSO, all provide data on this issue. Further data are available from the Annual Reports of the Registrar General.

13. A phrase taken from Pearse's remark made in a graveside speech for O'Donovan Rossa (referring to the English): 'The fools, the fools. They have left us our Fenian dead'.

14. Tone was a leader of the United Irishmen in the late 1790s, and is regarded by Republicans as 'the father of the Republic'. Pearse, and Connolly were theoreticians and leaders of the 1916 Rising—both were executed by the British. Carson was a far less charismatic figure, and a (Protestant) leader of the anti-Home Rule movement in the period before World War I.

15. This death was officially classified as 'Undetermined', and acts as further support for the claims concerning the inclusion and exclusion of political death which I made earlier. See also Asmal (1985).

References

Ackernecht, E.H. (1967) *Medicine at the Paris Hospital, 1794–1848* (Baltimore: Johns Hopkins Press).

Ackernecht, E.H. (1968) 'Death in the history of medicine', *Bulletin Of The History Of Medicine*, 42: 19–23.

Aldridge, R.B. (1969) 'Notes on childrens' burial grounds in Mayo', *Journal of the Royal Society of Antiquaries in Ireland*, 99: 83–7.

Alexander, M. (1980) 'The rigid embrace of the narrow house: Premature burial and the signs of death', *Hastings Centre Report*, 3: 25–31.

Anderson, C. (1949) 'Aspects of pathological grief and mourning', *International Journal of Psychoanalysis*, 30: 48–55.

Anderson, W.A.D. and Kissane, J.M. (1977) *Pathology* 2 vols. (7th ed.; St Louis: C.V. Mosby).

Antonovsky, A. and Bernstein, J. (1977) 'Social class and infant mortality', *Social Science And Medicine*, 11: 453–70.

Ariès, P. (1967) 'La mort inversée', *European Journal of Sociology*, 8: 2: 169–95.

Ariès, P. (1974) *Western attitudes toward death from the middle ages to the present* (Baltimore: Johns Hopkins University Press).

Ariès, P. (1983) *The hour of our death*, trans. H. Weaver (Harmondsworth: Penguin).

Ariès, P. (1985) *Images of man and death*, trans. J. Lloyd (Cambridge, Mass: Harvard University Press).

Armstrong, D. (1983) *The political anatomy of the body* (Cambridge University Press).

Armstrong, D. (1986) 'The invention of infant mortality', *Sociology of Health and Illness*, 8: 3: 211–32.

Arney, W.R. and Bergen, B.J. (1983) 'The anomaly, the chronic patient, and the play of medical power', *Sociology of Health and Illness*, 5: 1: 1–24.

Atkinson, J.M. (1978) *Discovering Suicide* (London: Macmillan).

Asmal, K. (1985) *Shoot to Kill? International lawyers' inquiry into the lethal use of firearms by the security forces in Northern Ireland* (Cork: The Mercier Press).

Bachofen, J.J. (1967) *Myth, religion and mother right*, trans. E. Mannheim (London: Routledge & Kegan Paul).

Backer, B.A., Hannon, N. and Russell, N.A. (1982) *Death and dying: individuals and institutions* (New York: John Wiley & Sons).

Baechler, J. (1979) *Suicides*, trans. B. Cooper (London: Basil Blackwell).

Baird, T.T. (1980) *You and your baby: Report of the advisory committee on infant mortality and handicap in Northern Ireland* (Belfast: HMSO).

Barley, S.R. (1983) 'The codes of the dead. The semiotics of funeral work', *Urban Life*, 12: 1: 3–31.

Bartley, M. (1985) 'Coronary heart disease a disease of affluence or a disease of industry', in P. Weindling (ed.) *The social history of occupational health* (London: Croom Helm).

Basman, J.V. (1971) *Grant's method of anatomy* (8th ed.; Baltimore: Williams & Wilkins).

Baudrillard, J. (1976) *L'échange symbolique et la mort* (Paris: Gallimard).

Bell, D. (1987) 'Acts of union: Youth subculture and ethnic identity among protestants in Northern Ireland', *British Journal of Sociology*, 38: 2: 158–83.

Bendann, E. (1930) *Death customs: an analytical study of burial rites* (London: Kegan Paul).

Benthall, J. and Polhemus, T. (eds) (1975) *The body as a medium of expression* (Harmondsworth: Allen Lane).

Benoliel, J.Q. (1978) 'The changing social context for life and death decisions', *Essence*, 2: (2): 5–14.

Beresford, D. (1987) *Ten men dead. The story of the 1981 Irish hunger strike* (London: Grafton Books).

Berger, P.L. and Luckman, T. (1967) *The social construction of reality* (Harmondsworth: Penguin).

Berthelot, J.M., Drulhe, M., Clément, S., Forné, J., M'bodj, G. (1985) 'Les sociologies et le corps', *Current Sociology* 33: 2.

Berthelot, J.M. (1986) 'Sociological discourse and the body', *Theory, Culture and Society*, 3: 3: 155–64.

Black, Sir Douglas *et al.* (1980) 'Inequalities In Health: report of a research working party' (London: DHSS).

Bland, R. (1979) 'Measuring social class', *Sociology*, 13: 283–91.

Blauner, R. (1966) 'Death and social structure', *Psychiatry*, 29: Nov: 378–94.

Blinderman, A. (1976) 'The coroner describes the manner of dying in New York City, 1784–1816', *The American Journal of Medicine* 61: 103–10.

Bloch, M. (1971) *Placing the dead. Tombs, ancestral villages and kinship organisation in Madagascar* (London and New York: Seminar Press).

Bloch, M. and Parry, J. (1982) *Death and the regeneration of life* (Cambridge University Press).

Bloor, M., Samphier, M. and Prior, L. (1987) 'Artefact explanations of inequalities in health: An assessment of the evidence', *Sociology of Health and Illness*, 9: 3: 321–64.

Bohannan, P. (1960) *African homicide and suicide* (Princeton University Press).

Boal, F.W. and Douglas, J.N.H. (eds) (1982) *Integration and division. Geographical perspectives on the Northern Ireland problem* (London: Academic Press).

Bowker, J. (1973) *Sense of God. Sociological, anthropological, and psychological approaches to the origin of the sense of God* (Oxford University Press).

Bowlby, J. (1961) 'Processes of mourning', *The International Journal of Psychoanalysis*, 42: 4–5: 317–40.

Boyd, W. (1943) *A Text-Book of Pathology* (4th ed. London: Henry Kimpton).

Brandon, S.G.F. (1967) *The judgement of the dead* (London: Weidenfeld & Nicholson).

Brewer, R.I. (1984) 'Some anomalies in social class coding and the official view of the professions', *Sociology*, 18: 3: 383–91.

Brim, O.G., Freeman, H.E., Levine, S. and Scotch, N.A. (1970) *The dying patient* (New York: Russell Sage Foundation).

Britten, J.D. (1979) *Practical notes on nursing procedures* (7th ed.; Edinburgh: Churchill Livingstone).

Britton, M. (1974) 'Diagnostic errors discovered at autopsy', *Acta Medica Scandinavica*, 196: 203–10.

Brodrick, N. (1971) *Report of the work of the committee on death certification and coroners* Cmnd 4810 (London: HMSO).

Budge, I. and O'Leary, C. (1973) *Belfast—approach to crisis: a study of Belfast politics 1613–1970* (London: Macmillan).

Burns, E.M., Isaacs, B. and Gracie, T. (1973) *Geriatric nursing* (London: Heinemann).

Burton, F. (1978) *The politics of legitimacy: struggles in a Belfast community* (London: Routledge & Kegan Paul).

Bynum, J. (1973) 'Social status and rites of passage: the social context of death' *Omega: Journal Of Death and Dying* 4: 4: 323–32.

Cabot, R.C. (1912) 'Diagnostic pitfalls identified during a study of 3000 autopsies', *Journal Of The American Medical Association*, LIX: 26: 2295–98.

Cameron, H.M. and McGoogan, E. (1981a) 'A prospective study of 1152 hospital autopsies I', *Journal of Pathology*, 133: 273–83.

Cameron, H.M. and McGoogan, E. (1981b) 'A prospective study of 1152 hospital autopsies II', *Journal Of Pathology*, 133: 285–300.

Canguilhem, G. (1978) *On the normal and the pathological*, trans. C.R. Fawcett. (Dordrecht: D. Reidel).

Canguilhem, G. (1971) *La connaissance de la vie* (2nd ed.; Paris: J. Vrin).

Central Statistical Office (1981) *Report on vital statistics* (Dublin: Stationery Office).

Chamboredon, J-C. (1976) 'La restauration de la mort', *Actes de la recherche en sciences sociales* 2: 2–3: 78–87.

Chaunu, P. (1976) 'Mourir à Paris (XVIe–XVIIe–XVIIIe Siècles)' *Annales-Économies Sociétés Civilisations*, 31: 1: 29–50.

Christian Burial (1983) *Irish Institute of Pastoral Liturgy*.

Clarke, R.S.J. (1982) *Graveyard inscriptions. Belfast*, vol. 1 (Belfast: Ulster Historical Foundation).

Clarke, R.S.J. (1984) *Graveyard inscriptions. Belfast*, vol. II (Belfast: Ulster Historical Foundation).

Clayton, P., Desmaris, L. and Winokur, G. (1968) 'A study of normal bereavement', *American Journal of Psychiatry*, 125: 168–78.

Cochrane, A.H. and Moore, F. (1981) 'Death certificates from the epidemiological point of view' *Lancet*, 3 Oct. 742–43.

Coleman, W. (1982) *Death is a social disease. Public health and political economy in early industrial France* (Madison: University of Wisconsin Press).

Condran, G.A. and Cheney, R.A. (1982) 'Mortality trends in Philadelphia: age and cause specific death rates 1870–1930', *Demography*, 19: 1: 97–123.

Connolly, S.J. (1982) *Priests and people in pre-famine Ireland. 1780–1845* (New York: Gill & Macmillan).

Curl, J.S. (1980) *A celebration of death. Introduction to some of the buildings, monuments and settings of funerary architecture in the western European tradition* (London: Constable).

Cutler, J. (1982) 'Cover up on asbestos victims' *New Statesman*, 104:2691:4.

Cutler, J. (1983) 'No need for change on asbestos victims', *New Statesman*, 105:2708:4.

Danforth, L.M. (1982) *The death rituals of rural Greece* (Princeton University Press).

Davis, C. (1980) 'Making sense of the census in Britain and The USA: The changing occupational position of nurses', *Sociological Review*, 28:3:581–609.

Davis, D. (1976) 'Deaths from coronary artery disease and coalworkers' pneumoconiosis' *British Medical Journal*, 2:925–27.

Delaporte, F. (1986) *Disease and Civilisation. The cholera in Paris 1832*, trans. A. Goldhammer (Cambridge, Mass: MIT Press).

De Vries, R.G. (1981) 'Birth and death: social construction at the poles of existence', *Social Forces*, 59:4:1074–93.

D.H.S.S. Northern Ireland (1982) *Northern Ireland Census 1981* (Belfast: HMSO).

D.H.S.S. (1984) *Registrar General of Northern Ireland. Annual Report. 1981* (Belfast: HMSO).

Dillon, M. and Lehane, D. (1973) *Political murder in Northern Ireland* (Harmondsworth: Penguin).

Donnelly, W. (1864) *Registration of deaths in Ireland* (Dublin: HMSO).

Douglas, J.D. (1967) *The social meanings of suicide* (Princeton University Press).

Douglas, M. (1966) *Purity and danger: an analysis of concepts of pollution and taboo* (London: Routledge & Kegan Paul).

Douglas, M. (1973) *Natural symbols: explorations in cosmology* (London: Barrie & Jenkins).

Douglass, W.A. (1969) *Death in Murelega: funeral rituals in a Spanish Basque village* (Seattle: University of Washington Press).

Durkheim, E. (1968) *Les formes élémentaires de la vie religieuse* (Paris: PUF).

Durkheim, E. and Mauss, M. (1963) *Primitive classification*, trans. R. Needham (London: Cohen & West).

Durkheim, E. (1952) *Suicide. A study in sociology*, trans. J.A. Spaulding and G. Simpson (London: Routledge & Kegan Paul).

Elias, N. (1978) *The civilizing process. The history of manners* (Oxford: Blackwell).

Elias, N. (1985) *The loneliness of the dying*, trans. E. Jephcott (Oxford: Blackwell).

Ellen, R.F. (1977) 'Anatomical classification and the semiotics of the body', in J. Blacking (ed.) *The anthropology of the body* (London: Academic Press).

Elliott, J.H.S. (1981) 'Recent developments in the law relating to coroners', *Northern Ireland Legal Quarterly*, 32:4:353–57.

Emery, J.L. and Marshall, A.G. (1965) *Handbook for mortuary technicians* (Oxford: Blackwell).

Engel, G. (1961) 'Is grief a disease?', *Psychosomatic Medicine*, 23:18–22.

Engel, G. (1977) 'The need for a new medical model: a challenge for biomedicine' *Science*, 196:129–36.

Etlin, R.A. (1984) *The architecture of death. The transformation of the cemetery in eighteenth-century Paris* (Cambridge, Mass: MIT Press).

Evans-Pritchard, E.E. (1934) 'Levy-Bruhl's theory of primitive mentality', *Bulletin Of The Faculty Of Arts, Cairo University*, 2:1:1–36.

Eyler, J.M. (1979) *Victorian social medicine: the ideas and methods of William Farr* (Baltimore: Johns Hopkins University Press).

Faber, K. (1923) *Nosography in modern internal medicine* (New York: Paul B. Hoeber).

Featherstone, M. (1982) 'The body in consumer culture', *Theory, Culture and Society*, 1:2:18–33.

Feifel, H. (1959) *The meaning of death* (New York: McGraw-Hill).

Figlio, K. (1977) 'The historiography of scientific medicine: an invitation to the human sciences', *Comparative studies in society and history*, 19:262–86.

Figlio, K. (1985) 'What is an accident?', in P. Weindling (ed.) *The social history of occupational health* (London: Croom Helm).

Firth, R. (1951) *Elements of Social Organisation* (London: Watts).

Flackes, W.D. (1980) *Northern Ireland a political directory. 1968–1983* (London: BBC).

Fortune, R. (1932) *Sorcerers of Dobu. The social anthropology of the Dobu Islanders of the Western Pacific* (New York: Dutton).

Foucault, M. (1970) *The order of things*, trans. A. Sheridan (London: Tavistock).

Foucault, M. (1972) *The archaeology of knowledge*, trans. A. Sheridan (London: Tavistock).

Foucault, M. (1973) *The birth of the clinic*, trans. A. Sheridan (London: Tavistock).

Foucault, M. (1977a) *Discipline and punish. The birth of the prison*, trans. A. Sheridan (London: Allen Lane).

Foucault, M. (1977b) *Language, counter-memory, practice*, trans. D. Bouchard (Ithaca: Cornell University Press).

Foucault, M. (1979) *The history of sexuality*, vol. 1, trans, R. Hurley (London: Allen Lane).

Foucault, M. (1980) *Power/Knowledge* C. Gordon (ed.) (Brighton: Harvester).

Fox, R.C. (1977) 'The medicalization and demedicalization of American society', in J.H. Knowles (ed.) *Doing better and feeling worse. Health in the US* (W.W. Norton).

Fox, R.C. (1980) 'The social meaning of death', *The Annals* (Philadelphia: American Academy Of Political And Social Science) 447.

Frazer, J.G. (1913) *The belief in immortality and the worship of the dead* (London: Macmillan).

French, S. (1975) 'The cemetery as a cultural institution: the establishment of Mount Auburn and the rural cemetery movement', in D. Stannard (ed.) *Death in America* (University of Pennsylvania Press).

Freud, S. (1957) 'Mourning and melancholia', in J. Strachey (ed.) *Standard edition of the complete psychological works of Sigmund Freud*, vol. 14 (London: Hogarth Press).

Freud, S. (1957) 'Thoughts for the times on war and death', in J. Strachey (ed.) *Standard edition of the complete psychological works of Sigmund Freud*, vol. 14 (London: Hogarth Press).

Fulton, R. (1976) *Death and identity*, revised ed. (Bowie: Charles Press).

Galtung, J. (1969) 'Violence, peace and peace research', *Journal of Peace Research*, 6:3:167–91.

Garfinkel, H. (1967a) 'Practical sociological reasoning. Some features in the work of the Los Angeles Suicide Prevention Center', in E.S. Schneidman (ed.) *Essays In Self Destruction* (New York: Science House).

Garfinkel, H. (1967b) ' "Good" organisational reasons for "bad" clinical records', in *Studies in ethnomethodology* (New Jersey: Prentice-Hall).

Geertz, C. (1960) *The religion of Java* (Glencoe: Free Press).

Gerth, H. and Mills, C.W. (1954) *Character and social structure* (London: Routledge & Kegan Paul).

Gervais, K.G. (1987) *Redefining Death* (New Haven: Yale University Press).

Giddens, A. (1979) *Central problems in social theory. Action, structure, and contradiction in social analysis* (London: Macmillan).

Glaser, B.G. and Strauss, A.L. (1965) *Awareness of dying* (Chicago: Aldine).

Glaser, B.G. and Strauss, A.L. (1968) *Time for dying* (Chicago: Aldine).

Gnoli, G. and Vernant, J-P. (1982) *La mort les morts dans les sociétés anciennes* (Cambridge: Maison De Sciences De L'Homme/Cambridge University Press).

Goffman, E. (1959) *The presentation of the self in everday life* (Harmondsworth: Penguin).

Goffman, E. (1970) *Stigma: notes on the management of spoiled identity* (Harmondsworth: Penguin).

Goffman, E. (1974) *Frame analysis. An essay on the organisation of Experience* (New York: Harper).

Goldthorpe, J.H. and Hope, K. (1974) *The social grading of occupations* (Oxford: Clarendon).

Goldthorpe, J.H. (1983) 'Women and class analysis: in defence of the conventional view', *Sociology*, 17:4:465–88.

Goody, J. (1962) *Death, property and the ancestors. A study of the mortuary customs of the LoDagaa of West Africa* (Stanford University Press).

Gorer, G. (1955) 'The pornography of death', *Encounter*, 5: Oct.: 49–53.

Gorer, G. (1965) *Death, grief and mourning* (London: Cresset).

Gordon, S.L. (1985) 'Micro-sociological theories of emotion', in Hell, H.J. and Eisenstadt, S.N. (eds) *Perspectives on sociological theory*, vol. 2 (Beverly Hills: Sage).

Grisham, J.W. and Nopanitaya, W. (1977) 'Cellular basis of disease' in W.A.D. Anderson and J.M. Kissane (eds) *Pathology* 2 vols. (7th ed.; St. Louis: C.V. Mosby).

Habenstein, R.W. and Lambers, W.M. (1963) *Funeral customs the world over* (Milwaukee: Bulfin).

Halbwachs, M. (1978) *The causes of suicide*, trans. H. Goldblatt (London: Routledge & Kegan Paul).

Halper, T. (1979) 'On death, dying and terminality: today, yesterday and tomorrow', *Journal Of Health Politics, Policy and Law*, 4:1: 11–29.

Hart, H.L.A. and Honoré, T. (1985) *Causation in the law* (2nd ed.; Oxford: Clarendon Press).

Harvard, J.J. (1960) *The detection of secret homicide* (London: Macmillan).

Hayes, R.J. (1970) *Sources for the history of Irish civilisation* (Boston: G.K. Hall).

Health Education Council (1987) *The health divide: inequalities in health in the 1980's* (London: Health Education Council).

Heath, A. and Britten, N. (1984) 'Womens' jobs do make a difference', *Sociology*, 18:4:476–90.

Hembright, T.Z. (1969) 'Comparison of information on death certificates and matching 1960 census records: age, marital status, race, nativity and country of origin', *Demography*, 6:413:23.

Hertz, R. (1960) *Death and the right hand. A contribution to the study of the collective representation of death*, trans. R. and C. Needham (London: Cohen & West).

Hertz, R. (1973) 'The pre-eminence of the right hand: a study in religious polarity', in R. Needham (ed.) *Right and left: essays in dual symbolic classification* (Chicago University Press).

Hertz, R. (1905–06) 'La réprésentation collective de la mort', *L'Année Sociologique.*

Herzlich, C. (1976) 'Travail de la mort', *Annales-Economies Sociétés Civilisations*, 31:1:197–217.

Hinton, J. (1972) *Dying* (Harmondsworth: Penguin).

Hoivik, T. (1977) 'The demography of structural violence' *Journal Of Peace Research*, 14:1:59–73.

Hopkins, K. (1983) *Death and renewal: sociological studies in Roman history*, vol. 2 (Cambridge University Press).

Huizinga, J. (1924) *The waning of the middle ages* (London: Edward Arnold).

Humphreys, N.A. (1887) 'Class mortality statistics', *Journal Of The Royal Statistical Society*, L:2:255–92.

Humphreys, S.C. (1981) *The family, women and death. Comparative studies* (London: Routledge & Kegan Paul)

Hunnisett R.F.(1961) *The medieval coroner* (Cambridge University Press).

Huntingdon, R. and Metcalf, P. (1979) *Celebrations of death: the anthropology of mortuary ritual* (London: Cambridge University Press).

Jervis, Sir J. (1957) *Jervis on the office and duties of coroners* (9th ed.), W.B. Purchase and H.W. Woollaston (London: Sweet & Maxwell).

Journal of The American Medical Association (1965) 'Of autopsies', *Journal of The American Medical Association*, 191:1075–78.

James, T.N. (1982) 'The development of ideas concerning the conduction system of the heart', *The Ulster Medical Journal*, 52:2:81–97.

Jewson, N.D. (1976) 'The disappearance of the sick man from medical cosmologies, 1770–1870', *Sociology*, 10:225–44.

Jones, I.G. and Cameron, D. (1984) 'Social class analysis: an embarrassment to epidemiology', *Community Medicine*, 6: 37–46.

Jones, P.H. (1945) *Cremation in Great Britain* (3rd ed.; London: Pharos Press).

Karsner, H.T., Rothschild, L. and Crimp, E.S. (1919) 'Clinical diagnosis as compared with necropsy findings in 600 cases', *Journal of The American Medical Association*, 73:666–69.

Kavanaugh, R. (1972) *Facing death* (Baltimore: Penguin).

Kearl, M.C. and Rinaldi, A. (1983) 'The political uses of the dead as symbols in contemporary civil religions', *Social Forces*, 61:3:693–709.

Klein, M. (1940) 'Mourning and its relationship to manic depressive states', *International Journal of Psycho-Analysis*, 21:125–53.

Knight, B.(1980) *Discovering the human body* (London: Heinemann).

Knight, B. (1984) *The post-mortem technician's handbook* (Oxford: Blackwell Scientific).

Knowelden, J., Keeling, J. and Nicholl, P. (1985) *Post neo-natal mortality* (London. HMSO).

Koran, L. (1975) 'The reliability of clinical methods, data and judgements, I', *New England Journal of Medicine*, 293:13:642–46.

Koran, L. (1975) 'The reliability of clinical methods, data and Judgements. II', *New England Journal of Medicine*, 293:14:695–701.

Kubler-Ross, E. (1970) *On death and dying* (London: Tavistock).

Kubler-Ross, E. (1975) *Death. The final stages of growth* (Englewood Cliffs: Prentice-Hall).

La Fontaine, J.S. (1985) 'Person and individual: some anthropological reflections', in M. Carrithers, S. Collins, and S. Lukes (eds) *The category of the person. Anthropology, philosophy, history* (Cambridge University Press).

Lane, R. (1979) *Violent death in the city* (Cambridge, Mass.: Harvard University Press).

Lantos, P.L. (1983) 'Changing images of the brain', *Psychological Medicine*, 13:2:255–66.

Ladurie, E. Le Roy (1979) *The territory of the historian*, trans. B. and S. Reynolds (Brighton: Harvester).

Leete, R. and Fox, J. (1977) 'Registrar General's social classes: origins and uses', *Population Trends*, 8: 1–7.

Lévi-Strauss, C. (1969) *Totemism* (Harmondsworth: Penguin).

Lienhardt, G. (1961) *Divinity and experience: the religion of the Dinka* (Oxford University Press).

Lindemann, E. (1944) 'Symptomatology and management of acute grief', *American Journal of Psychiatry*, 101:141–48.

Lofland, H.L. (1975) *Toward a sociology of death and dying* (Beverly Hills: Sage).

Loftus, B. (1986) 'Matters of life and death. Protestant and Catholic ways of seeing death in Northern Ireland', *Circa*, 26:Jan:14–18.

Loraux, N. (1982) 'Mourir devant Troie, tomber pour Athènes', in G. Gnoli and J-P. Vernant (eds) *La mort, les morts dans les sociétés anciennes* (Cambridge: Maison De Sciences De L'Homme/Cambridge University Press).

Lovell, A. (1983) 'A bereavement with a difference: a study of miscarriage, stillbirth, and perinatal death', *South Bank Sociology Occasional Papers* 4 (London: Polytechnic of the South Bank)

Lydall, J. (1982) 'The rituals of death in Hamar' *New Society*, 61:1028:174–76.

Malinowski, B. (1922) *Argonauts of the Western Pacific* (London: Routledge & Kegan Paul).

Mandelbaum, D.G. (1976) 'Social uses of funeral rites', in R. Fulton (ed.) *Death and identity* (Bowie: Charles Press).

Manning, P.K., and Fabrega, H. (1973) 'The experience of self and body. Health and illness in the Chiapas highlands', in G. Psathas (ed.) *Phenomenological Sociology. Issues and applications* (New York: John Wiley & Sons).

Manual of Funeral Directing (1970) (London: National Association Of Funeral Directors).

Manual of Funeral Directing (1981) revised ed. (London: National Association Of Funeral Directors).

Marris, P. (1974) *Loss and change* (London: Routledge & Kegan Paul).

Marris, P. (1958) *Widows and their families* (London: Routledge & Kegan Paul).

Marsh, G.H. and Laughlin, W.S. (1956) 'Human anatomical knowledge among the Aleutian Islanders', *Southwestern Journal of Anthropology*, 12:38–78.

Mauss, M. (1979) *Sociology and Psychology, Essays*, trans. B. Brewster (London: Routledge & Kegan Paul).

Mauss, M. (1985) 'A category of the human mind: the notion of person, the notion of self', in M. Carrithers, S. Collins, and S. Lukes (eds) *The category of the person. Anthropology, philosophy, history* (Cambridge University Press).

McDowall, M. (1983) 'Measuring womens' occupational mortality', *Population Trends*, 34:25–9.

McKeown, C. (1984) *The passion of peace* (Belfast: Blackstaff Press).

McKeown, M. (1972) *The first five hundred* (Belfast: *Irish News*).

McManners, J. (1981a) *Death and the enlightenment* (Oxford: Clarendon Press).

McManners, J. (1981b) 'Death and the French historians', in J. Whaley (ed.) *Mirrors of mortality* (London: Europa).

Medical Study Group of the Royal College of Physicians of London (1978) 'Death Certification and epidemiological research' *British Medical Journal*, 2:1063–65.

Merleau-Ponty,M. (1962) *Phenomenology of perception*, trans. C. Smith (London: Routledge)

Middleton, J. (1982) 'Lugbara death', in M. Bloch and J. Parry (eds) *Death and the regeneration of life* (Cambridge University Press).

Ministry of Health (1963) *Hospital building note number 20. Mortuary and postmortem room* (London: HMSO).

Mooney, J. (1888) 'The funeral customs of Ireland', *Proceedings Of The American Philosophical Society*, 25: 243–96.

Morley, J. (1971) *Death, Heaven and the Victorians* (London: Studio Vista).

Muir, R. (1924) *Text-Book of Pathology* (1st ed.; London: Edward Arnold).

Muir, R. (1933) *Text-Book of Pathology* (3rd ed.; London: Arnold).

Muir, R. (1941) *Text-Book of Pathology* (5th ed.; London: Arnold).

Murray, R. (1982) 'Political violence in Northern Ireland 1969–1977', in W. Boal and J.N.H. Douglas (eds) *Integration and Division* (London: Academic Press).

Murray, R. (1983) 'Reporting of Northern Ireland deaths in "The Times" 1969–1977', *Sociology*, 17:2:269–73.

NGA (1976) *The Last Post* (2nd ed.; Dublin: National Graves Association).

Oberschall, A. (1973) *Social Conflict and social movements* (Englewood Cliffs: Prentice-Hall).

O'Connor, Sr. M.C. (1942) *The art of dying well: the development of the ars moriendi* (New York: Columbia University Press).

O'Neill, J. (1985) *Five bodies. The human shape of modern society* (Ithaca: Cornell University Press).

Office of Population Censuses and Surveys (1980) *Classification of occupations* (London: HMSO).

Office of Population Censuses and Surveys (1982) 'Studies In Sudden Infant Deaths', *Studies On Medical and Population Subjects*, no. 45 (London: HMSO).

Park, R.E. (1967) 'The city: suggestions for the investigation of human behaviour in the urban environment', in R.E. Park *et al.* (ed.) *The city* (University Of Chicago Press).

Parkes, C.M. (1975) *Bereavement* (Harmondsworth: Penguin).

Parkes, C.M. (1965) 'Bereavement and mental illness', *British Journal of Medical Psychology*, 38:1–12.

Parry, J. (1982) 'Sacrificial death and the necrophagous ascetic', in M. Bloch and J. Parry (eds) *Death and the regeneration of life* (Cambridge University Press).

Parsons, T. (1951) *The social system* (London: Tavistock).

Parsons, T. (1963) 'Death in American society—a brief working paper', *American Behavioural Scientist*, 6:61–5.

Parsons, T. (1978) 'Death in the western world', in W.T. Reich (ed.) *Encyclopaedia Of Bioethics* (New York: Free Press).

Parsons, T. and Lidz, V. (1967) 'Death In American Society', in E. Schneidman (ed.) *Essays in self destruction* (New York: Science House).

Pearse, P.H. (1966) *Political writings and speeches* (Dublin: Talbot Press).

Peppers, L.G. and Knapp, R.J. (1980) *Motherhood and mourning. Perinatal death* (New York: Praeger).

Pine, V.R. (1975) *Caretakers of the dead. The American funeral director* (New York: Irvington).

Polhemus, T. (ed.) (1978) *The body reader. Social aspects of the human body* (New York: Pantheon).

Polson, C.J. Brittain, R.P. and Marshall, T.K. (1953) *The disposal of the dead* (London: English Universities Press).

Poole, M. (1983) 'The demography of violence', in J. Darby (ed.) *Northern Ireland. The background to the conflict* (Belfast: Appletree Press).

Presbyterian Church in Ireland (nd). *Services* (Belfast: Presbyterian Church in Ireland).

Pringle, D.G. (1983) 'Mortality, cause of death and social class in the Belfast urban area, 1970', *Ecology of Disease*, 2:1:1–8.

Prior, L. (1985a) 'The good, the bad and the unnatural. Some aspects of coroners' decisions in Northern Ireland', *The Sociological Review*, 33:1:64–90.

Prior, L. (1985b) 'Making sense of mortality', *Sociology of Health and Illness*, 7:2:167–90.

Prior, L. (1987) 'Policing the dead: a sociology of the mortuary', *Sociology*, 21:3:355–76.

Prior, L. (1988) 'The architecture of the hospital: a study of spatial organisation and medical knowledge', *British Journal of Sociology*, 39:1:86–113.

Radcliffe-Brown, A.R. (1922) *The Andaman Islanders* (Cambridge University Press).

Rawnsely, S. and Reynolds, J. (1977) 'Undercliffe cemetery Bradford', *History Workshop Journal* 4:215–21.

Riley, J.W. (1983) 'Dying and the meaning of death: sociological inquiries', *Annual Review of Sociology*, 9:192–216.

Robbins, S.L. Angell, M. and Kumar, V. (1981) *Basic Pathology* (3rd ed.; Philadelphia: W.B. Saunders).

Rose, S., Kamin, L.J. and Lewontin, R.C. (1984) *Not in our genes* (Harmondsworth: Penguin).

Royal College of Physicians and the Royal College of Pathologists (1982) 'Medical aspects of death certification', *Journal of Royal College of Physicians of London*, 16:4:4–14.

Rudinger, E. (ed.) (1977) *What to do when someone dies* (London: Consumers' Association).

Rudinger, E. (ed.) (1986) *What to do when someone dies*, revised ed. (London: Consumers' Association).

Sartre, J-P. (1957) *Being and nothingness* (London: Methuen).

Saunders, C. and Baines, M. (1983) *Living with dying. The management of terminal disease* (Oxford University Press).

Schneidman, E.S. (1976) 'The Death Certificate', in E.S. Schneidman (ed.) *Death: Current Perspectives* (Palo Alto: Mayfield).

Scott, M.J. *et al.* (1981) 'Perinatal death recording: time for a change?' *British Medical Journal*, 282:1070–74.

Scraton, P. (1984) 'The coroner's tale. The death of Jimmy Kelly', in P. Scraton and P. Gordon (eds) *Causes for concern. British criminal justice on trial?* (Harmondsworth: Penguin).

Shortland, M. (1985) 'Skin deep: Barthes, Lavater and the legible body', *Economy and Society*, 14:3:274–312.

Sigerist, H.E. (1970) *Civilisation and Disease* (University of Chicago Press).

Simmons, L.W. (1970) *The role of the aged in primitive society* (Archon Books).

Simpson, K. (1975) *Forensic Pathology* (7th ed.; London: Edward Arnold).

Simpson, M.A. (1979–80). 'The lady vanishes . . . or getting rid of the body', *Omega. A Journal of Death and Dying*, 10:3:261–63.

Singer, C. and Underwood, E.A. (1962) *A short history of medicine* (Oxford: Clarendon Press).

Smith, R. (1981) *Trial by medicine. Insanity and Responsibility in Victorian trials* (Edinburgh University Press).

Spencer, F. (1982) *A history of American physical anthropology 1930–1980* (New York: Academic Press).

Stannard, D.E. (1977) *The Puritan way of death* (New York: Oxford University Press).

Stannard, D.E. (1975) *Death in America* (University Of Pennsylvania Press).

Stanworth, M. (1984) 'Women and class analysis. A Reply to Goldthorpe', *Sociology*, 18:2:159–70.

Stepan, S. (1982) 'The idea of race in science: Great Britain 1800–1960' (Basingstoke: Macmillan).

Stevenson, T.H.C. (1928) 'The vital statistics of wealth and poverty' *Journal of the Royal Statistical Society*, 91:207–30.

Stone, L. (1979) *The family, sex and marriage in England 1500–1800* (London: Weidenfeld & Nicolson).

Strathern, A. (1982) 'Witchcraft, greed, cannibalism and death', in M. Bloch and J. Parry (eds) *Death and the regeneration of life* (Cambridge University Press).

Sudnow, D. (1967a) 'Dead on arrival', *TransAction*, 5:36–43.

Sudnow, D. (1967b) *Passing on: the social organisation of dying* (New Jersey: Prentice-Hall).

Szreter, S.R.S. (1984) 'The genesis of the registrar general's social classification of occupations', *British Journal of Sociology*, 35:4:522–46.

Taylor, S. (1982) *Durkheim and the study of suicide* (London: Macmillan).

The Church of England *The Offices according to the Church of England* (Oxford University Press).

Thomas, K. (1971) *Religion and the decline of magic* (London: Weidenfeld & Nicholson).

Thomas, L-V. (1968) *Anthropologie de la mort* (Paris: Payot).

Turner, B. (1984) *The body and society. Explorations in social theory* (Oxford: Blackwell).

Turner, V.W. (1969) *The ritual process* (London: Routledge & Kegan Paul).

Tylor, E.B. (1871) *Primitive Culture. Researches into the development of mythology, religion, art and custom*, 2 vols. (London: John Murray).

Unruh, D.R. (1979) 'Doing funeral directing', *Urban Life*, 8:2:247–63.

Van Gennep, A. (1960) *The rites of passage*, trans. M.B. Vizedom and G.L. Caffee with an introduction by S.T. Kimball (London: Routledge & Kegan Paul).

Veatch, R. (1976) *Death, dying and the biological revolution* (New Haven: Yale University Press).

Vizedom, M. (1976) *Rites and relationships: rites of passage and contemporary anthropology* (Beverly Hills: Sage).

Vovelle, G. and Vovelle, M. (1970) *Vision de la mort et de l'au-delà en Provence* (Paris: Armand Colin).

Vovelle, M. (1976) 'La redécouverte de la mort' *Pensée*, 189:3–18.

Vovelle, M. (1973) *Piété baroque et déchristianisation en Provence au XVIIIe Siècle* (Paris: Plon).

Warner, J.H. (1986) *The therapeutic perspective: medical practice, knowledge and identity in America 1820–1885* (Cambridge, Mass: Harvard University Press).

Warner, W.L. (1959) *The living and the dead* (New Haven: Yale University Press).

Watson, J.L. (1982) 'Of flesh and bones: the management of death pollution in Cantonese society' in M. Bloch and J. Parry (eds) *Death and the regeneration of life* (Cambridge University Press).

Weber, M. (1948) 'Science as a vocation', in H. Gerth and C. Wright Mills (eds) *From Max Weber: Essays in sociology* (London: Routledge & Kegan Paul).

Weindling, P. (ed.) (1985) *The social history of occupational health* (London: Croom Helm).

Weir, S. (1983) 'No weapon which deters rioters is free from risk', *New Society*, 65:1079:83–7.

Weisman, A.D. and Kastenbaum, R. (1968) *The psychological autopsy. A study of the terminal phases of life* (New York: Behavioural Publications).

Whaley, J. (1981) *Mirrors of mortality: studies in the social history of death* (London: Europa).

Wightman, W.P.D. (1971) *The emergence of scientific medicine* (Edinburgh: Oliver & Boyd).

Willis, R.A. (1950) *The principles of pathology* (London: Butterworths).

Willis, R.A. (1961) *The principles of pathology including bacteriology* (2nd ed.; London: Butterworths).

Wilson, G. (1939) 'Nyakyusa conventions of burial', *Bantu Studies*, 13:1–31.

Wilson M. (1957) *Rituals of kinship among the Nyakyusa* (London: Oxford University Press).

World Heath Organisation (1949) *International statistical classification of diseases, injuries, and causes of death* 2. vols., sixth revision (Geneva: World Health Organisation).

World Health Organisation (1957) *Manual of the international statistical classification of diseases, injuries, and causes of death* 2. vols., seventh revision (Geneva: World Health Organisation).

World Health Organisation (1977) *Manual of the international statistical classification of diseases, injuries and causes of death* 2 vols., ninth revision (Geneva: World Health Organisation).

World Health Organisation (1968) *Medical certification of cause of death. Instructions for physicians* (Geneva: World Health Organisation).

Wright, P. and Treacher, A. (1982) *The problem of medical knowledge. Examining the social construction of medicine* (Edinburgh University Press).

Wright, R.K. and Tate, L.G. (1980) 'Forensic Pathology. Last stronghold of the autopsy', *The American Journal of Forensic Medicine and Pathology*, 1:1:57–60.

Young, F.W. (1960) 'Graveyards and social structure', *Rural Sociology*, 25:446–50.

Young, R.M. (1970) *Mind, brain and adaptation in the nineteenth century* (Oxford: Clarendon).

Zonabend, F. (1973) 'Les morts et les vivants. Le cimetière de Minot de Chatillonais', *Études Rurales*, 52:7–23.

Zorbaugh, H.W. (1929) *The gold coast and the slum* (University of Chicago Press).

Zuckerman, S. (1963) *A new system of anatomy* (London: Oxford University Press).

OTHER WRITTEN SOURCES

Parliamentary Papers (PP)

1st Annual Report of the Registrar General in England, PP. 1839, 16, 1–127.

4th Annual Report of the Registrar General in England, PP. 1842, 19, 441–668.

Coroners' Inquests Ireland, PP. 1842, 38, 185–223.

Report on the sanitary condition of the labouring population of Great Britain. A supplementary report on the results of a special inquiry into the practice of interment in towns. PP. 1843, 12, 395–681.

Supplement to the 25th Annual Report of the Registrar General in England, PP. 1865, 18, 1–670.

1st Annual Report of the Registrar General in Ireland, PP. 1869, 16, 665–706.

35th Annual Report of the Registrar General in England, PP. 1875, 18, Part I, 1–405.

18th Annual Report of the Registrar General in Ireland, PP. 1882, 19, 891–1027.

44th Annual Report of the Registrar General in England, PP. 1883, 20, 891–1038.

74th Annual Report of the Registrar General in England, PP. 1913, 13, 493–577.

Public Records Office of Northern Ireland

Hospital Files
Hos 17/7/1/2
Hos 27/6/1

Hos 28/1/4/2
Hos 28/1/4/1
Hos 28/1/4/3
Hos 29/1/4/1

Crown and Peace Files

Ant 1/25
Ant 1/24
Belf 100/59/A/B/C
Belf 100/57/A/B
Dow 1/15
Dow 1/16
Fer I/i

Index